Erie Canal Bicyclist and Hiker Tour Guide
Second Edition, Revised

Erie Canal Bicyclist and Hiker Tour Guide

Second Edition, 2008 Revision

Harvey Botzman

Cyclotour Guide Books

2008

Erie Canal Bicyclist and Hiker Route Guide, 2nd Edition
© Harvey Botzman, 1996, 1999, 2004, 2008.

Published by
Cyclotour Guide Books, PO Box 10585
Rochester, NY 14610-0585
cyclotour@cyclotour.com. http://www.cyclotour.com

Other books by the author:
    'Round Lake Ontario: A Bicyclist's Tour Guide, 2nd Ed.
    'Round Lake Erie: A Bicyclist's Tour Guide, 2nd Ed.
    'Round Lake Michigan: A Bicyclist's Tour Guide, 2nd Ed.
    'Round Lake Huron: A Bicyclist's Tour Guide
    'Round Lake Superior: A Bicyclist's Tour Guide (2005)
    Finger Lakes Bicyclist's Tour Guide
    Long Distance Bicycle Touring Primer
An order form is at the end of this book.

Disclaimers:
The author; publisher; wholesale retail purveyor; library owner; of
    this book and its contents, and government units/agencies on
    whose roads you bicycle are not responsible for your riding
    habits, bicycle and any accidents which might occur. They
    encourage users of this Guide to wear a helmet; use a
    mechanically correct bicycle; use reflectors; use lights even
    during daylight hours; wear clothing which is readily visible to
    motorists, pedestrians and others; watch for other vehicles;
    position yourself and your bicycle correctly on a roadway or
    trail; and obey all traffic laws, rules and regulations.
Road and trail conditions change. The routes suggested herein
    may be altered due to road and trail maintenance; road and
    trail surface conditions; or your need to explore. Every effort
    has been made to provide accurate information.

Library of Congress Catalogue Card Number: 99-90016

ISBN: 1-889602-20-5 [Paper Bound]

ISBN: 1-889602-21-3 [Coil Bound]

10 9 8

To my parents

Samuel and Lillian Botzman

*Who allowed me to travel alone
on the trolley, at six years of age,
to visit my grandparents.
Thus starting me on the
path of travelling to experience
and participate in the world.*

Erie Canal Bicyclist & Hiker Tour Guide,
Second Edition, 2004 Revision

Harvey Botzman

Contents

Acknowledgements

My thanks to Gerry and Gail Robinson, my sister and brother in law. They thought my bicycle trips were strange but said, *write something!*

The encouraging influence of my nieces Randi Robinson; Bonnie Cimring, her husband Mark, greatnephews Alex, Jordan and Zachary. The business advice and traveling experiences of Joe and Sylvia Baron. Uncle Abraham and aunt Celia Aaroni's enthusiasm for this endeavor.

It was my friends and their children to whom I owe immense gratitude for their support, criticism and ability to take me away from staring at a computer monitor! Thanks, Ed, Martha, Eli and Emmy Awad; Jim, Becky, Jenny and Jimmy Parks; Jeff Schwartz; and others. Pat Townsend who spills coffee on my draft copies as she used her red pen to edit them. Rochester Bicycling Club members Richard DeSarra, Dick Burns, Bary Siegel, Todd Calvin, and others who'd say, "Let's ride!" And off I'd go!

The comments from cyclotourists who used my other books and can enjoy another tour: Steven, Ellen, Jared and Adam Branfman; and all those who have sent me post cards and letters.

Kristin Bennett of the Genesee Transportation Council deserve special mention.

Harvey Botzman

April 1, 2000
(June 20, 2004 2nd Rev.)
Rochester, New York

Preface

The Erie Canal was an engineering marvel during the 19th century. The original locks were made of stone blocks solidified together with *mud*. Not the mud of the earth but the mud of masons, cement. This was not the relatively high *tech* portland cement which we have today but a more rudimentary mortar. It has kept the original locks together for over 150 years.

This *Tour Guide* includes sections of the *Original, Old* (c. 1840), and *New* Erie Canal along the described routes. Fortunately for bicyclists and hikers the Original and Old Erie Canal have been subjected to the influence of preservationists. The Old Canal's towpath and right of way have have been converted into parks. Usually beautiful shaded, leveled and newly surfaced with stone dust or asphalt towpaths. Perfect for cyclotourists and hikers alike.

For many years I've cycled and hiked along the New York State Barge Canal System, as the Erie Canal is officially named. I've used my familiar road bike to traverse the asphalt, stone dust and dirt sections of the towpath and the adjoining roadways. With amazingly few flats. Many cyclists and hikers whom I've met have queried, "I wonder how far the path goes?" This *Tour Guide* answers that question.

It began as a simple description of the Erie Canal towpath between Oneida Lake and Tonawanda for friends and others who made inquiries to the Rochester Bicycling Club, the New York State Canal Corporation and the Genesee Transportation Council. It has progressively expanded to include the other parts of the New York State Barge Canal System—the Seneca/Cayuga Canal, the Oswego Canal and the Champlain Canal; the *new* (1840's expansion) Erie Canal; Canada's Chambly Canal North of Lake Champlain; and now a route along the Hudson River to New York City.

In truth, it was a delightful and challenging undertaking since no comprehensive land guide to this integrated working Canal System and the myriad local attractions in nearby cities, towns and villages existed.

TOUR PREPARATION

Tour Preparation Contents

Traveler Note

This chapter, *Tour Preparation*, has grown from 12 pages to 25 pages. You really do not need to carry these pages on your cyclotour or hike along the Canal.

If you purchased a coil bound copy of this *Tour Guide* then carefully bend back the end of the coil. Unscrew the coil binding, remove these pages. Screw the coil back into the holes. You've lost some weight! You can replace these pages when you return home from your cyclotour.

If you purchased a bound copy of this *Tour Guide*, then rip out these pages and paste them in when you return home.

Although most of the information contained in this Chapter applies to bicyclists, hikers should mine this Chapter for goodies.

Types of Bicycle Touring

I travel as a self-contained bicycle tourist. I cyclotour in this manner to view the world at its level as well as for economic reasons. The philosophical concept of self-reliance has a direct bearing on my mode of travel.

Other people cyclotour with only a credit card, an emergency repair kit, some snacks, and a few pieces of clothing. Still others travel with a sag wagon containing all their equipment, friends or family members. Some people travel alone others with family or friends. Many folks prefer to cyclotour with commercial or non-profit organized tours.

It really doesn't matter why or how you define your form of cyclotouring. You made a choice to travel by bicycle rather than by car or public transportation. You will meet people who state, ...*since I first rode a bicycle I've always wanted to bicycle tour.* You're cyclotouring and they're still waiting to bicycle tour!

In American and Canadian society we tend to define and classify what we do. In my mind bicycle touring is cyclotouring is bicycle touring. For others the following definitions of cyclotouring can help to sort out the type of bicycle touring which best meets their needs and wants.

Self-contained (self-reliant) Cyclotouring is when the bicyclist, (alone or with others) carries sufficient equipment to maintain the bicyclist(s) for the entire tour period. The equipment includes but is not limited to camping gear, clothing, personal gear, tools, and food. Obviously, consumables (food, *etc.*) will be replenished as the tour progresses.

Self-contained Small Group Cyclotouring is simply a group of people traveling together. The group can include one experienced bicycle tourist who's rôle is to teach the other group members bicycle touring skills.

Partially Loaded Cyclotouring is when the bicyclist carries emergency sleeping/camping equipment, basic repair equipment, a limited amount of clothing and personal items, snacks, or one meal's worth of food. A combination of commercial lodging and preparing one's own food or camping and eating in restaurants is considered as partially loaded cyclotouring.

Credit Card Cyclotouring is for bicyclists who want to be least encumbered with *stuff*! A credit card or debit card is necessary! Travelers checks will suffice! Only small panniers are needed. The panniers contain the minimum amount of clothing; a small repair kit; snacks (lunch?); a lock; a wallet with credit cards; and a small amount of cash! Meals are eaten in restaurants.   Lodging is at motels, b&bs or hostels. The cyclotourist travels by charging everything to the credit card or paying cash (obtained via ATMs). Hopefully the tourist doesn't forget to pay the bills!

Day Tripping is when an individual or a group travel for one day on a short round trip tour of a specific area. Usually these travelers carry the bare minimum amount of equipment and eat in restaurants.   Sometimes a day trip includes an overnight stay at commercial lodging.

Segment Cyclotouring is completing a long distance tour over a period of time with breaks to return home. The bicyclist starts each segment at the point where the previous segment was completed. Thus instead of bicycling the entire route along the Canal as one continuous cyclotour, the bicyclist might begin at Niagara Falls and cycle to Rochester on one weekend.   Then return home.   A few weeks later the cyclotourist continues touring starting in in Rochester and bicycling to Syracuse.   On a third weekend the bicyclist begins at Syracuse and rides to Utica; and so on.

Personal Sag Wagon Cyclotouring is a touring mode in which the food, camping and bicycle specific equipment is carried in a sag wagon. A spouse or friend functions as the sag wagon driver.   The bicyclist(s) carries the minimum amount of snacks, water, repair equipment, and some rain gear. Many times lodging for sag wagon bicycle tourists is at motels or b&bs rather than campsites. Bicyclist(s) and sag wagon meet at predetermined places for food, sightseeing, fun, and lodging.

Arranged Cyclotouring is when all long distance touring arrangements (with or without sag wagon support) are made by a non-profit or commercial bicycle tour company. Cyclotourists who have participated in arranged touring have had memorable experiences less the hassles associated with making all the arrangements themselves. They have enjoyed meeting and interacting with people who have similar interests.

Bikepacking is off road cyclotouring.   Usually the object is to establish a camping spot and Mt. bike on trails from that base camp.

Guerrilla Camping is finding a beautiful secluded place, off the road and using it as your camp site.   The guerrilla camper makes every effort to obtain permission to camp if there is an indication that the site is on private property.

Types of Hiking

Like cyclotouring, hiking has some specific definitions.

Hiking generally refers to locomoting using your feet rather than a bicycle or other wheeled vehicle.

Backpacking is a general term for hiking with an equipment loaded pack on one's back.

Backpacking specifically refers to hiking long distances with a fully loaded pack in uninhabited areas. The backpacker carries all the equipment necessary, including camping equipment, for an extended stay in the *backcountry* or in this case along the trail.

Long Distance Hiking refers to a hike of considerable distance usually with overnight stays. The long distance hiker may carry a fully loaded pack and camp along the way or simply a day pack and stay in commercial lodging or with friends.

Day Hiking is when individuals or groups take a round trip hike lasting a day or a part of a day. In general these hikes are shorter in both distance and time. The hiker carries a light weight *day pack* (frameless) with snacks, lunch, a first aid kit, some rain gear and other clothing, camera, etc.

This *Tour Guide* is designed for all bicyclists and hikers no matter how they define their mode of cyclotouring.

Experienced Cyclotourists

Friends, Family and the Passionate Cyclotourist

How to convince your non-cycling family members or friends to help you exercise your cyclotouring fantasy without breaking up the relationship!

    1. Make certain all family/friends have bicycles.

2. Plan your tour so that the first few overnight stops are 20-30 miles apart. This will allow you to spend time with your loved ones or friends while you tour.

3. The *passionate cyclotourist* bicycles to each overnight stop. At the overnight stopping point, the dedicated cyclist joins the other members of the touring group for an hour or two of recreational bicycling. Enjoy your vacation!

4. The passionate cyclist suggests to the other vacationers that one semi-dedicated bicyclist accompanies him/her on a portion of the next day's ride between overnight stops.

5. The sag wagon meets you and the co-rider at an intermediate point; picks up the co-rider who normally would not want to bicycle the entire distance between stops. You, the experienced cyclotourist, continues riding the entire distance to the next overnight stop.

6. Continue doing this for a few days and your family and friends will start enjoying *total* bicycle touring with you.

7. Alternatively, purchase a tandem!

Breakdown Cruise

At least two weeks before your tour begins take a short trial tour. Pack everything you *intend* to take on your long distance cyclotour. Include, in your panniers, what you *think* might be needed on your cyclotour. Ride twenty or thirty miles to a nearby campground. Stay overnight. Make notes on how you and your bike traveled.

When you return home, toss out everything which was superfluous to your weekend trip. Be vicious! Be heartless! "**Less is more**," Mies Van der Rohr said. Truer words were never stated in regard to cyclotouring. The less you load into your panniers the lighter your bike and the more enjoyable your tour will be!

Equipment

I'm frequently asked what I take on a tour. There are many bicyclists with more miles under their toes than me. They might carry more equipment than I do. My needs are very basic while cyclotouring. Your needs are different.

For aerodynamic and theft reasons, I try to have very few items *blowin' in the wind*!

The load is balanced, left and right sides, front and rear. Shift items between panniers to better balance the load. I use both sets of panniers because I'm small and light weight! If all the weight is on the rear wheels I lose some steering control.

One bicycle, kind of essential and I use an old one:
    18 speed, triple crank (24/40/52 x 13/34).
The panniers are packed as follows:

Right Rear Pannier	Left Rear Pannier
Tent	Stove inside a 1 qt. pan
Tent Poles	Fuel Bottle
Mattress Pad	First Aid Kit
Tools & Lights	Maps, misc. papers
Personal Items	Personal Items
1/2 "U" lock	1/2 "U" lock

    Sleeping bag on top of the rear rack.

Right Front Pannier	Left Front Pannier
Clothing	Food

Total weight = ~37 lb./17 kg. including panniers.

This pannier set up changes if I do not use front panniers. Then the rear panniers are balanced by a handlebar bag containing a limited number of heavy items: "U" lock, camera, snacks (fruit weights a lot), rain wear, towel, and bathing suit.

Hiking Specific Equipment

Shoes, Shoes, Shoes! The most crucial element for successful hiking. Purchase or use hiking shoes which are well broken in. Do not attempt to do more than a short half day trip in newly purchased shoes. Make certain that your hiking shoes fit correctly. A half size larger or smaller hiking shoe will present foot problems after a few miles of hiking.

For hiking on the Canal trails (stone dust, dirt and asphalt) a light weight hiking shoe which allows for your foot to breathe is a good choice. It should have a well defined tread pattern on the sole. A mid length (up to the ankle) hiking shoe is sufficient. Long distance backpackers might need additional ankle support if they are carrying a heavy pack. Many day trippers simply use sneakers but proper hiking shoes would make their hike a more pleasurable experience.

Socks are just as important as shoes. Socks specifically designed for hiking with extra cushioning material in various areas of the foot are available. They may not be necessary. Unfortunately socks are made in size ranges thus make certain that your socks fit both your foot and your shoes. It is a good idea to wash new socks before using them for a hike.

Always carry at least one extra pair of socks when hiking. Just sit down on the trail, remove your shoes and change your socks mid way through a day's hike along the Canal. Your return trek or the second part of your long distance hike will be a more comfortable experience.

Packs

A light day pack (1600-2900 cu in or L) will be more comfortable than a fanny pack. Don't overload it! Less is More!

If you are backpacking with full camping gear then a larger framed (internal or external) pack will be necessary. I would still try to keep everything light.

A large backcountry pack is probably not necessary for any trek along the Canals or River. Food, which can be bulky as well as heavy can be easily replenished daily. Clothing can be washed at Laundromats or in a pinch, using Canal or River water. Fuel for camp stoves, use a gasoline fueled camp stove and you'll be able to find fuel at any gas station.

When I hike the Canal for a week or more I only take a pint fuel bottle and refill it as necessary. Gasoline is heavy and no matter how good the seal on the fuel bottle is the gas smell still seems to surround my pack. The benefit is that flies and other insects tend to stay away.

Roads & Tow Path

State highways in New York State are smooth asphalt. Usually these roads have a striped paved shoulder of at least 4 ft. (1.2 m.) As roads are reconstructed a wider 10 ft. (16 m.) minimum paved shoulder will become the standard on State maintained roads.

State highways in Vermont and Québec are usually smooth asphalt with a small shoulder.

County and municipal roads in New York, Vermont and Québec are generally chip sealed.

County roads in New York usually have a 2-4 ft. (.6-1.2 m.) paved shoulder. County roads in Vermont and Québec sometimes have a shoulder.

Municipal roads may have a shoulder and then again they may not. If there is a shoulder it will be small and either gravel or mowed grass.

The Canal Tow Path is surfaced is with stone dust. Technically is stone <.125 in. (.32 cm.) in diameter. Generally the stone used is shale or ground metamorphic rock. Stone dust comes from two sources, quarries and street sweepings. The street sweepings have the added advantage of containing minute non-polluting amounts of salt left over from winter road salting. This small amount of salt inhibits the growth of vegetation on the Tow Path.

The Canal Corporation and its predecessor the NYSDOT prepare the Tow Path by excavating about two feet of the Canal levee.   Filling the excavation with large and then progressively smaller gravel mixed with clay and dolomite.

Usually a season goes by before the stone dust is laid over the base layers. This allows for the gravel/clay combination to settle. Depressions in the Path are filled in. The path is rolled again and finally a 5 in. (12 cm.) top layer of stone dust is applied, rolled and allowed to settle during a part of the summer. A second layer of stone dust is added later. The result is a smooth easily repaired surface on which to walk or bike.

If the stone dust layer was recently added to the Path then it will be loose. Biking through loose stone dust is sometimes compared to biking through mud. Bear in mind that within a week or two it will become compacted and a more appropriate surface.

If it is very dry then there will be more dust on your bike. A good spraying from a water hose will easily remove the dust from your bike and its components.

The stone dust which is kicked up tends to stay low and will not affect your respiratory tract.

Asphalt is used to surface the Tow Path in urban areas. You will notice that the condition of the asphalt sections of the Tow Path is generally worse than the stone dust sections of the Tow Path.

It is very expensive to maintain an asphalt multi-use trail the length of the Canal Tow Path. Tree roots, shifting sub-surface and other natural conditions easily erode the integrity of an asphalt surface. Additionally questions concerning who is politically responsible (the Canal Corporation or a municipality) for maintaining the Tow Path and you get the situation of little repair of the asphalt sections of the Trail.

Use of the Canal Tow Path is free. Funds for its construction and maintenance come from the Canal Corporation's parent, the New York State Thruway Authority (automobile tolls), the State budget and some Federal grants.

The Canal Corporation does maintain the Tow Path and the Canal to a very high standard. It is adding facilities such as port-a-potties, shelters, tables and benches as funds become available. Where you encounter eroded sections of the Trail recognize that repairs have to be scheduled. It is also your responsibly, as a user of the Canal Tow Path to inform the Canal Corporation of the problem. Tell the Lockmaster at the next lock, send the Corporation a post card or use the repair form in the appendix of this book.

Touring Ready

Bicycles

Your Bike vs. a Touring Bike

Many cyclotourists, including the author, use traditional road *sport touring* (*hybrid*) bicycles. These are fine bikes to use on the Canal Tow Path and its parallel roads.

For most cyclotourists their tried and true bike will suffice for this tour. Change the tires, put some racks and panniers on your bike and start pedaling!

It is *fit* not the type of bicycle which is important for successful cyclotouring (or any type of bicycling). An improper fit of your body to a bicycle will make your bicycle tour a horror. A proper fit of your body to a bicycle will make your tour a joy.

You can use any type of bike, with some modifications, for this or any other cyclotour. You can place racks, panniers, lights, fenders, different tires, and change the gearing on a hybrid, sport tourer, Mt. bike or even a racing bike and still successfully tour! Yes, purists! People do successfully tour on department and discount store bicycles.

Traditional touring bicycles with long chain stays and a full range of gears are a rare sight in bike shops. Only nine mass bike manufacturers make touring bikes. An additional fifteen or so custom builders make touring bikes. If you think you really need one, have your local bike shop order it.

The primary differences between a touring bicycle and a recreational bike or Mt. bike are in the chain stay length; head tube angle; frame flex; sufficient frame strength to carry a load; and having sufficient busses for attaching racks, water bottles, *etc.*

A touring bike usually has chainstays which are ~18 in./45.7 cm. or more in length. The head tube angle on a touring bike tends to be ~73°. Yes, all these technical specifications do make for a more comfortable long distance ride.

Bicycle manufacturers put all sorts of *do dads* on recreational bikes to make them appear as touring bicycles. The fact of the matter is that frame strength, frame flex, chain stay length, head tube angle and gearing are what really determine if a bicycle is a true touring bike!

Mt. Bikes

A Mt. bike makes a fine touring machine! Yes, traditional touring bike riders, they do! True, a few modifications are necessary to make a Mt. bike a more efficient touring bike. None the less, they make comfortable touring bikes.

A Mt. bike with a front suspension fork generally can not use front panniers. This means that all the weight of your *stuff* will be on the rear wheel. Use a handle bar bag and place some of the weightier items (U lock) in it to help balance the load.

Or change the front fork! If you do this, make certain that the new suspension fork has busses for attaching front racks. Several manufacturers now make special front forks specifically designed for attaching front racks. Front panniers really are not necessary if you limit the amount of *stuff* you take on your cyclotour! "Less is More!"

A number of rack manufacturers make special Mt. bike front and rear racks which can be used with front and rear suspended frames. Look through bicycle magazines for rack ads. Ask about these racks at your local bike shop.

Mt. bikes with short chain stays may present a problem with rear panniers. Your heels may continually strike the rear panniers as you pedal. If this occurs on your bike, move the panniers a few inches or centimeters rearward. Carefully pack your rear panniers with the heaviest items centered over the axle.

Mt. bike handle bars and handle bar mounted shifters are designed for constant shifting on difficult terrain. In general cyclotourists do not shift often but need to change their hand positions often to relieve numbness.

Don't go out and purchase a new set of shifters or handlebars! A simple and inexpensive Mt. bike modification is to add bar ends to a Mt. bike handlebar. These bar ends will allow you to use your current shifters and provide additional hand positions to relieve numbness. A new type of bolt on Mt. bike bar end even has the traditional dropped curved section. A number of cyclotourists use bolt on aero bars to provide even more hand positions.

Tires

I suggest that you use a set of the multipurpose touring tires mentioned at the end of this discussion. These multipurpose touring tires are efficient for negotiating smooth asphalt, stone dust and will allow you to successfully explore the rural dirt roads which strike your fancy along the way.

Slick no tread tires are not suitable for touring, even if you plan to race along the Canal! Occasionally you might have to go off the roadway and onto a gravel or grass shoulder. Slicks on such surfaces will provide a greater chance for you to wipe out!

A set of fairly wide, >28 mm. (~1 in.), touring or hybrid tires with a well defined (but not knobby) tread pattern will be well worth their premium price by having sufficient tread to slough off roadway irregularities. These types of tires are particularly suitable for this tour. Their well defined tread pattern will provide excellent traction and the smoother central road tread area will provide low rolling resistance.

Although Mt. bikes make fine touring machines for this tour, knobby treaded Mt. bike tires are not useful for traveling on asphalt or chip seal. Knobby tires have too much rolling resistance and wear out very fast touring on these road surfaces.

Gearing!

A triple chain ring with a relatively small inner chain ring is useful in some rolling hills areas. The only significant series of rolling hills along the route, where other *Canal* cyclotourists had a difficult time gaining significant momentum are on the Vermont sections of the Champlain Canal and along the Hudson River Route. Not really high hills but rather a series of closely spaced hills. A triple simply makes your riding more pleasurable.

Mt. Bike gearing usually provides a full range of choices for street and off road use. Mt. bikers might find that the higher gears used for road travel are not on their bike. One relatively easy way to obtain a more suitable gear configuration is to change the chain rings. Simply bolt on a large chain ring with more teeth (Don't forget to remove the current chain ring!). You might have wider steps between some gear stops but nothing which presents undue problems. Keep the small chain ring, you'll need it for the hills!

Given the chain rings on newer bikes (road and mountain), this might not be such a simple modification. Check with an experienced bicycle mechanic at a good bike shop before replacing the chain rings or freewheel.

Other Bits & Pieces

A first aid kit is a necessity.

Rain gear for the inevitable rain shower is a must.

Warm clothing for chilly mornings/evenings and after a rain shower will help prevent hypothermia.

Clothing is bulky and, surprisingly, weighs a lot. Do not take too much clothing. Laundromats are available in both small and big towns.

H_2O must be carried. Dehydration is the prime malady of bicyclists. Drink at least 8-12 fl. oz. (235-355 ml.) of water per half or three quarters of an hour. It is far better to drink more water than less water. You can add those high energy/electrolyte replacement substances/drinks to your water bottle but good old H_2O and some fruit will be just as effective for the majority of cyclotourists.

Equipment Lists

Do not take too much! **Less is more!** Excess weight due to excess equipment, clothing, tools, and food make a bicycle tour a drudgery rather than a pleasure. There are sufficient supply depots along the way. The Post Office & UPS are always available to send *stuff* home!

The *Equipment Lists* can help you plan and choose the items you need on your tour. The *Lists* are simply provided. You make the decision what to pack in your panniers. Base your equipment decisions on the type of cyclotouring you are doing—fully loaded to credit card—and your need for *stuff*. You will be able to purchase *stuff* along your route. You will be able to send home anything which is superfluous to your tour if you pack too much *stuff* in your panniers.

Balance your load, front and rear; right and left sides. Do not overload your bicycle.

Climate

The climate of the Erie Canal in Central and Western New York is different from that of Hudson Valley, Lake Champlain region and Oswego Canal. During the summer (June-September) the climate of all these areas is similarly perfect for bicycling. It is in the marginal months, March-April and October-November when the climate differences are most notable.

For perfect bicycle touring conditions plan to cyclotour during the April-September prime cycling season.

Wind! The bane of cyclists! Generally the wind blows from the Northwest or West.

The Erie Canal and the Seneca/Cayuga Canal are West-East Routes. The Oswego Canal, Champlain Canal and the

Hudson River run North-South.

As relatively open areas, the Canals and the River allow the wind to be channeled. Unlike the Great Plains there are trees, topographic and man made features along the routes which tend to block the wind's force.

Lake Champlain is a very large body of water which alters the climate of the surrounding land. Powerful winds can suddenly come off the Lake. These instantaneous winds might last for a few hours at best. The winds can be very strong one day but most likely the next day will be relatively calm, allowing you to travel in splendor. The winds coming off the Lake should not present any significant delays to your travels.

A climate factor called, *lake effect* influences the land mass surrounding large lakes creating micro-climate areas bordering a lake. Lake effect areas have a different climate than a location one or two miles away from the large body of water. You might notice these micro climates as the route verges away from the Lake. Lake effect also contributes to the betterment of humankind by creating ideal conditions for growing wine grapes and certain fruits like apricots.

Rain and Temperature:

In April and May the day time temperature range is 50-70°F (10-21°C) with rain a few days week. Rarely does it rain all day.

Days during June, July and August are sunny and clear with temperatures in the 73-85°F (23-30°C) range. It rains during the summer about once a week but rarely for more than an hour or two.   Evenings in late August can drop the temperature to the high 50s° F (teens° C.) Early September days usually are warm with clear cloudless skies.

In late September the day time temperatures begin to descend to the 60-70°F (12-21°C) range.   Mid-October brings precipitation similar to September with slightly chillier day time temperatures. The added bonus of fantastic Fall foliage in late September and early October makes the Canals, the Hudson Valley and Lake Champlain prime cycling destinations for locals and visitors from afar.

Snow is not unknown but rare in early March and late November. The snow during these months is heavy and wet. It usually disappears after a day or two as the temperature rises.

Don't think snow hinders bicyclists from using the routes bordering the Canals or Hudson River. Road cyclists switch to Mt. bikes with knobby tires or simply use the tires recommended for this tour. They'll put on a few more layers of clothing to ride all year long. Mt. bikers claim that snow is like mud except colder.

Fuel for Body and Mind

I carry very little food. Some pasta, dehydrated sauce mixes, cereal, snacks, fresh fruit, and two bottles of water. Food can be obtained readily in this area. Along the described route there are very few days when you will not pass at least one small local grocery or convenience store. Perishable products such as meat, cheese, milk or ice cream (the exception is yoghut) do not travel well in panniers. It is best to buy perishable products on a daily basis within a half hour of stopping to cook and eat them. Salmonella and other gastro-intestinal diseases can turn a delightful tour into a miserable experience. With a little common sense and care you should have few problems.

Without preaching, eating is important. Bicycling is a strenuous activity when you are touring everyday for a few weeks. Food and the correct foods to refuel and rebuild your depleted carbohydrate and protein supplies is of utmost importance.

I tend to eat more vegetables and carbohydrates (primarily pasta and rice) and less meat on my tours. These foods are relatively simple to store and prepare on the backpacking stove I use. I do eat my requisite beef, fish and chicken protein sources and they seem to taste even better mixed with farm fresh veggies.

Fresh vegetables and fruit can be bought at roadside stands. You will be missing a vital and satisfying culinary experience by not purchasing and eating fresh fruit and vegetables from the many farms and homeowners along the way.

Bananas and most citrus fruit, which tend to be staples of bicyclists, will have to be bought in grocery stores.

Take your fishing pole! Yup! There are fish in the Canals, Hudson River and Lake Champlain. Happy fish. You will encounter fisherpersons and they eat the fish they catch! Excellent trout, bass and other fish are found in the streams flowing into the Canals, Lake and River. If you are a fisherperson make certain that you contact the convention and visitors bureaus for information on fishing derbies.

If you are planning to catch your meal, check with the New York State, Vermont and Québec Departments of Environmental Conservation about eating certain species of fish. Oh! You need current fishing licenses for each jurisdiction.

Take a chance eating at what appears to be a non-imposing restaurant or tavern. In most cases, you will be pleasantly surprised with a fine, hearty meal and a friendly atmosphere. Similarly, the village bakeries (real bakeries, not the supermarket variety) have superb delights!

A notation is made in the text of grocery stores, convenience stores, gas stations, and the more permanent farm stands along the route. In urban and suburban areas only the last supply depots before entering a relatively long stretch of road where there are few stores are they noted.

Many campgrounds have small stores which cater to campers. Usually, their selection is limited. Bear in mind that the concessionaires stock what is needed most by the campers in a given park. If the park has a large number of RV campers then there will be fewer groceries. Most RV campers come to the park prepared and have little need for purchasing groceries. Make life easy for yourself, plan ahead, stop at a grocery which is within a half hour of your next meal. Use the *Food List* to help plan your needs.

Keep everything light. Try not to buy canned goods. Use dehydrated sauces and fresh foods which will be consumed in a day or two. Price will rarely be a factor for the small quantities you will need.

A short paragraph about dehydrated food. You are not going to be traveling in an area which is totally isolated from civilization. Only a few 50 mi. (80 km.) stretches of the route are relatively devoid of humanity. Trees, grains, fruits, deer, and cows being the dominant inhabitants. Expensive backpacker type dehydrated food packets are not necessary. Search your everyday grocery store for items like packets of sauces, veggie burgers in dehydrated form and pasta. Dehydrated foods—both those specifically designed for backpackers and those off the shelf in a grocery store— should be bought prior to the trip and tested for taste and preparation ease. There is nothing worse than looking forward to an easily prepared meal, making it and then discarding it for its foul taste.

You might find that pasta with locally made cheese is just as easy to prepare as an expensive box of macaroni and cheese. It probably will taste better, too!

Carrying food

Plastic freezer bags are the simplest and easiest way to carry foods. Freezer plastic bags, hold up better than regular plastic bags. You'll probably need a few different size bags.

Recently I've switched to carrying most of my food in plastic containers rather than plastic bags. I thought there would be a significant weight and space difference but that does not appear to be true. Plastic containers have the advantage of being easy to seal securely, not ripping open and being more moisture proof.

Recipes

Basic foods which are always in my panniers:

Pasta (spinach or avocado noodles); Rice, Cereal

Peanut (almond, cashew) butter

Jam, transferred to a plastic container, glass is heavy

Coffee, fresh ground, in a plastic container

Spice mixture (commercial packets) or in 35 mm film cans

Yogurt. Yogurt keeps for several days

Breakfast

Cereal w/yogurt & fresh fruit

Coffee

Eggs, milk and other perishable items should be bought and used within an hour of purchase. Pancake mix is fine but fat (oil) is usually needed. Fats become rancid very quickly in warm weather. Clean up is much more difficult with these foods and you want to start riding as soon as possible.

Lunch

Sandwiches

Peanut butter, jelly, cheese, fruit all on one sandwich.

Packaged or fresh cut luncheon meat from a grocery is fine but remember that luncheon meat spoils very quickly.

Purchase hard or semi-soft natural cheeses (cheddar, Swiss, parmesan) rather than soft or processed cheeses. The hard varieties will keep for several days.

Dinner

Pasta or rice

Salad if available; Lettuce and other vegetables are heavy and spoil baking in your panniers.

An easily prepared soup or stew can be made by dumping farm fresh vegetables along with a piece of chicken, ground beef or tofu into one pot and cooking everything.

Without the chicken (chicken stock spoils quickly) you can keep the soup overnight and use it for lunch the next day. If you make a vegetable soup and plan to use it for lunch the next day, boil it down to thicken the soup for over night storage and transport in you panniers. Of course you will need a container which seals securely. You can always thin the thickened soup with water. Cold vegetable soup is very good. Use a pinch or two of the herb sauce mixture.

Chicken, beef, fish, pork, etc. If I'm within a half hour of making dinner, I have the butcher put the meat into my plastic bag then that bag is placed into a second bag which is packed with ice (usually the butcher supplies free ice). Do not use any ice which has come in contact with uncooked meat.

I usually purchase chicken as it can be boiled with the pasta and I rarely use a wood fire.

Sauce

Sauces make meals interesting. Instead of carrying bottles or cans of pasta sauce use packets of different varieties of dehydrated sauce mixes (marinara, pesto, alfredo, Thai noodle, sweet and sour, *etc.*). These are found in almost any grocery store. A packet of sauce can be used for two or three meals! Roll over the packet top and place it in a small plastic bag to store for another dinner or lunch (sometimes I'll make the pasta meal for lunch and have sandwiches for dinner).

How to do it using only one pan! Drain the pasta but leave a bit of water in the pan. Add sauce mix, stir and eat! Yogurt and peanut butter can be added to pasta to make a sauce!

Real simple preparation for hearty meal. Little clean up.

Most commercial sauce mixes contain too much salt for my taste. I carry two or three different mixes in different 35 mm. film cans. Bulk spices can be found in grocery stores and natural food stores. You'll only need about .02 oz. (.5g.) of these bulk spices for five days of touring!

Curry Mixture

Gram marsala curry (contains cinnamon) or marsala curry
Coriander; cayenne pepper, dry mustard
+ peanut butter = Thai or Indonesian type of sauce.

Herbal Mixture

Basil, rosemary (just a little bit), thyme, oregano
+ yogurt = alfredo; or more basil + olive oil = pesto!

Mexican Mixture

Mexican, southwestern mix or chili mix, cayenne pepper
Adding chicken, peanut butter and some dark chocolate (hard to melt but possible) and you'll have chicken molé!

Gourmet eating at its finest!

Watch your calories; your carbohydrate, fat, and protein balance!

Drink sufficient water! Eat enough carbohydrates to refuel your bod. Do not BONK!

Packed & Ready to Go!

Tools

I'm a fanatic about tools. I probably bring too many. After being stuck in some desolate places without a nut or screw of the right size or thread I try to be prepared for almost anything.

In truth there is only one section of this route where you will be more than 75 mi. (120 km.) from a bike shop. The Post Office, UPS or a friendly motorist can easily transport a vital item to your campsite or lodging.

Although bicycle shops are located in major cities and towns, hardware stores and mass merchandisers abound. Most of these *substitute* bike shops will have something you can use for an emergency repair.

See the *Tool List* and make your own selection. Tools weigh a lot! A real lot! Use discretion. The newer multiple use tools are great, provided they meet your needs. Test the way your tools work before loading them into your panniers.

Combine tools; unscrew or cut off parts of tools you don't think you'll need.

A patch kit, pump, one tube, hex wrenches, and screw drivers are the bare minimum. A spare tire is unnecessary on this trip. If your tire degenerates to the point of no return, simply call the nearest bike shop and have them mail or UPS you a new one.

Personal Health & Safety

First Aid supplies are absolutely essential on a long distance tour. You can purchase ready made kits or you can assemble your own first aid supplies. Large and small adhesive gauze pads, a general bacterial agent, sun screen, general headache and muscle ache pills, adhesive tape, and a triangular bandage are the basic items. At some time on a tour you will probably use all of these items. It may take two or three years before you do but you will use them!

Be familiar with the danger signs associated with heat and muscle exhaustion, dehydration, hypothermia, and just being plain tired. Rest. Take care of yourself. Stop riding. If necessary go to a physician or hospital for treatment.

Helmet! Helmet! Helmet! Always wear one! Even on rural roads and urban bikeways. If you have something to protect, your brains, wear a helmet. Pros wear bike helmets, amateurs don't.

Bicycles must be equipped with a rear red reflector (a flashing red rear light is OK if it also is a passive red rear reflector); a front reflector and a front light; aural warning device; and other basic safety equipment.

During the day, the rear red flashing light should be on. It helps to make you more visible to motorists. It marks you as an experienced safety conscious bicyclist.

Wear bright clothing. When riding into the sun, wear clothing which will make you visible to automobile and truck drivers. A t-shirt with dark stripes or a patterned shirt is perfect. When riding with the sun at your back wear a top which will make you stand out from the scenery and sky. Use lots of reflective clothing during dusk, dawn and at night.

These safety items could save your life.

Lodging

All known bed & breakfasts and campgrounds are listed in the text with their complete address and telephone numbers. There may be some recently established lodgings which are not listed. Conversely, there may be some listed lodgings which no longer are in operation. These changes are the bane of tour guide writers and are unavoidable. I have tried to keep the listings up to date.

Consult the local tourist information office for a current lodging list if you have any questions.

Lodging facilities are not rated.

Use care to plan your overnight sojourns carefully. Some villages and hamlets along the way simply do not have formal places to sleep. Guerrilla campers have a distinct advantage in this regard.

Maps

The maps in this book provide more than sufficient information for you to cyclotour the routes circumnavigating and between each of the Finger Lakes. However you might want to obtain large scale (more detail) regional or county maps.

You can purchase large scale maps at most grocery or bookstores along the route or have your hometown bookstore order them. I recommend you cut up the large sheet regional maps. You only need the panels which show the area nearest the Lake which you will circumnavigating. You will save weight and space by cutting the large sheets. You can waterproof the map sections by coating them with *Map Seal.*

People

Meeting people and speaking to them is part of the joy and accessibility of cyclotouring. Unlike the Pacific Coast Bicycle Route, a touring bicyclist with is generally a rare sight around the Great Lakes. People will ask about your trip. People will offer help. Answer their queries with delight! Provide stories. Weave tales which will make them jealous.

Public Transit to Your Starting Point

A very efficient and enjoyable way to start your cyclotour is to travel to the Erie Canal via train, airline or an intercity bus. Of course if you live near by just cycle to the Canal. This *Guide* is designed so that a cyclotourist can begin and end at any point along the route. Directions to and from the major train stations, airports and bus terminals are provided in the text.

General Public Transit Rules

Due to recent security concerns check the carrier's web site and printed materials for new and changed rules concerning carriage of bicycles. Make certain you tell the carrier that you will be transporting a bicycle. Expect to show your bicycle to a security official <u>before</u> packing it into a bicycle box.

If you do not have a passport. I strongly suggest that you get one. It is the most accepted form of identification at common carrier terminals and stations.

Each carrier—airline, bus and train companies—have specific rules regarding the transport of bicycles. All carriers specify that bicycles must be boxed and shipped as baggage. Trains and the airlines will sell you a box at the terminal. Bus companies do not have boxes for sale at their terminals.

If you are traveling to the Erie Canal by train or an airline then purchase the carrier's box. These boxes are designed so that you simply have to turn the handlebars and remove the pedals to fit a standard sized upright bicycle into the box. Very simple! You **must** have your own tools. Bicycle tools are not available at any train stations or airplane terminals.

Using the carrier's bike box assures you that the carrier can not claim your box was too weak to hold a bicycle. Amtrak's bicycle boxes cost ~US$7.00; VIARail charges a standard CN $15.00; the airlines charge US$15.00 +.

Airlines

In general commuter airlines do not have facilities for the transport of bicycle boxes.

You will also have to pay an *extra* baggage charge on domestic United State & Canadian airline flights. This charge can be as high as US$ 80.00. A way of avoiding this ridiculous charge is to fly into Montréal or Niagara Falls, Canada from the United States or fly into a USA from Canada. On international flights, airlines are prohibited from charging exorbitant excess baggage charges for bicycles.

Trains

Long Distance Trains

Amtrak and VIARail do not charge extra for transporting your bicycle, just for the bike box itself.

You will not need either a folding bicycle or a Japanese *rinko bukuro* (bicycle bag, 2m.x2 m./6 ft.x 6 ft.) to use Amtrak in New York State.

Amtrak carries bicycles in baggage cars. This is significant! Not all Amtrak trains and stations have baggage facilities! Make certain that both your originating and terminating train and station have baggage facilities. Otherwise your bike will be at one station and you at another.

In conjunction with the New York State DOT, Amtrak has baggage car service on its New York City to Chicago *Lake Shore Express*. This train follows the Hudson River to Albany and then the Erie Canal between Albany and Buffalo.

Amtrak's *Adirondack* train from Schenectady to Plattsburgh; and its *Vermonter* (both Champlain Canal bound), New York City to Montréal, accept unboxed bicycles in their baggage cars. Amtrak is planning to expand its unboxed bicycle policy to all trains serving New York State as new equipment becomes available. Check to make certain that these two trains are carrying unboxed bicycles. At varying times they suspend this bicycle friendly service.

The New York Bicycling Coalition (www.nybc.net and local clubs are lobbying Amtrak to rapidly expand its unboxed bicycle carriage policies. Help out by sending the advocacy letters in the Appendix.

Fortunately for the cyclotourist coming to Erie Canal almost all Amtrak terminals along the route have baggage car facilities. Unfortunately, only one train (in each direction), *The Lake Shore Limited*, has baggage car service beyond Schenectady.

VIARail travelers will have to embark at Brampton, near Hamilton or at Montréal and make their way to either the Erie Canal at Tonawanda or the Chambly Canal at Sur de la Richelieu QC. Then they can use the use the Champlain Canal to reach the

Erie Canal at Waterford. The route from Montréal to the Chambly & Champlain Canals is provided in this *Guide*. Some VIARail and GO local trains between Brampton and Montréal allow unboxed bicycles to be carried in the passenger cars. Check the VIARail & GO schedules.

Commuter Trains

If you are arriving at one of New York City's Airports you can take the Long Island Railroad or Subway to Manhattan (the main business area) or The Bronx (northern most part of NYC) and begin your tour from there.

The bicycle route from New York City's Newark Airport is not provided.   You will have use NJ Transit Buses or PATH commuter trains to reach Manhattan.

The Metropolitan Transit Authority (MTA), operators of NY Metro area commuter trains allow bikes on trains during non-rush hours. You do need a permit which is available by mail or at Pennsylvania Station.

GO Trains are commuter trains operating in Ontario Province. Generally, bicycles are permitted during non-rush hours.

Bus

Bus travel presents a different problem. Bus line offices do not stock bicycle boxes. You will have to do one of the following:

1. Obtain a bicycle box from a bike shop;

2. Go to Amtrak or an airline and obtain a box from those carriers;

3. Construct your own box from two or more smaller boxes;

4. Put your (unboxed) bike into the baggage compartment when the driver's back is turned. Many drivers suddenly disappear with the implication that you should do this heinous crime!

As of the publication of this *2nd Edition*, only Rochester has bike racks on all its local buses. Albany, Utica, Syracuse and Buffalo are planning to place these wonders on their buses.

Tandem and long wheel base recumbent bicyclists must check the carrier's rules and regulations. In General these *over size* bicycles can be transported on public transport if they are boxed. Which means more disassembly of the bicycle. A bit of astute questioning and making certain that you receive the answer in writing might be necessary.

Ah! To be back traveling in Africa (Peace Corps '66-'69) where bikes are simply placed on top of the bus or lashed to the wall of the train's baggage car. How simple! And rarely were the bikes damaged.

How to Box Your Bike

The first time I boxed my bike I did it at home. I inserted extra cardboard into the box to reinforce the long sides of the box. I double sealed all edges using reinforced packing tape. I loaded the bike filled box into my station wagon and brought it to the terminal the day before my departure. It took an interminably long time to do all this >2½ hours. What a chore! Make life simple for yourself. Pack the box at the terminal. Allow an extra 45 minutes to pack the box. I'm down to 15-20 minutes *bike into box* packing time now!

1. Before you start on your cyclotour take pictures of your bicycle with and without panniers. Open the panniers and take some pictures of the contents of the panniers. If any damage occurs in transit you might need these pictures to assert your claim.

2. Public Transit terminals do not have bicycle tools. You will need the following tools (depending on the bolts on your bike.
    Cone wrench (pedals)
    6 mm hex wrench (stem/pedal bolt)
    Hex wrenches to loosen the brakes & for the new types of pedal & stem bolts.
    A roll or two of 2" wide filament reinforced packing tape
    Clothes line (for tying the handlebars to the top tube; and a crank arm to a chain stay).

3. Obtain a bicycle box.

4. Clearly mark the following information on four sides of the bike box. Use a black permanent marker. Write in big letters and numerals.
    Destination:
    Departure date:
    Train or Flight number:
    Ticket number:
    Your name:
    ↑ Pointing to the top.

5. Remove both pedals using a cone wrench. The pedals or cranks on new bikes are sometimes removed using a hex wrench. Tape or tie one crank (if not removed) to a chain stay. Put your pedals into one pannier.

6. Loosen the brake cables; loosen the stem; turn the stem or remove it so as to align the handlebars with the top tube. Wrap or tie the handlebars to the top tube or front rack.

7. Wheel the bike into the bike box.

Box Ready!

8. Secure the bike by wedging your sleeping bag and a pannier between the bike and the box sides. Do not overload the box with heavy panniers. Carry the other panniers on to the train, plane or bus.
9. Seal the box with 2" reinforced packing tape.
10. Bring the filled bike box to the baggage room and obtain a baggage claim check. Keep the baggage claim check with you. You will not be able to claim your bike without this claim check.

Time needed to disassemble your bike and pack the bike box = 20-45 minutes.

At Your Destination
Claim your bicycle!
I have to preface this discussion of damage claims with the fact that my bike has never been damaged traveling via Amtrak and only once on a plane trip. Amtrak stores bikes in an upright position in its baggage cars. Airlines and bus lines store bikes on their side in baggage holds.

Check the exterior of the bicycle box for possible in transit damage. If you see any damage, to the exterior of the bike box, immediately take a picture of the damage <u>and</u> show the damage to the baggage personnel before you open the box.

Open the bike box. Check your bike for any damage or missing items. If damage occurred, immediately show it to the baggage personnel <u>and</u> complete the damage claim form.

After assembling your bike, take a short ride in the terminal to make certain there was no non-visible damage to the gearing, frame, wheels, etc. If you determine that there is some damage, immediately show it to the baggage personnel and take a picture of the damage. Ask for and complete the damage claim form.

Find a local bicycle shop (look in the phone book.) Purchase the part. Copy the receipt and make copies of your completed claim form. Send a copy of the receipt with the original claim form to the carrier. Mail home, the original receipt and one copy of the claim form. It takes 2-6 weeks for most airlines, bus lines or Amtrak to begin to settle baggage damage claims. Enjoy your cyclotour.

Postal Addresses

The proper form of addressing letters is important for your mail to arrive at its destination. The postal systems in both the USA and Canada are very automated. Barcodes are placed automatically on the bottom of envelopes and post cards. Even your handwritten addresses are machine, optical character recognition read.

The clearer you address your letters the faster they speed to their destination. Print! Addresses should be printed in capital letters without punctuation.

Zip codes and Postal Codes

N = Number; L = Letter

USA Zip Codes consist of five or nine numbers:

NNNNN or NNNNN-NNNN

Canadian Postal codes consist of a combination of two groups of numbers and letters separated by a space.

NLN LNL

Use two or three letters to abbreviate roadways and the State or Province.

street = ST; avenue = AVE; road = RD; drive = DR; boulevard = BLVD; *etc.*

In Québec the French version of some roadways is used: boulevard = BOUL; avenue = AV; chemin = CH.

New York = NY; Vermont = VT; Québec = QC.

A return address is placed in the upper left corner of the envelope.
The stamp goes on the upper right corner.
The addressee's address is centered on the envelope.
A ½ in. (1.25 cm.) blank space must be left at the bottom of the envelope or post card.

RETURN NAME
ADDRESS   Postage
CITY ST NNNNN

                    NAME
                    ORGANIZATION
                    STREET
                    CITY ST NNNNN
                    NATION

Information Sources

Glossy tourist brochures with all sorts of information and discount coupons will be joyfully supplied by tourist information bureaus. I suggest that you write for them.

I have had to search, dig and cajole regional and local planners; transportation agencies; county and municipal officials for valid bicycling route information. I've biked around each Lake in both directions; biked between each Lake; and car/bike checked the route. A very time consuming and expensive endeavor, which is exactly why you purchased this book! You can simply cyclotour to your heart's mighty beat!

You should request bicycling information if only to make tourism officials aware that people do want to bicycle in their locality. Always request bicycling specific information and local maps. Mention that you obtained the address from *Erie Canal Bicyclist & Hiker Tour Guide* by Harvey Botzman. It helps!

New York State is in the process of developing a full fledged bicycling packet. The State Bicycle Coordinator will send you a number of goodies, unobtainable elsewhere.

The Canal Corporation has a very generalized map (in nice colors) of the entire New York State Canal System. I suggest that you contact them too.

If you use all the routes in this *Guide* you will pass through more than 36 New York; 3 Vermont' 2 Québec; and 1 Ontario county.. To conserve space and weight, County Tourism Offices (TO), regional Convention and Visitors Bureaus (CVB), or Chambers of Commerce (CofC) are listed below. These County and regional agencies are arranged according to the route going from West to East and South to North along the Canals. A separate set of listings is for the Hudson River route. The text usually notes when you cross a County border. Municipal (city, town and village) information sources are listed in the text.

Do be careful as you cross a County border. Police may be hiding behind a billboard and if you're speeding, a ticket will be proffered. Passports are not needed when crossing County borders!

These information source listings are arranged first by State/Province. County listings are alphabetical by Canal/River route. Municipal and other local information sources are listed in the text.

Abbreviations used in these listings: TO = Tourism Office; CVB = Convention & Visitors Bureau; CofC = Chamber of Commerce.

State, Provincial and Canal

New York State Canal Corp., PO Box 189, Albany NY 12201, 800 422-6254, www.canals.state.ny.us

New York State Div. of Tourism, 32 S. Pearl St., Albany NY 12245, 800 225-5697, www.iloveny.com

Ontario Min. of Tourism, Queens Park, Toronto ON M7A 2E5, 800 668-2746, www.travelontario.net

Tourisme Québec, CP 979, Montréal QC H3C 2W3, 877 266-5687/514 864-3838, www.bonjourquebec.com

Vermont Dep't. of Tourism, 6 Baldwin St., Montpelier VT 05633 800 837-6668, www.vermontvacation.com

County Tourist Information

Erie Canal

Albany County CVB, 25 Quackenbush Sq., Albany, NY 12207, 800 258-3582/518 434-1217, www.albany.org

Cayuga County CofC, 131 Genesee St., Auburn NY 13021, 800 499-9615/315 255-1658, www.tourcayuga.com

Erie County (Buffalo-Niagara CVB), 617 Main St., Buffalo NY 14203, 800 283-3256/716 852-0511, www.visitbuffaloniagara.com

Fulton County CofC, 2 N. Main St., Gloversville NY 12078, 800 676-3858/518 725-0641, www.fultoncountyny.org

Genesee County CofC, 220 E. Main St., Batavia NY 14020, 800 622-2686/716 343-7440, www.geneseeny.com

Herkimer County CofC, 28 West Main St., PO Box 129, Mohawk NY 13407, 315 866-7820, www.herkimercountychamber.com

Livingston County CofC, 4560 Millennium Dr., Geneseo NY 14454, 800 538-7365/585 243-4160, www.FingerLakesWest.com

Madison County TO, Brooks Hall, Rte. 20, Morrisville NY 13408, 800 684-7320/315 684-7320, www.madisontourism.com

Monroe County (Greater Rochester VA), 45 East Ave.., Rochester NY 14604, 800 677-7282/585 546-3070, www.visitrochester.com

Montgomery County 366 W. Main St., Amsterdam NY 12010, 800 743-7337/518 842-8200, www.montgomerycountyny.com

Niagara County TO, (Buffalo-Niagara CVB), 617 Main St., Buffalo NY 14203, 800 338-7890/716 282-8992, www.visitbuffaloniagara.com , www.niagara-usa.com

Oneida County CVB, I-90 Exit 31, Utica NY 13503, 800 426-3132/315 724 7221, www.oneidacountycvb.com

Onondaga County CVB, 572 S. Salina St., Syracuse NY 13202, 800 234-4797/315 470-1910, www.VisitSyracuse.org

Ontario County TO, 248 S. Main St., Canandaigua NY 14424, 877 386-4669/585 394-3915, www.visitfingerlakes.com

Orleans County TO, 14016 Rt. 31W, Albion NY 14411, 800 724-0314/585 589-3198, www.orleansny.com/tourism

Oswego County TO, 46 East Bridge St., Oswego NY 13126, 800 248-4386/315 349-8322, www.oswegocounty.com

Rensselaer County TO, 1600 7th Ave., Troy NY 12180, 518 270-2959, www.rensco.com

Saratoga County CofC, 28 Clinton St., Saratoga Springs NY 12866, 800 526-8970/518 584-3255, www.saratoga.org

Schenectady County CofC, 306 State St., Schenectady NY 12305, 800 962-8007/518 372-5656, www.schenectadychamber.org

Seneca County TO, 1 DiPronio Dr., Waterloo NY 13165, 800 732-1848/315 539-1759, www.visitsenecany.net

Wayne County TO, 9 Pearl St., PO Box 131, Lyons, NY 14489, 800 527-6510/315 946-5469, www.waynecountytourism.org

Hudson River Route

Albany County CVB, 25 Quackenbush Sq., Albany NY 12207, 800 258-3582/518 434-1217, www.albany.org

Bronx Tourism Council, 198 E. 161st St., Bronx NY 10451, 718 590-2766, www.ilovethebronx.com

Columbia County TO, 401 State St., Hudson NY 12534, 800 724-1846/418 828-3375, www.columbiacountyny.org

Dutchess County TO, 3 Neptune Rd., Poughkeepsie NY 12601, 800 445-3131/845 463-4000, www.dutchesstourism.com

Greene County TO, PO Box 527, Rte. 23B, Catskill NY 12414, 800 355-5587/518 943-3223, www.greenetourism.com

New York City CVB, 810 7th Ave., New York NY 10019, 800 692-84748/212 484-1222, www.nycvisit.com

Orange Co. TO, 30 Matthews St., Ste. 111, Goshen NY 10924, 800 762-8687/845 291-2136, www.orangetourism.org

Putnam Co. CVB,111 Old Rte. 6, Carmel NY 10512, 800 470-4854/845 225-0381, www.visitputnam.org

Queens County TC, 120-55 Queens Blvd., Ste. 309, Kew Gardens NY 11424, 718 263-0546, www.discoverqueens.info

Rensselaer County TO, 1600 7th Ave., Troy NY 12180, 518 270-2959, www.rensco.com

Rockland County TO, 18 New Hempstead Rd., New City NY 10956, 800 295-5723/845 708-7300, www.rockland.org

Ulster County TO, 10 Westbrook Ln., Kingston NY 12401, 800 342-5826/845-3566, www.ulstertourism.info

Westchester County CVB, 222 Mamaroneck Ave., White Plains NY 10605, 800 833-9282/914 995-8500, www.westchestertourism.com

Champlain Canal Route

Addison County CofC, 2 Court St., Middlebury VT 05753, 800 733 8376/802 388-7951, www.midvermont.com

Albany County CVB, 25 Quackenbush Sq., Albany NY 12207, 800 258-3582/518 434-1217, www.albany.org

Chittenden County/Lake Champlain Regional TO, 60 Main St., Ste. 100, Burlington VT 05401, 877 686-5253/802 863-3489, www.vermont.org , www.lakechamplainregion.com

Chambly TO, 514 658-1200.

Clinton County TO/Champlain Shores VCB, 7061 Rte. 9, Plattsburgh NY 12901, 518 563-1000, www.goadirondack.com or www.northcountrychamber.com

Essex County/Lake Placid CVB, 216 Main St., Lake Placid NY 12946, 800 447-5224/518 523-2445, www.lakeplacid.com

Franklin County (VT) CofC, 2 N. Main St., St. Albans VT 05478, 802 524-2444, www.vermontvacation.com

Grand Isle County/Champlain Islands CofC, PO Box 213, North Hero VT 05474, 800 262-5226/802 372-8400, www.champlainislands.com

Haut-Richelieu, Off. du Tourisme et des Congrèss du; 31 Rue Frontenac, Saint-Jean-sur Richelieu QC J3B 7X2, 888 781-9999/450 542-9090, www.tourismehautrichelieu.org

Lake Champlain VC, 94 Montcalm St., Ticonderoga NY 12883, 866 843-5253,

Tourisme Montréal, CP 979, Montréal QC H3C 2W3, 877 266-5687/514 864-3838, www.tourisme-montreal.org

Montérégie, ATR de la , 989 rue Pierre-Dupuy, Longueuil QC J4K 1A1, 514 674-5555, www.tourisme-montreal.org/monteregie

Rensselaer County TO, 1600 7th Ave., Troy NY 12180, 518 270-2959, www.rensco.com

Rutland Region CofC, 256 N. Main St., Rutland VT 05701, 800 756-8880/802 773-2747, www.rutlandvermont.com

Saint-Hyacinthe, Bur. de tourisme et des congrès; 2090 rue Cherrier, Saint-Hyacinthe, QC J2S 8R3, 800 849-7276/450 774-7276, www.tourismesainthyacinthe.qc.ca

Saratoga County CofC, 28 Clinton St., Saratoga Springs NY 12866, 800 526-8970/518 584-3255, www.saratoga.org

Warren County TO, 1340 State Rte. 9, Lake George NY 12845, 800 365-1050/518 761-6366, www.visitlakegeorge.com

Washington County TO, County Municipal Center., Fort Edward NY 12828, 888 203-8622/518 746-2290, www.washingtoncounty.org

How to Read the Route Guide Entries

It's really easy! The entire route is divided into route segments of
~50 mi. (~80 km.)

The route descriptions are written as if you are proceeding from
West to East along the Erie Canal and Seneca/Cayuga
Canal; South to North along the Champlain Canal and
Oswego Canal; and North to South along the Hudson River.

At the beginning and end of each route section you will see,
besides normal chapter titles, the following barred route
heading:

Westbound travelers read the mileage on the <u>left</u> side of the page
downwards from the top of the page.

W to E	**Albion to**	E to W
mi. (km.) Read ↓	**Fairport**	mi. (km.) Read ↑

Eastbound travelers read the mileage
on the <u>right</u> side of the page
upwards from the bottom of the page.

The first line of an entry gives the cumulative distance in miles
and kilometers (in parentheses) in either direction and a
location intersection. Usually it is in the form of:

9.4 (15.1)   O'Neil Rd. @ Tow Path   45.2 (73.1)

Every effort has been made to be accurate in the distances noted.
Mistakes might occur! If so, please send me a post card
noting the error.

The distances are cumulative. You will have to do the subtraction
to find the distances between entries.

The second line of each entry usually gives directions, Turn,
Continue, Stop, Look, *etc.* and where to go. *E. g.*, Turn South
on to Rt. 31. Cardinal compass directions are used as if
proceeding from **West to East** along the Erie Canal and
Seneca/Cayuga Canal; **South to North** when going using
the Champlain Canal and Oswego Canal; and **North to
South** along the Hudson River Route. Left and right
directions are rarely used.

Turn North on to O'Neil Rd., ride across the bridge.

Special Instructions for Travelers
Going Opposite to the Way the Directions are Written

Travelers proceeding <u>Opposite to the way the directions are written</u> must *<u>reverse</u>* the direction provided in a text entry.
Turn North
should be read as:
Turn **South**.
by travelers going
East to West along the Erie & Seneca/Cayuga Canals;
North to South along the Champlain Canal and Oswego Canal;
South to North along the Hudson River Route.

This only becomes a problem if you have absolutely no sense of direction. Travelers rapidly get used to reading the mileage (kilometage [*sic*]) on the right side of the page and mentally reversing the directions. Use builds expertise!

Getting lost has always been a treat for me. I've discovered new and interesting routes, places and most importantly people. Think of it as part of the adventure of traveling.

The entries for cities, towns or villages with specific services appears like this:

Ft. Ann

Info.:
Cycling & Hiking Info.:
Services & Facilities:
Lodging:
Attractions:

If there is no information then a category does not appear. State and Provincial abbreviations are not included when it is obvious which state or province applies.

Bed & breakfast and campground accomodations listings are complete with addresses and telephone numbers.

Motels are noted simply as *motel* without any other information. For motel accommodations you will have to use a phone book or write to the information source.

Restaurants are listed as, restaurant without a name.

If every bit and piece of information in my files was listed in this *Guide,* it would be more than 700 pages long and weigh over 1¾ lb. (79 kg.). Thus a bit of research before you depart will allow you to follow the *Less is More* rule!

Of course you could be a *wanderlust* cyclotourist and let your front wheel lead you to wherever!

Dip Your Wheel & Begin Your Trek!

Route Segments			
Route Segment	Mi.	Km.	Page
Niagara Falls/Buffalo to Tonawanda	11	18	48
Tonawanda to Albion	45	74	60
Albion to Fairport	47	76	70
Fairport to Seneca Falls	53	86	88
Seneca Falls to Fayetteville Lake Oneida North Lake Oneida South	54 [45] [33]	87 [73] [53]	112
Fayetteville to Utica	47	76	132
Utica to Fort Plain	42	67	146
Fort Plain to Albany	69	111	157
Total Main Erie Canal Route	368	592	
Top O' The Finger Lakes Route	86	138	102
Oswego Canal Route	32	52	126
Albany to Whitehall Loop: Ft. Edward to Lake George	67 [55]	108 [88]	174
Whitehall to Westport	55	89	186
Westport to Plattsburgh	48	77	192
Plattsburgh to Saint-Jean-Sur-Richelieu	51	82	198
Saint-Jean-Sur-Richelieu to Montréal	36	58	204
Vermont - Lake Champlain	156	252	208
Tortal Champlain Canal Route	413	665	
Albany to Rhinebeck	60	96	218
Rhinebeck to Bear Mt.	53	85	226
Bear Mt. to New York City, Manhattan	51	82	234
Geo. Washington Bridge to Bear Mt.	34	55	242
Bear Mt. to Kingston	51	82	245
Kingston to Albany	58	93	249
Total Hudson River Routes	307	494	
Distances in [ ] are not included in totals.			

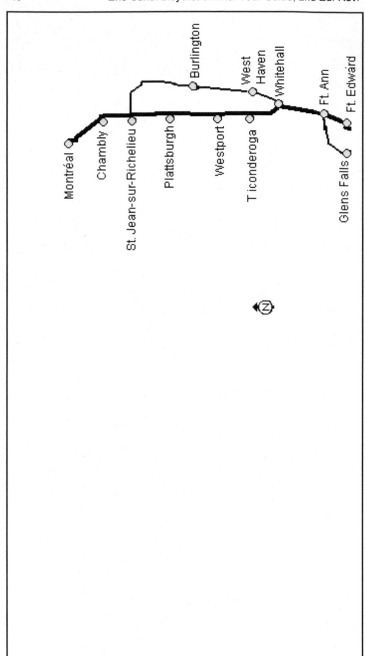

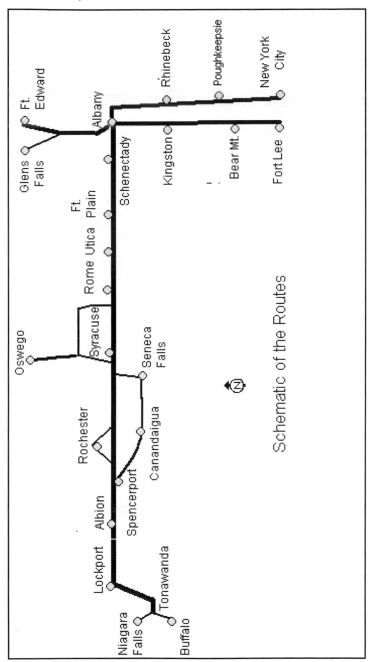

Schematic of the Routes

Buffalo to Tonawanda
Niagara River Route

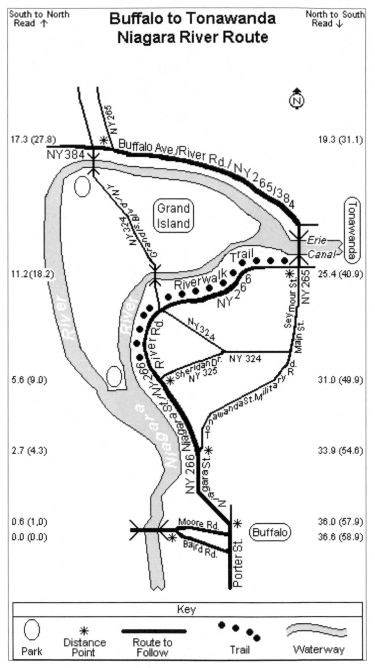

South to North Read ↑

North to South Read ↓

17.3 (27.8)   19.3 (31.1)

11.2 (18.2)   25.4 (40.9)

5.6 (9.0)   31.0 (49.9)

2.7 (4.3)   33.9 (54.6)

0.6 (1.0)   36.0 (57.9)

0.0 (0.0)   36.6 (58.9)

Grand Island

Tonawanda

Erie Canal

Trail

Riverwalk

Buffalo Ave./River Rd./NY 265/384

NY 384

NY 265

Grand's Blvd./NY

NY 324/NY

River Rd.

NY 266

Niagara St./NY 266

NY 266 Niagara St.

Niagara St.

NY 324

Sheridan Dr.

NY 325

NY 26 6

Seymour St.

NY 265

Main St.

Sherry Rd.

Tonawanda St. Military

Moore Rd.

Baird Rd.

Porter St.

Buffalo

Niagara River

River

Key

| Park | Distance Point | Route to Follow | Trail | Waterway |

NIAGARA FRONTIER

At the western edge of the Erie Canal, Tonawanda Creek opens on to the Niagara River allowing boats to traverse the Great Lakes and the industrial heartland of North America.

It is here, on the *Niagara Frontier,* where we start this 900 mile (1450 kilometer) cyclotour. It is here that in 1824, Governor Clinton poured water from the Hudson River, and by extension the Atlantic Ocean, into the swirling waters of the Niagara River and the Great Lakes.

You never heard of Tonawanda? Ah! You have heard of its more famous neighboring municipalities, Buffalo and Niagara Falls. Tonawanda is equidistant from its neighbors. We begin in Niagara Falls and Buffalo because you will most likely arrive in these major cities to begin your cyclotour. Public transportation—trains, planes, and intercity buses—all have terminals in Niagara Falls and Buffalo.

Buffalo, NY & Fort Erie, ON

Info.: Erie County and Buffalo CVB, 617 Main St., Buffalo NY 14203, 800 283-3250, www.buffalocvb.com

Area code: 716. Zip code: various.

Fort Erie, Ontario is across the Niagara River from Buffalo. It is a pleasant city with a great 18th century Fort. Period costumes and demonstrations of 18th and 19th century military life are regularly enacted at the Fort.

Fort Erie Tourism, 200 Jarvis St., Fort Erie ON L2A 2S6; 905 871-8525.

Cycling and Hiking Info.: Bicycle Maps: *Bicycle Route Guide: Buffalo/Niagara Falls Area* available from the Greater Buffalo CVB. *Bicycle & Exercise Paths, Town of Amherst.* Town Clerk, Town Hall, 5583 Main St., Williamsville NY 14221, 631-7045.

Bicycle Shops and Camping Stores: There are numerous bicycle and camping equipment stores in this area. Most are in the suburbs. Bike shop and camping store in downtown Buffalo near the Hostel.

Bicycle Clubs: www.bluemoon.net/~skibby has the most complete listing of this area's bicycling activities. Big Wheels Bicycle Club, 22 Amber St., Buffalo 14420; Buffalo & Erie County Bicycling Club, 524 Vine Lane, Amherst 14228; Niagara Frontier Bicycle Club, PO Box 211, Amherst 14426, 632-2820, www.nfbc.com, Western NY Recumbent Riders, www. bluemoon.net/~padelbra/the_recumbenteers.htm; Western NY Mt. Bike Assoc., www.wnymba.org.

Hiking: Foothill Trail Club, 100 Ayer Rd., Williamsville 14221; Finger Lakes Trail Conference (FLTC), PO Box 18048, Rochester 14618. The FLTC is an extensive network (800 mi., 1290 km.) of trails transversing New York State from the Pennsylvania border & Buffalo to the Catskill Mountains.

Facilities: All. Retail stores and banks abound in and around Buffalo. General shopping is primarily in suburban shopping malls. Several hospitals.

Attractions: Bicycling: You will want to take a trip to The Burgwardt Bicycle Museum, 3943 N. Buffalo Rd. (Rtes. 240/277), Orchard Park 14127, 662-3853. The Museum is 11 mi (18 km) South of the Buffalo-Depew Amtrak Station. A *Metro* bus does go to Orchard Park.

Riverwalk Park and Bikeway extending from downtown Buffalo to Tonawanda & the Canal.

Hikers and bikers going from Downtown Buffalo to the Canal (Tonawanda) and Niagara Falls should use the Riverside Trail along the Niagara River.

Sports: Baseball, harness racing, hockey, lacrosse, & football.

Culture: Albright-Knox Art Gallery has a great collection of modern paintings; Science Museum & Planetarium; Buffalo Symphony; Zoo; Botanical Gardens; Theodore Roosevelt Inaugural National Historic Site, Allentown National Historic District.

The world's only Kazoo factory is in East Aurora, 6 mi (10 km) from The Burgwardt Bicycle Museum in Orchard Park. A local *Metro* bus goes to East Aurora.

Architecture: Frank Lloyd Wright homes (5); Frederick Law Olmstead parks; art deco buildings; & grain elevators.

Universities and colleges.

Waterfront: Naval and Servicemen's Park has a military museum, submarine, destroyer and cruiser on exhibit. The waterfront's huge grain elevators are reminders of the City's historic role as a grain milling center. An archeological dig near the Naval Park has uncovered the original Erie Canal *commercial dock*.

Lodging: Erie Co. & Buffalo CVB, 800 BUFFALO.

Hostel: Hostelling International/AYH, 667 Main St., Buffalo, 14203, 852-5222.

Chain and locally owned motels. The least expensive motels are closest to the airport. There are no campgrounds in Buffalo.

B&Bs: Western New York Bed & Breakfast Association, PO Box 1006, Buffalo 14213; Beau Fleuve B&B Inn, 242 Linwood Ave., Buffalo 14209, 882-6116; Betty's, 398 Jersey St., Buffalo 14213, 881-0700; Bryant House, 236 Bryant St., Buffalo 14222, 885-1540; E.B.'s B&B, 781 Richmond Ave., Buffalo 14222, 882-1428.

Public Transportation:
BUS: Intercity Buses stop at the Transportation Center in Downtown Buffalo. Greyhound: 855-7531. Trailways: 852-1750.

An extensive system of local public bus and light rail transit is provided by the Niagara Frontier Transportation Authority, Transportation Center, Ellicott & N. Division Sts, Buffalo 14203, 716 855-7211. Ask for the *System* and the *Metro Self Guided Tours* maps. *Metro* buses go to Tonawanda, Niagara Falls, Orchard Park and East Aurora. Bikes on buses may be a problem!

RAILROAD Baggage service on Amtrak Trains is a necessity for cyclotourists (unless you have a folding bike). Not all trains or all stations (throughout the Amtrak system) have baggage car service. On the Niagara Frontier only the Buffalo-Depew Amtrak Station has baggage service, 683-8440. (The Buffalo-Exchange St. downtown station, 856-2075 does NOT have baggage service.) After assembling your bicycle & claiming other baggage ask someone how to get to Dick Rd. It's much easier to ask someone than for me to write the directions. Its only 2 short blocks away! Directions to the Canal and Niagara Falls are provided below. Bike shop in Depew.

Before you leave Depew you might want to take advantage of your location and visit The Burgwardt Bicycle Museum, 3943 N. Buffalo Rd. (Rtes. 240/277), Orchard Park 14127, 716 662-3853. The Museum is 11 mi. (18 km.) South of the Buffalo Depew Amtrak station. From Depew take Rt. 78 South—>Rt. 187 South—>Rt. 20A West—>Rt. 277 in Orchard Park. The world's only kazoo factory is in East Aurora (B&B here too) which is on Rt. 20A East of Rt. 187.

Route Note

A crucial decision has to be made at this point on your tour: To visit Niagara Falls or Buffalo before beginning your Canal cyclotour/hike. Directions are provided for these *side trips* as well as going directly to Tonawanda and the Canal.

Directions from the Buffalo airport and the Buffalo-Depew Amtrak station to the Canal and Niagara Falls are provided below.

S to N	**Buffalo Depew Amtrak & Airport**	N to S
mi. (km.) Read↓	**Direct to Canal**	mi. (km.) Read↑

00.0 (00.0)   Buffalo-Depew Amtrak Station   12.1 (19.5)
Ride North on Dick Rd.
Mileage is from the Amtrak station.
The Buffalo-Depew Amtrak Station, 683-8440, is directly

South of the Airport. Thus we start at the Amtrak Station and go to the Airport from where we will trek to Tonawanda, the Canal, and Niagara Falls.

1.0 (1.6)   Airport @ Rt. 33/Genesee St.   11.1 (17.8)
Turn West on to Rt. 33/Genesee St.
Dick Rd. is .8 mi (1.2 km) from the Airport entrance.

1.8 (2.9)   Dick Rd. @ Rt. 33   10.3 (16.6)
Turn North on to Dick Rd.
Amtrak & air travelers join here. Mileage is from the Amtrak Station.

3.2 (5.2)   Wehle Rd. @ Dick Rd./Cayuga St.   8.9 (14.3)
Dick Rd. changes its name to Cayuga St. after it crosses Wehle Rd. Continue riding North on Cayuga St.

4.0 (6.4)   Rt. 5/Main St. @ Cayuga St.   8.1 (13.0)
Turn West on to Rt. 5.
Turning East here brings you into Williamson where there are bike shops & malls.

4.5 (7.2)   Rt. 277/N. Union St. @ Rt. 5   7.6 (12.2)
Turn North on to Rt. 277/Union St. which changes its name to N. Forest Rd. but the Rt. 277 signs are clear.

5.9 (9.5)   Rt. 324/Sheridan Rd. @ Rt. 277   6.2 (10.0)
Turn West on to Rt. 324/Sheridan Rd.

8.8 (14.2)   Rt. 62/Niagara Falls Blvd. @ Rt. 324   3.3 (5.3)
Continue riding on Rt. 324/Sheridan Dr. one more block to Eggert Rd. to go to the beginning of the Canal and the Niagara River. If you are planning to go to Niagara Falls this is a more pleasant route along the Niagara River.
Here is a more direct but busy way to go to the Falls: Turn North on to Rt. 62 and ride to the Falls! Its a 20 mi (32 km) ride from this point along busy Niagara Falls Blvd./Rt. 62.   Niagara Falls Blvd./Rt. 62 crosses the Canal 3.5 mi (5.6 km) north of Sheridan Rd.

8.8 (14.2)   Eggert Rd. @ Rt. 324   3.3 (5.3)
Turn Northwest on to Eggert Rd.

10.7 (17.2)   Rt. 425 @ Eggert Rd.   1.4 (2.3)
Eggert Rd. melds into Rt. 425.   Continue riding Northwest on Rt. 425 under the highway overpass to Colvin St.

11.0 (17.7)   Colvin Blvd. @ Rt. 425   1.1 (1.6)
Turn West on to Colvin Blvd. Ride 1 block to Young St.

The Mighty Falls

11.1 ((17.9)   Young St. @ Colvin Blvd.   1.0 (1.6)
Turn Northwest on to Young St.

11.9 (19.1)   Rt. 356 (State St.) @ with Young St.   .2 (.3)
Almost there! Turn on to Rt. 265 and at the bridge you
will see an entrance to the the bicycle path which goes
under the bridge and along the south shore of the Canal.
Enter the bike path! Ride West, towards the Niagara
River.

If you want to go to Niagara Falls from this point, specific
directions are given on page 36.

12.1 (19.5)   Niagara River @ Erie Canal   0.0 (0.0)
Whew! We begin from this point!

S to N	**Canal Direct to Buffalo Airport &**	N to S
mi. (km.) Read↓	**Buffalo-Depew Amtrak**	mi. (km.) Read↑

Niagara Falls

Info,: There are two Niagara Falls. One in Ontario, Canada and
one in New York State, USA.
Area Codes: Niagara Falls, Canada: 905.
Niagara Falls, USA: 716.
Zip & postal codes vary.
Niagara Falls CVB, 4673 Ontario Ave., Niagara Falls ON L2E
3R1, 905 356-6601.
Niagara Region Tourist Council, 2201 St. David's Rd., PO Box
1042, Thorold ON L2V 4T7, 905 984-3626/416 641-8788.
The Niagara Parks Commission, PO Box 150, Niagara Falls ON
L2E 6T2, 905 356-2241.

Niagara County Tourism, 139 Niagara St., Lockport NY 14094,
     800 338-7890/716 439-7300, www.niagara-usa.com
Niagara Reservation State Park, PO Box 1132, Niagara Falls, NY
     14303, 716 278-1770. The NY *Falls* park!
Cycling/Hiking Info.: Bike shops and camping/hiking equipment
     stores are on both sides of the border. See phone book.
Niagara Frontier Bicycle Club, P. O Box 211, Amherst NY 14426,
     716 283-4006.
Foothills Trail Club, 6709 Woodside Pl., Niagara Falls, NY 14304;
     Finger Lakes Trail Conference, PO Box 18048, Rochester,
     NY 14618.
Services: All. Hospital.
Attractions: Niagara Falls, both USA and Canada, are tourist
     cities with a wide variety of attractions. The opportunities for
     tourism are too numerous for me to list here. Check the
     freebee newspapers.   A discount coupons for many
     attractions are available at the official government tourist
     information kiosks.   Be very careful not to be charged for
     booking tourist attractions or accommodations at non-
     government official tourist information stores.
Special Side Trip: Shaw Festival in Niagara on the Lake, ON.
     This trip is entirely on the smooth well maintained Niagara
     Recreationway which parallels (separate for the first 11 mi.
     (18 km.)) the Niagara Parkway. You will be riding on top of
     the Niagara Escarpment until one mile (1.6 km.) before
     Niagara on the Lake. Simply take the Niagara Recreationway
     (maps available at any tourist information booth in Niagara
     Falls, ON) to its northern terminus which is Niagara on the
     Lake. CofC, 143 King St., PO Box 1043, Niagara on the Lake
     ON L0S 1J0, 905 468-4263. Shaw Festival, PO Box 774,
     Niagara on the Lake ON L0S 1J0, 905 468-4263.
Lodging: This is a major tourist destination, book lodging at least
     one day in advance. Both sides of the Falls have numerous
     motels and hotels at all price ranges.The further you are from
     the Falls, the lower the price.
Hostel: Niagara Falls Hostel, 4699 Zimmerman Ave., Niagara
     Falls ON L2E 3M7, 905-357-0770.
B&Bs: NY: Manchester House, 653 Main St., Niagara Falls NY
     14301, 285-5717; Park Place, 740 Park Place, Niagara Falls
     NY 14301, 282-4626; Rainbow House B&B, 423 Rainbow
     Blvd. S., Niagara Falls NY 14303, 800 724-3536/282-1135.
     ON: B&Bs in Niagara Falls, Canada are too numerous to list!
     Write to the CVB for a complete list.
There are several private campgrounds on both sides of the Falls.
     The closest is Niagara Falls KOA, 2570 Grand Island Blvd.,
     Grand Island NY 14072, 800 8 642-4272/716 773-7583.

Public Transportation
Niagara Falls, **NY**
BUS Intercity, city & suburban buses stop at the International Transportation Center in downtown Niagara Falls, NY. Usually an intercity bus from the US going to Toronto will also stop in Niagara Falls, ON.

The local bus system is operated by the Niagara Frontier Transportation Authority, International Transportation Center, 4th & Niagara Streets, Niagara Falls, NY 14303, 285-9119. Ask for a *System Map* & for information about *Bikes on Buses.*

Tour buses also operate from the Transportation Center.

Niagara Falls, NY Bus Station to the Falls: It's easier for you to simply follow the signs to the *Falls* or ask someone for directions to the *Falls* than for me to attempt to give you directions. Alternatively simply follow the roaring sound of the *Falls.*

RAILROAD Amtrak baggage service, a necessity for cyclotourists, is not available at the Niagara Falls, NY Amtrak station. A tragedy! The nearest station with baggage car service is at the Buffalo-Depew station 28 mi. (45 km.) Southeast of from the Rainbow Bridge. Directions from the Buffalo-Depew Station to the Canal and Niagara Falls are given in the Buffalo section.

Write Amtrak to correct this situation (President, Amtrak, 60 Massachusetts Ave. NE, Washington, DC 20202). However you can take a train from Niagara Falls, NY to Toronto (direct); Vancouver, Chicago, Detroit (connecting trains are meet in Aldershot, ON); New York City or Boston.

Niagara Falls, **ON**
BUS: Intercity buses from Canada and the US stop 1 block from the Whirlpool Bridge (within .5 mi (.8 km) of the *Falls*) at the Bus Station. The VIA & GO rail station is across the street.

Most tourists & residents use the *Niagara Parks People Mover* to make their way around Niagara Falls, ON. Among other things, your bike will be safely esconded in you room.

RAILROAD: VIA Rail, 800 561-9181. The station is opposite the Bus station 1 block (.5 mi, .8 km) from the Casino. VIA Rail-Amtrak trains stop in Niagara Falls, ON. Trains to Toronto, Windsor, and Sudbury, ON; Vancouver, BC; Detroit, MI & Chicago, IL make connections in Aldershot, ON.

If you are in Niagara Falls and reading this, remember that this tour *reality* begins and ends at the Canal! All directions are given from points on the Canal. You are now NORTH of the Canal.

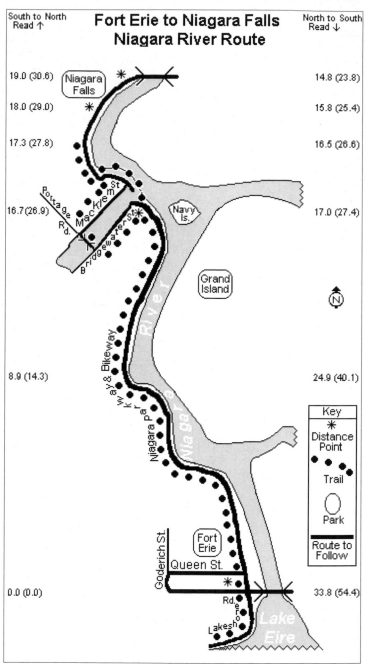

Fort Erie to Niagara Falls
Niagara River Route

South to North
Read ↑

North to South
Read ↓

19.0 (30.6)   Niagara Falls   14.8 (23.8)

18.0 (29.0)   15.8 (25.4)

17.3 (27.8)   16.5 (26.6)

Portage Rd.   MacKle   m   St

16.7 (26.9)   Navy Is.   17.0 (27.4)

Bridgewater St.

Grand Island

8.9 (14.3)   Niagara parkway & Bikeway   24.9 (40.1)

Niagara River

Key
✳ Distance Point
•••• Trail
◯ Park
▬ Route to Follow

Goderich St.   Fort Erie

Queen St.

0.0 (0.0)   Rd   eo   33.8 (54.4)

Lakesh   Lake Eire

S to N	**Erie Canal to**	N to S
mi. (km.) Read↓	**Niagara Falls**	mi. (km.) Read↑

00.0 (00.0)   The Canal @ NY 384   11.8 (19.0)
Cross the Canal via the Bridge. At the Southeast pier of
the Bridge is the entrance to the Canal Towpath. Ride
on to the Towpath. Turn West, go .25 mi. (.4 km.) to the
intersection of the Niagara River and the Canal. We
begin our journey from that point.

4.9 (7.9)   Williams St. @ NY 384/BR 5   6.9 (11.1)
Cyclotourists from Niagara Falls Airport join us here.
NY 384 changes its name to River Rd.
To confuse bicyclists, NY 384 has the BR 5 designation
as well as NY 62/Niagara Falls Blvd. which is north of
this point. Just follow the regular road route numbers!

10.8 (17.4)   Buffalo St. @ NY 384   1.0 (1.6)
Rainbow Blvd./NY 384 becomes Buffalo Ave.

11.4 (18.3)   Rainbow Blvd. @ NY 384/1st St.   .4 (.6)
NY 384 melds Changes its name to Rainbow Blvd. and
becomes a four lane street.

11.7 (18.8)   NY 384/1st St. @ Niagara St.   .1 (.1)
Turn South on to 1st St.

11.8 (19.0)   NY 104/62/384/BR 5   0.0 (0.0)
               @ Rainbow Bridge
Ride straight on to Niagara St./NY 384

Bike Route 5

This intersection is the western most point of New York State Bike
Route 5. A New York State Bike Route is maintained by the
State Department of Transportation rather than a County or
Municipality. Bike Route highways are usually major two and
four lane roads with at least a 8 ft. (2.5 m.) separately striped
paved shoulder and *Bike Route* signs at regular intervals.

Bike Route 5 (BR 5) is the main East-West improved State
highway for bicycles. It parallels or is the closest major road
to the Canal for much of its length. Bike Route 5 is not a
separate numbered State bikeway, instead it is a part of
several different numbered State highways.

This *Route Guide* will designate roadways by their usual highway
route number/names. We will use the BR (Bike Route)
designation only where applicable.

At this point, BR 5 is St. NY 62/Niagara Falls Blvd. which goes to
the Niagara Falls Airport and eventually crosses the Canal in

the Town of Tonawanda. We will be using a more scenic road to get you to the beginning of the Canal in Tonawanda.

11.8 (19.0)   Rainbow Bridge   0.0 (0.0)
Cross over the Bridge and see the *Falls* from the Canadian side. Customs and Immigration will simply ask you a few questions. However, if you have a list of your belongings (use the **Equipment Lists**).have the Customs officer stamp the list. It will make your return to the US/Canada less of a hassle if problems arise.

S to N	**Niagara Falls to**	N to S
mi (km) Read↓	**Canal**	mi, (km.) Read↑

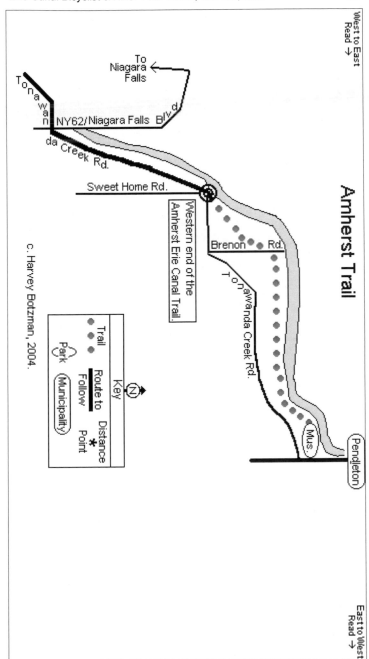

West to East Read →

To Niagara Falls

Tonawanda Creek Rd.

NY62/Niagara Falls Blvd.

Sweet Home Rd.

Western end of the Amherst Erie Canal Trail

Brenon Rd.

Tonawanda Creek Rd.

Amherst Trail

Mus.

Pendleton

c. Harvey Botzman, 2004.

Key

N

Trail

Park

Route to Follow

Municipality

Distance Point

★

East to West Read →

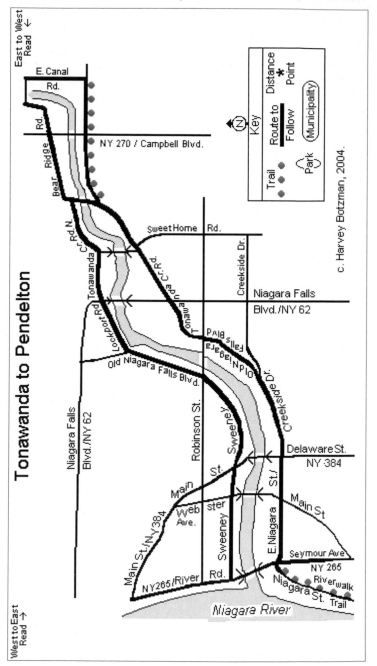

WESTERN NEW YORK

W to E	Niagara River to	E to W
mi. (km.) Read↓	Albion	mi. (km.) Read↑

Tonawanda

Info.: On the South shore of Tonawanda Creek is the Tonawanda Town & Village, Erie County. On the North shore of Tonawanda Creek is North Tonawanda Village, Niagara County. In rural areas *creek* is pronounced *crik*! Area Code: 716. Zip code: various.
Tonawandas CofC, 15 Webster St., N. Tonawanda NY 14120, 692-5120, www.the-tonawandas.com; Kenmore-Tonawanda CofC, 3411 Delaware Ave., Kenmore NY 14217, 874-1202, www.ken-ton.org
Cycling/Hiking Info.: Bike shop.
Lodging: Motels (on NY 62). B&B: Grand Canal, 5217 Tonawanda Creek Rd. N. Tonawanda 14120, 694-6119.
Public Transportation: Local bus only, Niagara Frontier Trans. Auth., Buffalo, 285-9319.

0.0 (0.0)   Niagara River @ Canal Tow Path   45.6 (73.4)
Travel East on the Canal Tow Path (CPT)
Here we begin!
You'll have to go a bit south along the River to get a wheel dipping picture! You've probably toured Niagara Falls and are ready to ride into the countryside.

.2 (.4)   Young St./NY 384 @ Delaware St.   45.4 (73.1)
Exit tow path and cross Ellicott Creek on the NY 384 Bridge. This is the 2nd Bridge over the Creek within a very very short distance.

.5 (.8)   Niagara St. @ Delaware St./NY 384   45.1 (72.6)
Turn East on to Niagara St.

3.2 (5.2)   Ellicott Creek Park @ Niagara St.   42.4 (68.2)
Continue traveling on Niagara St.

4.0 (6.4)   Old Niagara Blvd. @ Niagara St.   41.6 (66.9)
Simply a street name change. It's really annoying not to say confusing when streets change their name as they go over municipal borders.

4.8 (7.7)   Tonawanda Cr. Rd.   40.8 (65.7)
@ Old Niagara Blvd.

At the cemetery Old Niagara Blvd. changes its name once again to Tonawanda Creek Rd.   It also makes a right turn! Keep riding 'round the turn.

5.0 (8.0)   NY 62 @ Tonawanda Creek Rd.   40.3 (65.3)
Cross NY 62/Niagara Falls Blvd.   Continue riding on Tonawanda Creek Rd.
Niagara Falls Airport travelers exit/enter the *Main Canal Route* here. To go to the Airport go Northwest on Rt. 62 for approximately 11 mi. (18 km.)

6.5 (10.5)   Sweet Home Rd.   39.1 (62.9)
              @ Tonawanda Cr. Rd.
Entrance to Bike Path. A beautiful paved path along the Canal in the Town of Amherst.

Amherst
Info.: Amherst CofC, 716 632-6905.
Area Code: 716. Zip code: 14228.
Cycling & Hiking Info.: *Town of Amherst Bike and Exercise Paths Map,* available from the Town of Amherst, Recreation Dept., Town Hall, 631 7135. Bike shop, camping supply store.
Lodging: Motels.   Camping: Amherst Marine Center, 1900 Campbell Rd. @ Erie Canal Tow Path, 691-6707 (showers and possible emergency camping).
Attractions: The Amherst Mus., 3755 Tonawanda Creek Rd., E. Amherst, 689-1440, is at the end of the bike path. Ten 19th century buildings on 35 acres adjacent to the tow path.   Fine lunch point and a friendly group of curators and docents.   Amherst Marine Ctr., Campbell Rd. @ Canal Tow Path rents canal cruiser/campers. The State University at Buffalo is in Amherst.

12.0 (19.3)   New Rd. @ Bike Path   33.6 (54.1)
Turn North on to New Rd.
If you want to visit the Amherst Mus., .25 mi. (.4 km.) turn West on Tonawanda Creek Rd.

12.2 (19.7)   Pendleton Hamlet   33.4 (53.8)
              @ New Rd./E. Canal Rd.
Continue riding North on New Rd. which changes its name to Congress St. and then East Canal Rd.
Pendleton Hamlet: Convenience type grocery store.
                         Note
During 2004 the route from Pendleton to Lockport is being reconstructed by the Canal Corp.

14.8 (23.8)   Fiegel St.   30.8 (49.6)
                @ E. Canal Rd./Congress St.
If you found the hill on E. Canal Rd. a bit too much for
you, cross the Canal here & ride North on Bear Ridge
Rd.! Bear Ridge Rd. will take you directly North into
Lockport..

15.7 (25.3)   Robinson Rd. @ E. Canal Rd.   29.9 (48.1)
Turn West, cross the Canal to Bear Ridge Rd. or
continue traveling North on E. Canal Rd. to go to
Lockport.

15.8 (25.4)   Bear Ridge Rd. @ Robinson Rd.   29.8 (48.0)
Turn North on to Bear Ridge Rd.

17.4 (28.0)   Summit St. @ Bear Ridge Rd.   28.2 (45.4)
Turn East, cross the Canal. You are now in Lockport.

17.5 (28.2)   State Rd. @ Summit St.   28.1 (45.2)
Turn North on to State Rd.

18.5 (29.8)   South Transit Rd./NY 78   27.1 (43.6)
                @ State Rd.
Turn East on to South Transit Rd. to reach West Ave.

18.6 (30.0)   West Ave./Walnut St.   27.0 (43.5)
                @ S. Transit Rd.
Cross the Bridge,
This is the meeting place of the Canal and NY Rtes.
31/93/78.
    Look on the West side of Lock area for the access
ramp to the tow path. It will be a steep *hill* going from the
street level all the way to the bottom of the Lock area
with a level area between Locks 34 & 35 near the power
house Canal Museum.
    This *hill* is the result of glaciers!   The Niagara
Escarpment must be climbed. Lockport was chosen as
the site for these Locks and the 40 ft. (12 m.) difference
in elevation due to the slightly softer sandstone and other
sedimentary layers underlying the Escarpment granite. If
you look carefully at the blocks which form the Locks you
will see small imbedded coral fossils!
    Yes, this is the beginning of the Canal Tow Path (**CTP**)
heritage trail and it is a great ride down the lock path and
all the way to Palmyra!   But don't forget to visit the
museum and locks.
    You are between Locks 34 & 35. The Lock area entry
way and *hill* is here!   Half a mile (.8 km.) West on
Niagara St. is the Historical Society.

Lockport

Info.: Eastern Niagara CofC, 41 Main St., Lockport NY 14094, 716 433-3828.

Area code: 716. Zip code: 14094.

Bicycle Info.: Bike Shop, in Plaza above Lock 35.

Services: All. Hospital.

Canal Site: Locks 34 & 35 as well as the original Erie Canal flight of five (5) locks. Canal Museum at between Locks in the old power house. Self guided walking tour of the Lock area with permanent descriptive placards. Excursion Boat: Lockport Locks & Canal Tours, PO Box 1197, Lockport, 693-3260.

Lodging: Motels, Lockport Inn, very bicycle friendly. B&Bs: Hambleton House, 130 Pine St., 439-9507; Maplehurst, 4427 Ridge Rd., 434-3502. National Centennial House, 111 Ontario St., 434-8193.

Other attractions: Historic District.

19.3 (31.0)   Upson Park @ Clinton St./NY 78   26.3 (42.3)
Upson Park is at the base of the Lock area.

E to W Traveler Route Note

Westbound travelers who want to avoid a relatively steep climb up the Niagara Escarpment in the lock area. can exit into Upson Park. Travel East to the first bridge crossing the Canal (Adams St. bridge) and cross to the South side of the Canal. A moderately sloped paved path paralleling the Canal will bring you to the top of the Lock area in downtown Lockport.

Or simply follow the City streets paralleling the North side of the Canal to the Lock area and downtown Lockport.

25.5 (41.0)   Hartland Rd. @ Canal Tow Path   20.1 (32.2)
Continue traveling on the CTP.

An alternate road route is provided below for folks who want a bit of a change. The distance between Gasport & Middleport using either the CTP or roads is the same.

Gasport

Services & Facilities: Laundry, restaurants.

Lodging: B&B: Country Cottage, 7745 Rochester Rd. (Rt. 31), Gasport NY 14067, 716 772-3351.

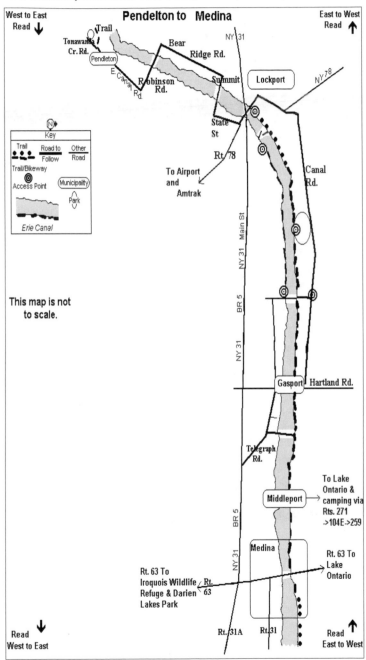

| W to E | **Alternative Road Route** | E to W |
| mi. (km.) Read↓ | **Gasport to Middleport** | mi. (km.) Read↑ |

25.6 (41.1)   Telegraph Rd. @ Hartland Rd.   20.0 (32.2)
Turn East on to Telegraph Rd.

26.5 (42.6)   Bolton Rd. @ Canal   19.1 (30.7)
Continue traveling on Telegraph Rd.

27.0 (43.5)   Root Rd. @ Canal   18.6 (29.9)
Cross the Canal on the Holt Rd. Bridge. You will be able
to pick up the stone dust **Canal Tow Path** on the North
side of the Canal. If you really don't like stone dust,
continue riding on Telegraph road. It junctions with NY
31/ BR 5 in 1.6 mi. (2.5 km.).
E to W travelers: This alternate road route is provided for
folks who want a bit of a change. The distance between
Middleport and Gasport using either the CTP or roads is
the same.

| W to E | **Alternative Road Route** | E to W |
| mi. (km.) Read↓ | **Gasport to Middleport** | mi. (km.) Read↑ |

| W to E | **Main Erie Canal Tow Path Route** | E to W |
| mi. (km.) Read↓ | **Middleport to Albion** | mi. (km.) Read↑ |

30.9 (49.7)   Stone Rd./NY 271   14.7 (23.7)
@ Canal Tow Path

Middleport

Services: Restaurants.
Lodging: Canal Country Inn, 4021 Peet St., Middleport
14105, 716 735-7572. Camping: Wildwood Lake Cpgd., 3
mi. (5 km.) North at 2711 County Line Rd., Medina 14103,
716 735-3310; Golden Hill State Park, 9691 Lower Lake
Rd., Barker 14012, 716 795-3885, 9 mi. (14 km.) North
(end of County Line Rd.) on Lake Ontario with a great
historic lighthouse complex).

31.6 (50.85) County Line Rd.   14.0 (22.5)
@ Canal Tow Path
Border Crossing. Have visa's ready!
Info.: Niagara County, Orleans County, Genesee
County. Although Genesee County is not directly on the
Erie Canal Route, several side trips from our route go to
destinations southward into Genesee County.

35.1 (56.5)   Gravel Rd./NY 63   20.5 (16.9)
               @ Canal Tow Path
               Continue traveling on the CTP.

Medina

Info.: Medina Area CofC, 433 Main St., Medina NY 14103, 585 798-4287.
Area code: 585. Zip code: 14103.
Services: All. Hospital. Of particular note, Cora's Bakery and the Cookie Store.
Lodging: Motels. Very small legal camping area (free at the Canal.
Attractions: Mule drawn canal packet boats: Apple Grove Inn (also a motel & dinner theatre), Rt. 31E, 798-2323; Canal front park. Private hunting preserve.
Side Trips: 5 mi (8 km) directly South on Rt. 63 is Iroquois National Wildlife Refuge, PO Box 517, Casey Rd., Alabama 14003, 607 948-5445.
Darien Lake Theme Park & Cpgd., 9993 Alleghany Rd., Darien Center 14040, 599-4644. Rock concerts are held at the Theme Park during the summer. Darien Center is 18.6 mi. (30 km.) directly South on Rt. 63. Darien Lakes St. Pk. (camping), Harlow Rd., Darien Center 14040, 547-9242.

39.6 (69.8)   Knowlesville Rd.   6.0 (9.7)
               @ Canal Tow Path (CTP)
               Continue traveling on the CTP, it will take you directly into Albion.
               If the Tow Path is too rough for you, exit the tow path and ride North on Knowlesville Rd. The next two entries provide a road route to Albion which is basically parallel to the CTP.

40.2 (64.7)   Eagle Harbor-Knowlesville Rd.   5.4 (8.7)
               @ Knowlesville Rd.
               Turn East on to Eagle Harbor Rd.

45.3 (72.9)   Main St./NY 98 @ Canal Tow Path   .3 (.5)
               @ West State St./Albion-Eagle Harbor Rd.
               Turn South on to NY 98/Main St.
               As you enter Albion, Albion-Eagle Harbor Rd. changes its name to West State St.

Route Notes

E to W: The Canal Tow Path is stone dust from Albion to Lockport. An alternative road route between Albion and

Medina is provided in the two entries immediately above this note. The CTP can be used. The mileage is the same either way you travel. Hikers stay on the Tow Path.

Albion

Info.: Greater Albion CofC, 101 North Main St., Albion NY 14411, 585 589-7727.

Area code: 585. Zip code: 14411.

Bike Info.: No bike shop. Stop into the CofC and the County Supervisor's Office (Court House) and tell them you're bike touring along the Canal. Very bike & hiking supportive County.

Services: All. County Clerk (fishing licenses).

Lodging: Motel. B&B: Friendship Manor, 349 South Main St., 589-7973; Sweet Apple Guest Home, 1745 Oak Orchard Rd., 682-3311.

   Waterport [6 mi. (9.5 km.) North of Albion.],   Area code: 716. Zip code: 14571. B&Bs: Cedar Valley, 13893 Park Ave., 682-3253; Leonard's Landing, Archbald Rd., 682-4294; Lizzie's Lodge, 14339 NY 18 (9 mi (14.5 km North), 682-3316. Camping: Lakeside Beach St. Pk., NY 18 @ NY 279, 682-4888, 9.5 mi. (15 km.) North on Lake Ontario.

Attractions: Courthouse Square Hist. Dist. Cobblestone Society Mus., NY 98 @ 104, Childs, NY (3 mi., 5 km. North), 589-9013.

45.6 (73.4)   NY 31 @ NY 98/Main St.   00.0 (00.0)
Use the **Canal Tow Path** to continue travelling East or West.

If the **Tow Path** is too rough for you or you need a change, turn on to NY 31/BR 5.

W to E	**Albion to**	E to W
mi. (km.) Read↓	**Niagara River**	mi. (km.) Read↑

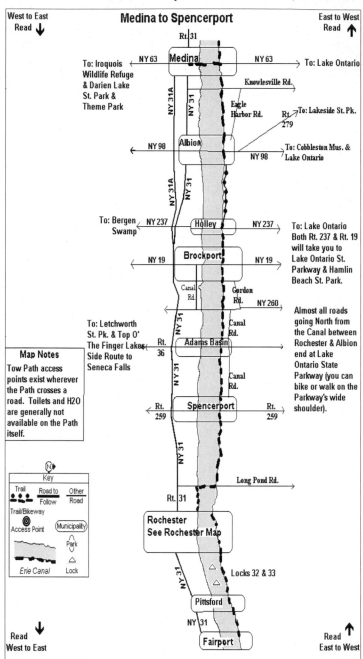

Medina to Spencerport

West to East
Read ↓

East to West
Read ↑

Rt. 31

To: Iroquois
Wildlife Refuge
& Darien Lake
St. Park &
Theme Park

NY 63   Medina   NY 63   To: Lake Ontario

Knowlesville Rd.

NY 31A   NY 31

Eagle
Harbor Rd.   Rt.   To: Lakeside St. Pk.
279

NY 98   Albion   To: Cobbleston Mus. &
NY 98   Lake Ontario

NY 31A   NY 31

To: Bergen   NY 237   Holley   NY 237   To: Lake Ontario
Swamp   Both Rt. 237 & Rt. 19
will take you to
Lake Ontario St.
NY 19   Brockport   NY 19   Parkway & Hamlin
Beach St. Park.

Canal   Gordon
Rd.   Rd.

NY 260

Almost all roads
going North from
the Canal between
Rochester & Albion
end at Lake
Ontario State
Parkway (you can
bike or walk on the
Parkway's wide
shoulder).

To: Letchworth
St. Pk. & Top O'
The Finger Lakes   Rt.   Adams Basin   Canal
Side Route to   36   Rd.
Seneca Falls

NY 31

Canal
Rd.

Rt.   Spencerport   Rt.
259   259

NY 31

Map Notes

Tow Path access
points exist wherever
the Path crosses a
road. Toilets and H2O
are generally not
available on the Path
itself.

Long Pond Rd.

Rt. 31

Key

Trail   Road to   Other
Follow   Road

Trail/Bikeway

Access Point   Municipality

Erie Canal   Park

Lock

Rochester
See Rochester Map

NY 31

Locks 32 & 33

Pittsford

NY 31

Read ↓   Read ↑
West to East   East to West

Fairport

GENESEE COUNTRY

Comprising an area twenty five miles on either side of the Genesee River and extending from Lake Ontario to the Pennsylvania border is the rich farm land, forests, rural communities, small cities, and urban area Rochester of the Genesee River Valley. The North-South oriented Finger Lakes begin here.

The Tow Path's level surface belies the hilly contours of the land 15 mi. (24 km.) South of the Canal. North of the Canal the topography smooths out as it encounters the Lake Ontario plain.

This is an ideal section for you to explore the countryside North and South of the Canal Tow Path. Most of the roads which run from West to East and parallel to the Canal traverse rolling hill farm land. These roads usually end at a road which will bring you back to the Canal. You've created your own loop!

Take almost any road going North from the Canal and the very worst thing that can happen is that you'll end up at Lake Ontario!

The Canal itself runs in a slight southwesterly direction from Albion until Rochester. Prior to 1925 an impressive aqueduct transported the Canal over the Genesee River in the heart of Rochester's downtown. The Canal now skirts the City itself. Alas, motor cars now traverse the aqueduct's Canal bed.

One of the more intriguing sights you will see in this section and throughout Western New York are Cobblestone houses, barns and churches. Take a close look at those bridges over the Canal, many lift up!

Explore! Tour!

W to E	Albion to	E to W
mi. (km.) Read↓	**Fairport**	mi. (km.) Read↑

00.0 (00.0)   NY 31/BR 5 @ NY 98   46.1 (74.2)
If you are hiking/biking on the Canal Tow Path, continue
to do so! Want a change? Bike through Albion to Rt. 31/
BR5 and go East to Holley or West to Medina.

Albion

Info.: Greater Albion CofC, 101 North Main St., Albion
NY 14411, 716 589-7727. See last page of the Western
New York chapter for details.

9.2 (14.8)   Rt. 237 @ Canal Tow Path (CTP)   36.9 (59.4)
                  @ Rt. 31/BR 5
Continue traveling on the Canal Tow Path.

Holley

Info.: Area code: 585. Zip code: 14470
Sevices: Convenience store, restaurants.
Attractions: Holley Depot Train Mus., 638-8188.
Side Trip: The Bergen Swamp is a 1900 acre unique
ecological National Historic Landmark. To visit the
Swamp you have to call the caretaker. Caretaker,
Bergen Swamp, 6646 Hessenthaler Rd., Byron 14422,
548-7304. To reach the Swamp travel South on NY 237
to NY 262. Turn East on NY 262 and go to Hessenthaler
Rd. One way distance: 11 mi. (18 km.)

10.5 (16.9)   Border Crossing   34.6 (58.4
Visa's are not necessary! Monroe County, Livingston
County, Orleans County, Genesee County.

13.5 (21.7)   NY 19 @ CTP/NY 31/BR 5   32.6 (52.5)
Continue traveling on the CTP or
Turn South on to NY 19 to go into:

Brockport

Info.: Hilton-Parma CofC, 1266 Hilton-Parma Rd., Hilton
NY 14468. Area code: 585. Zip code: 14420.
Bike Info.: Bike Shop on Main St. Rochester Bicycling
Club, 420-2953 (see Rochester listings).
Services: All. Bus with bike racks to Rochester.
Lodging: Motels. B&Bs: Clarkson Corners, 3734 Lake
Rd., 637-0340; The Portico, 3741 Lake Rd., 637-0220;
Victorian B&B, 320 Main St.; White Farm, 854 White Rd.,
637-0459; Sandy Creek Manor House, 1960 Redman

Rd., Hamlin, NY 14464, 964-7528/. Camping: Hamlin
Beach St. Pk., Hamlin 14464, 964-2462, on Lake Ontario
is 10 mi. (16 km.) North.
Attractions: Canal Lift Bridge, State College.

13.5 (21.7)   NY 19 @ CTP or NY 31/BR 5   32.6 (52.5)
Continue traveling on the Canal Tow Path.
The Tow Path is much nicer than NY 31/BR 5 from here
until Palmyra.
If you do not want to use the stone dust Canal Tow Path
you can use the following rural road route instead of
heavily trafficked NY 31/BR 5.

W to E	**Rural Road Route**	E to W
mi. (km.) Read↓	**Brockport to Spencerport**	mi. (km.) Read↑

13.7 (22.0)   Rt. 19/Main St. @ Canal, South side   33.2 (53.4)
Go into the Brockport Canal Park on the Southeast side
of the Canal.

14.0 (22.5)   Canal Park @ State St./Canal Rd.   32.9 (52.9)
At the eastern end of the Canal Park the walkway meets
State St./Canal Rd.
Travel East on State St. which becomes Canal Rd.

15.8 (25.4)   NY 260 @ Canal Rd.   31.1 (50.0)
Turn North on to Rt. 260, go over the Canal.

16.2 (26.1)   Gordon Rd. @ NY 260   30.7 (49.4)
Turn East on to Gordon Rd..   Gordon Rd. is the first
street after the Canal.

18.3 (29.5)   Gallup Rd. @ Gordon Rd.   28.8 (46.3)
Continue straight   on Gordon Rd. which changes its
name to Town Line Rd. at Gallup Rd.

19.6 (31.5)   Washington St./NY 36   26.5 (42.5)
              @ Town Line Rd.
Turn South to the Canal.
Adams Basin

W to E	**Rural Road Route**	E to W
mi. (km.) Read↓	**Spencerport to Brockport**	mi. (km.) Read↑

Commuters on the way home.

20.1 (32.3)   Washington St./NY 36   26.0 (41.8)
               @ Canal Tow Path (CTP)
Continue traveling on the CTP.

Adams Basin

Lodging: Canalside Inn, 425 Washington St., Adams
Basin 14410, 352-6784 (may be closed). On the Canal
Tow Path. Ask the owners about the interesting history
of Adams Basin.

Attraction: Due South (2 mi., 3.6 km.) on Washington
St. is Northhampton County Park (Group camping only).

Top O' the Finger Lakes Route begins at this point on the Erie
Canal Route. See the Route's chapter for information.

Side Trip: To Letchworth St. Pk., Castile 14427, 493-3600,
surrounds the Genesee River Gorge through two counties
(Livingston and Wyoming) South of the Canal. The Gorge is
said to rival the Grand Canyon and is particularly beautiful in
the Fall and mid summer. The Park has an active program
of Mt. Biking on its Trails, the Finger Lakes Trail (mainly a
hiking/equestrian trail and is part of the x-USA North Country
Trail). The Genesee Greenway (Lake Ontario to the
Pennsylvania border) runs trhough the Park. Camping.

To go to Letchworth St. Park: Turn South on to Rt. 36, ride 14.5
mi. (23.3 km.) South to Caledonia. Continue riding South on
Rt. 36 for an additional 12.5 mi. (20.1 km.) to the Park
entrance just North of Mt. Morris Village. This is a relatively
flat, not as in Florida flat, route. Total one way distance = 27
mi., (43 km.)

21.1 (34.0)   Union St./Rt. 259 @ CTP   25.0 (40.2)
Continue traveling on the CTP.

Spencerport

Bike Info.: Bike shop (Sugars, 352-8300) in shopping plaza ~.5 mi. (.8 km.), North of the Canal on Union St.
Services: All. Bus with bike racks to Rochester.
Lodging: Daisy House, 3965 Union St., North Chili, 14624, 889-2497.
Attractions: Waterways U.S.A. Canal Cruises, S. Union St. @ Canal, 800 692-8375; Victorian Doll Museum, 4332 Buffalo Rd. (NY 33), North Chili 14514, 247-0130.

24.7 (39.8)   Elmgrove Rd. @ Canal Tow Path   21.4 (34.4)
Continue traveling on the Tow Path.

26.4 (42.5)   Long Pond Rd. @ CTP   19.7 (31.7)
W to E: To continue traveling eastward on the Tow Path you must go to the South side of the Canal. Using the bridge cloverleaf, exit the Tow Path at the western edge of the Long Pond Rd. bridge. Travel over the Canal to its South side. You do not have to cross Long Pond Rd.! The paved section begins here. If you prefer (Ha! Ha!) riding on stone dust/dirt stay on the North side of the Canal where the path really becomes a path!
E to W: To continue traveling westward on the Tow Path you must go to the North side of the Canal. Using the bridge cloverleaf, exit the Tow Path at the eastern edge of the Long Pond Rd. Bridge (you'll see a path which is between the *condos* and Long Pond Rd.) Travel over the Canal to the North side. The stone dust surface begins again.

28.1 (45.2)   Lyell Ave./NY 31/BR 5 @ CTP   18.0 (29.0)
Continue traveling on the Tow Parh
You have entered the western edge of Rochester. The downtown area is seven miles from this point using the Tow Path and the Riverside Trail. Large grocery, excellent bakeries, hardware store and a motel are about 1 mi. (1.6 km.) West along Lyell Ave./NY 31.

Travelers Note

Instances of resident/bicyclist trouble between Lyell Ave. and Lock 33 have been reported. In general you have nothing to worry about. The Canal Tow Path is patrolled by the police. Simply be aware of your surroundings and the people, bicyclists and pedestrians whom you encounter on this section of the Tow Path. Stop to enjoy the scenery, Canal and Genesee River channels.

30.6 (49.2)   Brooks Ave. @ CTP   15.5 (25.0)

Continue traveling on the Tow Path.
Rochester Airport entrance/exit. Airport arivees should note their mileage when turning on to the Path.
    The Rochester Airport is .5 mi. (.8 km.), West of the Canal. To go to the Airport, exit the towpath on the North side of the Brooks Ave. underpass and travel .5 mi. (.8 km) West to Buell Rd. (stop light intersection.) Cross Brooks Ave./NY 208, and use the sidewalk to enter the Airport. Travel through the parking area to the terminal. Using these directions you'll avoid going up a steep hill to the departure area. There is an elevator to the ticket area.

30.8 (49.6)   Aviation fuel tanks & a Holiday Inn   15.3 (24.6)
              Southwest of Brooks Ave.
These tanks are mentioned (they're quite ugly) to remind westbound cyclotourists/hikers who want to take a plane home that the next intersection is the Airport.

31.9 (51.3)   Genesee River @ CTP   14.2 (22.9)
              Viaduct/Arched Bridge @ CTP
Turn North & follow the trail along the Genesee River.
The Tow Path makes a sharp turn at an overhead viaduct (arched bridge) as it meets the Genesee River.
From the Bridge over the Canal on the West side of the River, looking East, you can see the intersection of the Canal and the Genesee River.

                    Genesee Greenway
This is the intersection of the Genesee Valley Greenway and the Erie Canal Trail (Erie Canal Recreationway). The Greenway is only paved between the Canal and Scottsville Rd. (~5 mi./8 km. South). It does continue southward for ~100 mi./160 km. along an old canal bed and railroad bed to the Pennsylvania border. It is beautiful but you do need a mountain bike with a well defined treaded tire to traverse the Genesee Greenway.

32.1 (51.7)   Pedestrian Bridge (West bank)   14.0 (22.5)
              @ Canal Tow Path (CTP)
Turn East on to the pedestrian bridge over the Genesee River!
This bridge is named for Wally Nielsen who was an active member of the Rochester Bicycling Club. He advocated for and wrote the first book on converting abandoned railroad rights of way to recreational trails.

32.4 (52.1)   Pedestrian bridge (East Bank)   13.7 (22.0)
              @ Canal Tow Path Jct. Riverside Trail

Route Notes

Eastbound Through Travelers: Upon leaving the Pedestrian Bridge bear right and continue riding due East along the paved path parallel to the Canal. Do not make southbound turns to go over any of the small bridges you see unless you're very adventurous or want a unique picture or experience.   These bridges will simply take you across the Canal to high grass, isolated areas of Genesee Valley Park.

Westbound Through Travelers return to the main route, at this point, from the loop trip to Rochester.

W to E	**Fairport to**	E to W
mi. (km.) Read↓	**Albion**	mi. (km.) Read↑

West to East Straight Thru Directions are continued after the Rochester Loop

Rochester Loop

The Riverside Trail along the East bank of the Genesee River is a scenic way to enter Rochester. The cyclotourist and hiker are brought directly into downtown Rochester.

This Loop Trip is provided to allow you to tour Rochester. It is a 10 mi. (16 km.) loop returning you to the Tow Path at Winton Rd.. W to E distance indicator: 35.3 mi. (56.8 km.) on the main Erie Canal Route.

Note that it is possible to take a bus from various points along this route to go into Rochester or return to the Canal. See Public Transit information below.

Rochester

Info.: Greater Rochester Visitors Assn., 45 East Ave., Rochester, 14604, 585 546-3070, www.visitrochester.com. Don't forget to request a bicycle map and a bus map!

Area code: 585. Zip code: various.

Bicycling Info.: Rochester Bicycling Club; PO Box 10100, Rochester NY 14610, www.rochesterbicyclingclub.com ; Genesee Valley Cycling Club (racing), Flower City Cycling Club; Rochester Area Triathletes.

Over 12 bike shops in Rochester and its suburbs. The bike shops closest to the route are noted. If you need repairs or equipment determine where you are and then consult a phone book or a passing cyclist for directions to the nearest bike shop.

Hiking Info.: Friends of the Genesee Valley Greenway, PO Box 42, Mt. Morris 14510, 585 658-2569, www.fogvg.org

Finger Lakes Trail Conference, PO Box 18048, Rochester 14618, www.fingerlakes.net. This is an extensive network of trails traversing New York State from the Pennsylvania border to the Catskills.

Adirondack Mountain Club, Genesee Valley Chapter, PO Box 18558. Rochester NY 14618, 987-1717, www.gvc-adk.org.

Rochester Orienteering Club, 377-5650; Genesee Valley Hiking Club; Webster Trails; Victor Trails; Crescent Trail hiking schedules are published newspaper.

Camping equipment stores are in suburban shopping malls; one is in Rochester on Lyell Ave.

Services: All. Hospitals. Shopping is primarily in the suburban malls. Colleges & University.

Lodging: Rochester motels and hotels vary in price from about $35.00-$135.00. The least expensive motels are in the suburbs or around the Airport. There is no hostel and the

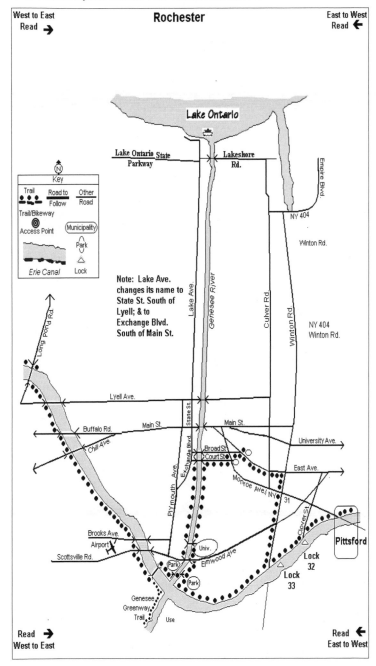

West to East
Read →

Rochester

East to West
Read ←

Lake Ontario

Lake Ontario State Parkway

Lakeshore Rd.

Empire Blvd.

NY 404

Winton Rd.

Key

Trail

Road to Follow

Other Road

Trail/Bikeway

Access Point

Municipality

Park

Erie Canal

Lock

Note: Lake Ave. changes its name to State St. South of Lyell; & to Exchange Blvd. South of Main St.

Genesee River

Lake Ave.

State St.

Culver Rd.

Winton Rd.

NY 404 Winton Rd.

Long Pond Rd.

Lyell Ave.

Buffalo Rd.

Main St.

Main St.

University Ave.

Chill Ave.

Broad St.

Court St.

East Ave.

Monroe Ave./ NY 31

Plymouth Ave.

Exchange Blvd.

Clover St.

Pittsford

Brooks Ave.

Airport

Univ.

Lock 32

Scottsville Rd.

Elmwood Ave

Park

Lock 33

Genesee Greenway Trail

Park

Use

Read →
West to East

Read ←
East to West

colleges do not rent to non-students.

B&Bs: *Dartmouth House, 215 Dartmouth St., 14507, 271-7872; Wynderly, 132 Windemere Rd., 14610, 224-0788; B&B at 428 Mt. Vernon, 428 Mt. Vernon Ave., 14620, 271-0792. Contact the Visitors Assn. for a current list.

Camping: Lock 33, Edgewood Ave., Brighton (~6 mi. S. of downtown Rochester has a camping area for through travelers. Formal campgrounds: Plan to camp East, West or South of Rochester & travel about 15-25 mi. (25-40 km.), to downtown. Guerilla campers can camp a County park, a City park (definitely not recommended) or along the Erie Canal. Lock 33 is your best & safest place to camp.

Attractions: Culture: George Eastman House/International Mus. of Photography, 271-3361, was the Kodak founder's mansion; Strong Mus. 454-7639, (children's mus. & American cultural history); Strassenburg Planetarium/Rochester Mus. and Science Ctr. 271-1880; Memorial Art Gallery; Frederick Douglass Mus.; GEVA Theatre, 232-4382; Susan B. Anthony Nat'l. Hist. Site, 235-6124; High Falls Hist. Area; Rochester Philharmonic, 454-2620, performs at the Finger Lakes Arts Center in Canandaigua during the summer (See Top O' the Finger Lakes Route).

Architecture: The Landmark Society, 133 South Fitzhugh St., 14608, 546-7029, has a complete list & booklet of the area's architecturally significant buildings.

Gardens: Garden Ctr. of Rochester, Highland Pk., 473-5130 has a brochure detailing all significant gardens in Rochester & the Finger Lakes.

Seneca Park Zoo, 467-9453, a natural habitat based Zoo.

Many neighborhood festivals during the summer.

Sports: Rhinos soccer, Red Wings baseball, Nighthawks lacrosse, all at Frontier Field. Buffalo Bills football training camp at St. John Fisher College. Amerks hockey.

Cruises: Canal: Corn Hill Navigation, 262-5661; Lake Ontario: Riverview Cruise Lines, 865-4930.

Public Transportation: Airport: On the western edge of the City along the Erie Canal, Brooks Ave. @ Tow Path, W to E, distance indicator: 30.6 mi. (49.2 km.)

Intercity Buses: Trailways, 232-4912; Greyhound, 232-3092. Terminal: Chestnut/Monroe Ave. at Broad St.,

Local Bus Information: Regional Transit Service (RTS), 654-0200. All RTS buses have bicycle racks. During non-rush hours when buses are empty, bikes may go inside the bus if more than 2 bicycles have to be accommodated. The driver has to telephone the bus dispatcher. Several RTS bus routes operate to and from the Canal. Notably, the Monroe Ave.

(Pittsford & JCC (Lock 33), Clinton Ave., East Ave., Plymouth Ave. and Genesee St. routes. There are also suburban routes which operate to/from Downtown to villages on the Canal but only during weekday rush hours You'll need to consult a bus map and a schedule. Buses operate like spokes from a wheel, emanating from downtown Rochester. A little known secret is the University of Rochester shuttle bus from the Eastman Theater in downtown to the University near the intersection of the Genesee River and Canal.

For hikers, taking a bus from downtown to the Canal after sightseeing is a valid option.

W to E	**10 mi. (16 km.) Loop Tour of**	E to W
mi. (km.) Read↓	**Rochester**	mi. (km.) Read↑

00.0 (00.0)   East Bank/West Bank Genesee River   9.3 (15.0)
@ CTPPedestrian Bridge
Turn North on to the Riverside Trail which parallels the Genesee River.

.5 (.8)   Elmwood Ave. @ Riverside Trail   8.8 (14.1)
Trail underpass (it goes under Elmwood Ave.) leading into Genesee Valley Park.

1.0 (1.6)   Riverside Trail   8.3 (13.4)
@ University of Rochester stadium (E. bank)
@ Brooks Ave. (W. bank of River)
Pedestrian bridge. The E. bank path branches & goes down to the River here. I suggest you ride along the River bank, it's a delightful ride.

1.6 (2.5)   Ford St. Bridge @ Riverside Trail   7.7 (12.4)
Trail goes under this bridge. Landmarks: housing project, E. bank. Paved pier, W. bank.

2.5 (4.0)   Riverside Trail Head   6.8 (10.9)
@ South Ave., East Bank of River
Cross South Ave., travel due East on Woodbury Blvd. Landmarks: GEVA Theatre opposite Washington Pk.
@ Court St., West Bank of River
Turn East on to the Court St. bridge & cross the River. At South Ave., turn South and go to the East bank Riverside Trail Head and continue following the directions.

2.8 (4.5)   Monroe Ave./NY31/BR 5   6.5 (10.5)
@ Woodbury Blvd.
Turn North, travel past the metal sculpture & Manhattan Square Park. Landmark: Strong Mus.

3.0 (4.8)   Broad St. @ Monroe Ave./Rt. 31   6.3 (10.1)
Turn (right) on to Broad St.. A Big white building is on
one corner, the metal sculpture & park is on the other
corner. Monroe Ave. changes it's name to Chestnut St.
here. Intercity Bus Station: 1 block North on Monroe
(across the street from the Xerox building).

3.5 (5.6)   South Union St. @ Broad St.   5.8 (9.3)
Turn North. Only way to go! Broad St. ends here.

3.7 (6.0)   East Ave. @ S. Union St.   5.6 (9.0)
Turn East on to East Ave.

4.0 (6.4)   S. Goodman St. @ East Ave.   5.3 (8.5)
Loop continues straight. Going South here will bring you
to Park and Monroe Aves.
Science Ctr. & Mus./Planetarium on the southeast
corner. The Art Gallery is one block North on Goodman
St. @ University Ave.

4.3 (7.0)   Westminster St. @ East Ave.   5.0 (8.0)
Loop continues straight. Geo. Eastman House/ Mus. of
Photography is on the North side of East Ave.

4.8 (7.7)   Culver Rd. @ East Ave.   4.5 (7.2)
Continue traveling on East Ave.
Turning North here, then West on the next street,
University Ave. takes you to Towner's Bike Shop (271-
4553).
Turning South here will bring you to Rochester's Park
Ave. neighborhood with its many outdoor cafes. Going a
bit further South will bring you to Monroe Ave./Rt. 31
where you can board a bus to return you to the Canal.

5.8 (9.3)   Winton Rd. @ East Ave.   3.5 (5.6)
Turn South on to Winton Rd.

9.3 (15.0)   Canal Tow Path @ Winton Rd.   00.0 (00.0)
Enter Canal Tow Path from the West side of Winton Rd.
The entrance is just past the Jewish Home and Meridian
Centre office park but before the bridge going over the
Canal. Pedallers Bike Shop (334-1083.)

W to E	**10 mi (16 km) Loop Tour of**	E to W
mi. (km.) Read↓	**Rochester**	mi. (km.) Read↑

Notes

Canal Cruise

W to E	**Erie Canal Route**	E to W
mi. (km.) Read↓	**Albion to Fairport**	mi. (km.) Read↑

East to West Traveler Note
East to West Through Directions are continued
after the Rochester Loop.

A 10 mi. (16 km.), loop route to downtown Rochester begins here at Winton Rd. Westbound cyclists will find this the best way to tour Rochester.

Hikers will want to continue westward to the Genesee River and then take the Riverside Trail into the City. Alternatively hikers might want to take a bus into the downtown area from Pittsford or Edgewood Ave. and then return to the Tow Path via the Riverside Trail. The point is, read the Rochester information section before starting to hike downtown from this point.

35.3 (56.8)   Winton Rd.   10.8 (17.4)
          @ Canal Tow Path (CTP)
W to E Rochester Loop travelers rejoin us here.
E to W cyclotourists/hikers. a Loop tour of Rochester is on the next two pages. You can take the Loop or continue traveling on the Canal Tow Path.
Hikers should particularly note the local bus information in the Rochester Info. section. and in the Loop text.

36.0 (58.0)   Edgewood Ave. @ Lock 33/CTP   10.1 (16.3)
Continue traveling on the CTP. Landmarks: Lock 33 and the Jewish Community Center. The portage underpass is really a pain at this Lock. Carefully cross Edgewood Ave.
A bus to downtown at the JCC. Camping at this Lock.

37.3 (60.0)   Clover St. @ Lock 32/CTP   8.8 (14.2)

Clover St. is a very busy street. Use underpass.
W to E traveler note: Turning North on to Clover St./Rt. 65 & riding for .75 mi. (1.2 km.) will bring you to Monroe Ave./Rt.31. There are motels and a bike shop (Park Ave. Bikes) at this intersection. Turning West on Monroe for .5 mi. (.8 km.) will bring you shopping plazas & a bike shop. Continuing East on Monroe for 1.5 mi. (2.4 km.) will bring you back to the Canal.

37.9 (60.9)   Old Canal Path @ CTP   8.2 (13.2)
There is a barely discernable path which follows the Old Erie Canal to a lock above the large grocery store mentioned above. If you need supplies, I suggest that you try to find this path it is quicker, shorter & safer (but with a rougher trail surface) than using the Clover St. or Monroe Ave. exits to go to this shopping area.

38.5 (62.0)   Monroe Ave. @ CTP   7.6 (12.2)
W to E: Use care! There is a gate at the end of the hill. You will go off the Tow Path at this point, on Brook Rd. Turn right (East) when you reach the Brook Rd. At the end of the Brook Rd., turn right (South), towards the Canal, you'll see the Path once again and continue traveling East on the Tow Path.
E to W: You will bear away from the Canal and go off the Tow Path. Turn left (West) on to the first street, Brook Rd. On your left in <.1 mi. (<.2 km.) you will see the entrance to the Tow Path. If you find yourself in a residential area after .3 mi. (.5 km.), turn around and look for the entrance again.
E to W traveler note: Turning on to Monroe Ave./Rt. 31 (carefully cross Monroe Ave. to ride on the right side of the road) and riding North for 1.5 mi. (2.4 km) will bring you to shopping plazas & motels. Continuing on Monroe Ave. for another .5 mi (.8 km) will bring you to a bike shop (Park Ave., 381-3080) and motel at the intersection of Monroe Ave. @ Clover St. Turn South on to Clover St./Rt. 65 and ride .75 mi. (1.2 km.) to the Tow Path. Continue Riding North on Monroe Ave. to reach downtown Rochester, ~3 mi. (~4.9 km.)

39.0 (62.0)   Schoen Place @ CTP   7.1 (11.4)
Continue traveling on the Tow Path.
You must walk your bike through pedestrian busy Schoen Place.

Pittsford

Info.: Mayor, Village Hall, 21 Main North St. Pittsford NY 14534. Area code: 585. Zip code: 14534.
Bike Info.: Tow Path Bike Shop (381-2808).
Services: Restaurants and stores.
Lodging: Motel (Schoen Pl.) B&B: Oliver Loud's Inn, 1474 Marsh Rd. (further along the CTP), 248-5200.
Attractions: Canal Cruises: Corn Hill Navigation, 262-5661. Many 19th century buildings.

Tow Path Surface Change: Going East the CTP becomes a hard pack smooth stone dust surface after Schoen Place in Pittsford. Westbound, asphalt.

45.6 (73.4)   Rt. 250/Main St. @ Canal Tow Path   .5 (.8)
Continue traveling on the CTP.
Unique lift bridge over the Canal.

Fairport

Info.: Dock Master, Village Hall, Fairport 14450.
Area code: 585. Zip code: 14450.
Bike & Hiking Info.: Bike shop.
Services: Restaurants and shops, hardware store.
Lodging: Speak with the dock master to use the public shower (primarily for mariners). B&Bs: Woods Edge, 151 Bluhm Rd., 223-8877; Strawberry Castle, 1883 Penfield Rd., Penfield 14526, 385-3268.
Attractions: Canal cruises: The Fairport Lady, 10 Liftbridge Lane W., 223-1930; Colonial Belle, 5 N. Main St., 377-4600. Lift bridge over Canal.

46.1 (74.2)   Turk Hill Rd. @ CTP   0.0 (0.0)
Continue traveling parallel to the Canal.
The Tow Path leads directly on to an unnamed street. Continue traveling parallel to the Canal. There will be very little traffic and you will pass the Perinton Public Works Dep't. At the end of the street the towpath suddenly runs directly on the Canal's shore line. Don't be dismayed! Continue following the shore line. It's actually a beautiful section.

W to E	**Fairport to**	E to W
mi. (km.) Read↓	**Albion**	mi. (km.) Read↑

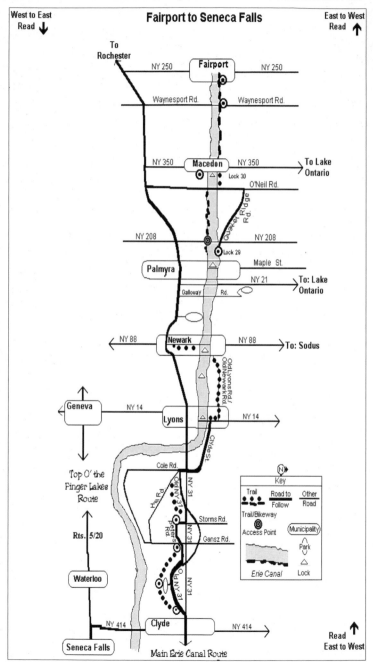

Fairport to Seneca Falls

West to East
Read ↓

East to West
Read ↑

To Rochester

NY 250 — Fairport — NY 250

Waynesport Rd. — Waynesport Rd.

NY 350 — Macedon — NY 350 → To Lake Ontario

Lock 30

O'Neil Rd.

Quaker Ridge Rd.

NY 208 — NY 208

Lock 29

Palmyra — Maple St.

NY 21 → To: Lake Ontario

Galloway Rd.

NY 88 ← Newark — NY 88 → To: Sodus

Old Lyons Rd./Old Newark Rd.

Geneva ← NY 14 — Lyons — NY 14 →

Clyde St.

Cole Rd.

Top O' the Finger Lakes Route

Hill Rd.

Old NY 31

NY 31

Storms Rd.

Peters Rd.

NY 31

Gansz Rd.

Rts. 5/20

Old NY 31

NY 31

Waterloo

NY 414 — Clyde — NY 414 →

Seneca Falls

Main Erie Canal Route

Read ↑ East to West

Key

Trail　Road to Follow　Other Road

Trail/Bikeway

Access Point　Municipality

Erie Canal　　Park　　Lock

BREAD BASKET

In the 19th century central and western New York was the bread basket of America. The Canal contributed to the development of the rich aluvial plains and soils left by departing glaciers. The soil was enriched by the deposits of forest organic material. Rocks and sand were left by the departing glaciers. The small round stones, cobblestones, piled by farmers as fences or on the sides of fields were used by the Canal's masons to produce a unique architectural style, cobblestone houses, barns and warehouses. The quarries provided the basic stone blocks for the Canal; the sand for the mortar.

More importantly the Canal brought prospective farmers from the crowded cities of the Atlantic Coast. In classic frontier economics some of the trees which were cleared from the land were sent to local sawmills and then by barge to Albany and the cities of the Atlantic coast. Some sawmill owners realized that a finished product would garner more profit than raw lumber. Thus the establishment of furniture manufacturers both to supply local needs and bring value added revenue from the coast to the Canal's shoreline.

As the mid-West became more important and efficient in grain production farmers switched to other commodities—seed production to sell to urbanites and agriculturalists alike.

With the capital acquired from the strong agricultural base of the mid 19th century a manufacturing segment of the economy developed to produce farm equipment and eventually other machines. The many rivers and falls cascading over the drumlins provided the power to create an industrial heartland.

Along with the rising standard of living came people to work in those burgeoning factories.

In turn a series of permutations on standard religions. The religiosity of transplanted Europeans was in keeping with the Seneca and other Native American traditions which demarcated numerous places in this area as having special powers.

W to E	**Fairport to**	E to W
mi. (km.) Read↓	**Seneca Falls**	mi. (km.) Read↑

0.0 (0.0)   NY 250/Main St. @ Canal   53.7 (86.4)
Continue traveling on the CTP through the Village. An
underpass allows you to bypass busy NY 250/Main St.
Working lift bridge over the Canal.
Fairport: Info. etc. in previous chapter.

.3 (.5)   Barrier @ CTP   53.4 (85.9)
Simply disregard the barrier, go around it, and continue
on the Tow Path. Hopefully it has been removed.

.5 (.8)   Turk Hill Rd. @ Tow Path   53.3 (85.7)
Just past the Turk Hill Rd. underpass will be a street.
The Tow Path leads directly on to this unnamed street.
Continue traveling along this street, parallel to the Canal.
There will be very little traffic and you will pass the
Perinton Public Works Dep't. At the end of the street the
towpath suddenly runs directly on the Canal shore. Don't
be dismayed!   Continue following the shore line.   It's
actually a beautiful section.

3.2 (5.1)   Wayne County Line @ Canal Tow Path   51.4 (82.7)
Monroe County - Wayne County border.

Wayne County

Public Transportation: WATS, on NY 31 & other major roads,
bikes can be transported if partially disassembled, 315 946-
5617.

Attractions: Lake Ontario Fishing Derbies; County Fair; Each
Town has a fair or festival during the summer.

Wayne County Tow Path Trail (WCT): In the 1970's Wayne
County developed a Heritage Tow Path Trail along the *Old
Canal.*   It has a stone dust/cinder and dirt surface.
Eventually it became overgrown with grass. It is mowed
about three times a year. In general it is a very level Tow
Path trail.   It is not a perfectly smooth surface having
weathered since the '70s. However it is marked with large
signs at each point it crosses a road. It is free of bushes
and large pot holes! It is best traversed using a Mt. bike with
wide tires or by hiking.

As the County receives funds it is upgrading the Heritage Trail
and improving its surface with either asphalt or stone dust.

Most exciting for both hikers and mt. bikers is the *Old* Erie Canal
sections of the WCT. These sections diverge from and then
rejoin the main trail forming a seamless trail system. The

main WCT parallels the *New* Canal and Route 31. Both trail access points and the trail route is marked on the map for this section.

Lodging: Private campgrounds and some camping in County Parks; B&Bs; motels, .

At various points along the Wayne County Tow Path Heritage Trail are parks. Interestingly, the County allows camping at some of these parks. The Park sign says: "Permit required for camping call Wayne County Department of Parks, 7212 NY 31 West, Lyons, NY 14489, 315 ." The very pleasant Parks Department clerk told me, "No one has ever asked for a permit! Can I send you a copy of the Parks Law?" The point is, this is free camping in beautiful, well maintained, secluded parks and no permit form exists! You can write for a copy of the Wayne County Parks Law but let's keep this a cyclotourist/hiker secret! If you are planning to camp simply be discreet. Park facilities are limited: vault toilets, tables, and some have H_2O others don't. Keep them clean. I doubt anyone will even know that you are camping in a Wayne County Park which permits camping. Ninety-nine percent of Wayne County residents don't know that camping is permitted! Helmets off for a progressive County!

3.9 (6.2)   Wayneport Rd. @ CTP/WCT   50.6 (81.4)
You have just traveled through a small trailer park.
Cross Wayneport Rd. and continue on the CTP/WCT.
If you want to use NY 31/BR 5, turn South on to Wayneport Rd. and travel .5 mi. (.8 km.) to NY 31 then on to NY 31/BR 5. The distance to Lock 30 via Rt. 31 or the Tow Path is about the same.

8.8 (14.1)   Lock 30 @ WCT/NY 350   45.8 (73.7)
Tow Path Surface Note
Three routes are provided for travelers between Macedon and Palmyra: Rural Road Route, Single Track Trail Route and the main Erie Canal Route.

Macedon

Bike Info.: Home of Terry Bicycles (office and warehouse facilities only).

Services & Facilities: Restaurants, hardware store, gas station, grocery, convenience store, and motel.

Attractions: Lumberjack Festival.

Lodging: Camping at the Canal marina, a short distance from the Lock.

W to E	**Rural Road Route**	E to W
mi. (km.) Read↓	**Macedon to Palmyra**	mi. (km.) Read↑

8.8 (14.1)   Railroad St. (Lock 30 Park)   45.8 (73.7)
              @ NY 350
Turn South on to NY 350.

9.0 (14.5)   NY 31/BR 5 @ NY 350   45.6 (73.3)
Turn East on to NY 31. Use the wide paved shoulder.
Direct/Fast Route to Palmyra: Use NY 31/BR 5. NY 31
has a wide shoulder and little daytime traffic.

9.4 (15.1)   O'Neil Rd. @ NY 31/BR 5   45.2 (73.1)
Turn North on to O'Neil Rd., ride over the Canal.

9.5 (15.2)   Quaker Ridge Rd. E. @ O'Neil Rd.   45.1 (72.6)
Turn East on to Quaker Ridge Rd.. This is a narrow road
which parallels the Canal. It is not flat, it has some
moderate rolling hills.

12.6 (20.3)   Lock 29 @ Quaker Ridge Rd. E.   42.4 (68.2)
Enter the Lock area by going over the grass. Cross over
the Lock on the Lock gates. This is a very beautiful lock
with a waterfall and County park (vault toilets, no
camping).

W to E	**Rural Road Route**	E to W
mi. (km.) Read↓	**Palmyra to Macedon**	mi. (km.) Read↑

W to E	**Single Track Trail Route**	E to W
mi. (km.) Read↓	**Macedon to Palmyra**	mi. (km.) Read↑

8.8 (14.1)   Lock 30 East End   45.8 (73.7)
              @ Lock Water Gate
This Route is for adventurous bikers and hikers. A single track trail exists on the North side of the Canal. It is overgrown and rough.
Continue traveling on the North side of the Canal. Just past Lock 30's East water gate, on North side of the Canal, you'll see the foot path. It is best to walk the first 10 yds. (11 m.) if you are mt. biking.

9.4 (15.1)   O'Neil Rd. @ WCT/CTP   45.2 (72.7)
Cross O'Neil Rd. Use care. The vegetation makes auto sight lines obscure the trail crossing.
   Bicyclists will have to push or carry their bikes up a small enbankment to the road.
After crossing O'Neil Rd., continue traveling on the single track trail until it suddenly divides! Yes! two paths for one!
      The North fork of the trail follows the *Old* Canal, the South fork follows the *New* Canal. However, both are very very rough, over grown and beautiful, best left for hikers. If you decide to become very adventurous you'll end up at the same place (same mileage too)—Lock 29.
A more level WCT route exists.

12.6 (20.3)   Lock 29 @ Quaker Ridge Rd. E.   42.4 (68.2)
Enter the Lock area by going over the grass. Cross over the Lock on the Lock gates. This is a very beautiful lock with a waterfall and County park (vault toilets, no camping).

W to E	**Single Track Trail Route**	E to W
mi. (km.) Read↓	**Palmyra to Macedon**	mi. (km.) Read↑

W to E	**Main Erie Canal Route**	E to W
mi. (km.) Read↓	**Macedon to Palmyra**	mi. (km.) Read↑

8.8 (14.1)   Lock 30 East End   45.8 (73.7)
               @ Lock Water Gate
Cross the Lock over the water gates.   Follow the
Lockmaster's directions.
Follow the signs to the Canal Tow Path. To continue on
a smooth Tow Path to Palmyra you have to exit the Lock
area on to Rt. 350.
Travel South on Rt. 350 to Rt. 31. Turn East on Rt. 31
and travel to O'Neil Rd.

9.4 (15.1)   O'Neil Rd. @ WCT/CTP   45.2 (72.7)
Cross NY 31/BR 5 at O'Neil Rd. Use care. A curve
obscures bicyclists & pedestrians.
Go into the large parking lot on the East side of O'Neil
Rd. near the Canal. At the eastern end of the parking lot,
near the Canal you'll see a Wayne County Erie Canal
Heritage Trail (WCT) sign and the paved/stone dust Trail.

11.3 (18.2)   NY 208/Yellow Mills Rd. @ WCT   43.3 (69.7)
Continue riding on the Tow path or go North over the
Bridge to Quaker Rd. (see Rural Road Route) or go
South to use NY 31/BR 5.

12.2 (19.6)   Lock 29 Park   42.3 (68.1)
               @ CTP/WCT
               @ NY 31/BR 5
Travelers Note
The Erie Canal Tow Path Trail essentially ends at Lock
   29. From here until Fayetteville, East of Syracuse you
   will be traveling on a mixture of rural roads and State
   highways.
There are plans to improve and extend the official Tow
   Path Trail to at least Clyde. The Trail will then follow
   the Heritage Trail Route which is provided in this text.
Where trails/tow paths (improved & unimproved) exist
   they are noted in the text and the routes along the
   trails/tow paths are provided.

Bicyclists: To go East into Palmyra you must exit the
Lock 29 Park and use NY 31/BR 5. It is a very short mile
(kilometer and a half) to downtown Palmyra.
Hikers: At the eastern edge of the Lock 29 Park, South
of the Canal is the entrance to the WCT. This trail path
is most suitable for mt. bikes and hikers. The trail runs

on the South side of the Canal for .7 mi. (1.1 km.) and stops at Maple Ave./Church St. near downtown Palmyra. Turn South on Maple Ave./Church St. to go into Palmyra.

E to W Traveler Note
Three routes are provided for travelers between Palmyra and Macedon: Rural Road Route, Single Track Trail Route and the Canal Tow Path Route. Each has its own joys and characteristics. The Canal Tow Path Route has an asphalt surface.

You can also use Rt. 31/BR 5 to go to Macedon & Rochester but the Tow Path is much nicer and just as fast. There is a negligible difference in distance no matter which route you use.

13.0 (21.0)   Maple Ave./Church St.   41.5 (66.8)
              @ Main St./NY 31/BR 5
Turn East on to Main St./NY 31/BR 5
Hikers and bikers using the Tow Path should come up to Main St. from the Canal.
There is somewhat of a single track path on the North side of the Canal. It is too overgrown to be passable for long distance bikers and hikers. It is used by local single track bicyclists, fisherman, birders and hikers.

Palmyra
Info.: Historic Palmyra, PO Box 96, Palmyra NY 14522, 315 597-6981; Wayne County Business Council, PO Box 337, Palmyra NY 14522; 315 597-4468.
Area code: 315. Zip code: 14522.
Services: Restaurants, grocery & convenience stores; hardware, clothing and general merchandise stores.
Attractions: 19th Century buildings on Main St. & around town. Alling Coverlet Museum, 122 William St., 597-2212; Palmyra Hist. Museum, 132 Market St., 597-4794; Hill Cumorah Visitors Center (Mormon Church founding site) 603 Rt. 21 S., 597-5851.
Lodging: Cobblestone Corners Farm, 3313 Jeffery Rd., 597-6809, about 2.5 mi. (3.2 km.) North of Palmyra off Rt. 21; Canaltown, 119 Canandaigua St., 597-5553.

13.6 (21.9)   NY 21 @ NY 31/BR 5/Main St.   40.9 (65.8)
Continue traveling on NY 31/BR 5/Main St.
A single track path exists on the North side of the Canal.
Taking NY 21, South will bring you to the Top O' The Finger Lakes Route at Canandaigua; taking NY 21, North, will bring you to Lake Ontario.

15.8 (25.4)   Galloway Rd. @ NY 31/BR 5   38.7 (62.3)
Continue traveling on NY 31.
.5 mi (.8 km) along Galloway Rd. to Swift's Landing
County Park (camping allowed, no H_2O, long drop toilets)
on the original Canal. There are a few hills on this road.

19.8 (31.9)   Wide Waters Park @ NY 31/BR 5   34.7 (55.8)
Continue traveling on NY 31.
County Park, camping allowed but not advised.

21.6 (34.8)   NY 88 @ NY 31/BR 5   32.9 (52.9)
Turn North on to NY 88 and then East on to Van Buren
St. which parallels the Canal.
If you want to make some time continue traveling on Rt.
31/BR 5 to Lyons.
Going South on NY 88, connects you with the Top O' The
Finger Lakes Route at Phelps.

Newark

Info.: Town Hall, Newark NY 14513.
Area code: 315. Zip code: 14513.
Bike Info.: Bike shop in shopping plaza area on Rt. 31.
Services: All.
Lodging: Chapman's Blue Brick Inn, 201 Scott St., 331-
3226, in village; Quality Inn Motel on Canal.
Attractions: Hoffman Clock Mus. at Newark Public
Library; Fireman's carnival in early June.

22.1 (35.5)   Lock 28B @ Van Buren St.   32.4 (52.1)
                NY 31 @ N. Clinton St.
Continue traveling on Van Buren St. or NY 31
Travel East to Lyons; West to Palmyra.
You can return to NY 31/BR 5 via the bridge over the
Canal/North Clinton St.. The distance using NY 31 or Old
Lyons Rd. to go to Lyons is about the same, 4.7 mi (7.6
km), only the road is different!

22.9 (36.9)   Old Lyons Rd. @ Van Buren St.   30.8 (49.6)
Turn East on to Old Lyons Rd.
Or continue traveling on NY 31.

24.5 (39.4)   County House Rd.   29.2 (47.0)
                @ Old Lyons Rd.
Bear left to continue on Old Lyons Rd. which changes its
name to Old Newark Rd.! County House Rd. will lead
you to NY 31.

25.6 (41.2)   Lock 28A @ Old Newark Rd.   28.1 (45.2)
Continue on Old Newark Rd. or cross the Canal to NY 31.
Canal Corporation dry dock and Lock. An interesting collection of Canal boats used for maintenance of the waterway.

26.8 (43.1)   NY 14 @ Water St./Layton Ave.   26.9 (43.3)
As you enter the Lyons, Old Newark Rd. changes its name to Water St.. Water St. becomes Layton Ave.. Continue traveling straight to Rt. 14/Geneva St. past Lock 27.
Traveling South on Rt. 14, will connect you with the Top O' The Finger Lakes Route at Geneva.

Lyons

Info.: Wayne County Tourism, 9 Pearl St., Lyons NY 14489, 800 527-6510/315 946-5470.
Area code: 315. Zip code: 14489.
Bike Info.: No bike shop.
Services: Restaurants, grocery & convenience stores, hardware store, antique shops and County offices.
Lodging: B&Bs: Kreiss Farm, 2097 Highland Fruit Farm Rd., (.5 mi. (.8 km.)) North of Lock Berlin, 946-9448; Roselawne, 101 Broad St., in village, 946-4218; *Lyons/ Wayne Motels 7761 Rt. 31, just W. of the Village, 946-9024.
Attractions: Lock 27; Peppermint Days (mid July); Saturday farmers' market.

27.1 (43.6)   Rt. 14/Geneva St. @ Layton St.   26.6 (42.8)
Turn North on to NY 14/Geneva St., ride 2 blocks to Clyde St.
NY 14 leads North to Sodus Point on Lake Ontario, 14 mi. (22.5 km.).
NY 14 leads South to Geneva, 11 mi. (17.7 km.), and Seneca Lake with its wineries as well as connecting with the Top O' The Finger Lakes Route. The Seneca/Cayuga Canal beginning in Geneva and ending in Clyde links the Erie Canal with Lake Seneca. The Main CTP route meets this Canal at Clyde and Seneca Falls.

27.3 (43.9)   Clyde St. @ NY 14/Geneva St.   26.4 (42.5)
Turn East on to Clyde St.

28.0 (45.1)   NY 31/BR 5 @ Clyde St.   25.7 (41.3)
Cross NY 31 to Cole Rd..

Stop! Look at this intersection! Old Rt. 31 runs parallel to new NY 31. Between Hill St. and Old Rt. 31 there is a sign with the Wayne County Erie Canal Heritage Trail behind it. You can ride on this Trail all the way to Clyde! This is a relatively smooth mowed grass trail which might be improved with a stone dust or asphalt surface by the time this book is published. If it is not improved, use the Rural Road Route directions or simply take NY 31/BR 5, to Clyde. The distances are about the same anyway you travel!

Travelers Note

The Main Canal Route continues after the
Lyons to Clyde Heritage Trail Route and
Lyons to Clyde Rural Road Route.

W to E	**Lyons to Clyde**	E to W
mi. (km.) Read↓	**Heritage Trail Route**	mi. (km.) Read↑

Note: You can go between the Rural Road Route, New NY 31/ BR 5 and the Heritage Trail Route at will by using the cross streets. Hikers might prefer to use the Heritage Trail; bikers the Rural Road Route.

0.0 (0.0)	Cole Rd. @ NY 31	6.2 (10.0)
	Travel East on the Heritage Trail	
.4 (.6)	Warncke Rd.	5.8 (9.3)
.8 (1.3)	Sunderville Rd.	5.4 (8.7)
1.9 (3.1)	Peters Rd.	4.3 (6.7)
2.4 (3.8)	Lock Berlin Park	3.8 (6.1)
	Facilities: historic lock, vault toilets, no H_2O or camping.	
2.5 (4.0)	Peters/Gansz Rd.	3.7 (5.9)
3.1 (5.0)	Black Brook County Park	3.1 (4.9)
	Shelter, vault toilets, no H_2O, camping allowed.	
5.2 (8.4)	Driveway	1.0 (1.6)
	Turn South (short end of the driveway!) on to Old Rt. 31	
6.2 (10.0)	NY 31/BR 5 @ Old Rt. 31	0.0 (0.0)
	Turn East on to NY 31	

E to W	**Clyde to Lyons**	W to E
mi. (km.) Read↓	**Heritage Trail Route**	mi. (km.) Read↑

W to E	**Lyons to Clyde**	E to W
mi. (km.) Read↓	**Rural Road Route**	mi. (km.) Read↑

Note: You can go between the Rural Road Route, New NY 31/ BR 5 and the Heritage Trail Route at will by using the cross streets.
Hikers might prefer to use the Heritage Trail; bikers the Rural Road Route.

28.0 (45.1)   NY 31/BR 5 @ Cole Rd.   25.2 (41.3)
W to E: Cross NY 31 to Cole Rd. Turn on to Old NY 31 which runs parallel to new NY 31.
E to W: Cross NY 31 to Clyde St.

28.4 (45.7)   Warncke Rd. @ Old NY 31   25.3 (40.7)

29.2 (47.0)   Sunderville Rd. @ Old NY 31   24.5 (37.8)

29.3 (47.1)   Old Rt. 31 @ New NY 31/BR 5   24.4 (39.3)
Cross New NY 31 and continue riding on Old NY 31.

31.0 (49.9)   Storms Rd./Peters Rd.   22.7 (36.5)
               @ Old Rt. 31
Turn Southeast on to Storms road & carefully cross New NY 31/BR 5; Storms Rd. becomes Peters Rd. on the South Side of New NY 31.
Travel East on Peters Rd.

31.5 (50.7)   Lock Berlin Park @ Peters Rd.   22.2 (35.7)
Facilities: Lock, tables, vault toilets, no H_2O or camping.

31.6 (50.8)   Gansz Rd. @ Peters Rd.   22.1 (35.6)
Turn North to New NY 31/BR 5.

31.7 (50.9)   Gansz Rd. @ New NY 31/BR 5   22.0 (35.4)
Turn East on to New NY 31/BR 5.

32.2 (51.8)   Old NY 31 @ New NY 31/BR 5   21.5 (34.6)
Turn South on to Old Rt. 31.

32.4 (52.1)   Black Brook County Park @ Old Rt. 31   21.3 (34.2)
Facilities: Shelter, vault toilets, camping allowed, no H_2O,

38.6 (62.1)   NY 31/BR 5 @ Old Rt. 31   15.1 (24.3)
Turn East on to NY 31/BR 5.

W to E	**Clyde to Lyons**	E to W
mi. (km.) Read↓	**Rural Road Route**	mi. (km.) Read↑

W to E	Main Erie Canal Route	E to W
mi. (km.) Read↓		mi. (km.) Read↑

40.0 (64.4)   NY 414 @ NY 31/BR 5   13.7 (22.0)
Turn South on to NY 414.
Stock up on snacks if you are going to Seneca Falls.
There are no stores on NY 414.

Clyde

Services: Restaurants, small grocery, hardware store.
Lodging: B&B: Clyde Athletic Club, 131 Glasgow St.,
Clyde NY 14433, 800 484-6760/315 923-2226.
Attractions: Grape Hill Lilac Park; WPA Murals on walls
of Post Office; Fireman's Carnival, mid-August.

Travelers Note: To continue on the Erie Canal,
        use the Clyde to Port Byron Route.

If you want to visit the National Woman's Hist. Site & the
Seneca-Cayuga Canal at Seneca Falls use the Top O'
the Finger Lakes Route from Clyde. Turn South on NY
414, and travel 14 mi. (23 km.), to Seneca Falls.

The more direct route is to go to Port Byron.   Both
Routes meet at Port Byron.

W to E	Erie Canal Route	E to W
mi. (km.) Read↓	Clyde to Port Byron	mi. (km.) Read↑

0.0 (0.0)   NY 414 @ NY 31/BR 5   15.4 (24.8)
Travel East on NY 31/BR 5.
Clyde

6.1 (9.8)   NY 89 Jct. NY 31/BR 5   9.3 (14.9)
Continue traveling on NY 31.
Savannah:: Restaurant, convenience store.

9.4 (15.1)   NY 31 Jct. NY 89   6.0 (9.6)
Turn East on to NY 31.

15.4 (24.8)   NY 38 @ NY 31   0.0 (0.0)
Port Byron.

W to E	Erie Canal Route	E to W
mi. (km.) Read↓	Port Byron to Clyde	mi. (km.) Read↑

40.9 (65.8)   Cayuga St. @ NY 414   12.8 (20.6)
   W to E Travelers: Through travellers to Seneca Falls
   travel due South on 414.
   To visit beautifully situated Lock 26. Turn on to Cayuga
   St. (Y intersection) Follow the signs to the boat launch
   then turn South on Tyre Rd./Deveraux Rd. At Lock Rd.
   turn East, go through the quarry area to Lock 26.

52.7 (84.8)   Rtes. 5/20 @ NY 414   1.0 (1.6)
   W to E Travelers: Turn East on to Rtes. 5/20/414 to go
   to Seneca Falls via Top O' The Finger Lakes Route.
   E to W Travelers: Turn North on to NY 414 to continue
   traveling on the Erie Canal Main Route; Continue traveling
   West on Rtes. 5/20 to travel on the Top O' The Finger
   Lakes Route

53.7 (86.4)   NY 89 @ Rtes 5/20/414   0.0 (0.0)

Seneca Falls

Info.: Seneca County Tourism, Waterloo NY, 315 539-1759,
   www.visitsenecany.net AC: 315. Zip: 13148.
Services: All.
Lodging: Motel.   B&Bs: The Guion House (in village), 32
   Cayuga St., 568-8129; Waterloo House, 45 Virginia St.,
   Waterloo (3 mi. (5 km.), West of the Seneca Falls, 13165 ,
   568-9456.
Camping: Cayuga Lake St. Pk., 2 mi. (3 km.), East of Seneca
   Falls on Garden St. & NY 89, 2678 Lower Lake Rd., 568-
   5163; Cayuga Lake Cpgd, NY 89S, PO Box 107 Waterloo
   13165, 568-0919; Oak Orchard Marina & Cpgd., NY 89N (on
   the edge of Montezuma Nat'l. Wildlife Refuge), PO Box 148,
   Reading Center 14876, 607 535-9969.
Attractions: Women's Rights Nat'l. Hist. Pk., 136 Fall St., 568-
   2991; Erie Canal Cruise Lines, 114 W. Bayard St., 586-
   8500. Starting point for Cayuga Lake Winery Trail, PO Box
   123, Fayette 13065, 800 684-5217.

W to E   **From Top O' The Finger Lakes Route**   E to W
          To Main Canal Route: Seneca Falls to Fairport
mi. (km.) Read↓   **Seneca Falls to Clyde**   mi. (km.) Read↑

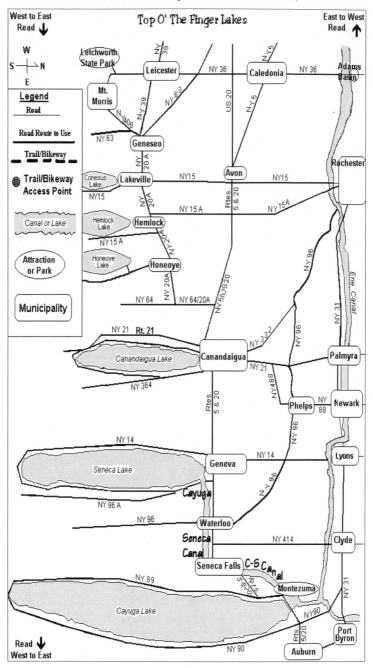

TOP O' THE FINGER LAKES ROUTE
SENECA-CAYUGA CANAL

This route is included to accommodate folks who want to travel along the Seneca-Cayuga Canal. Several users of *'Round Lake Ontario: A Bicyclist's Tour Guide,* requested this route too. The Finger Lakes have become a popular place to bicycle and we've published *Finger Lakes Bicyclist's Tour Guide* to accommodate those hearty bicyclists who like to test their mettle.

The area between each of the Finger Lakes is generally marked with hill topography. Going North to South the land descends in elevation. North of the Finger Lakes the land has moderate hills, thanks to the ice age formation of drumlins. In general the drumlin hills are severe on the North and Western sides with long sloping South and East sides. Nothing to worry about along this Route the roads used are basically rolling hills. The wineries which dot the Finger Lakes region will make your travels more amusing.

This Route extends from Spencerport to Seneca Falls, 85 mi. (138 km.) making a southern loop to the Main Erie Canal Route. The Top O' the Finger Lakes Route/Seneca-Cayuga Canal is between 5 mi. (8 km.) and 35 mi. (56 km.) South of the Main Erie Canal Route.

In general traveling North on almost any North-South road will take you back to the Erie Canal. The major North-South connecting roads between the two routes and realistic directions are provided.

The directions for the route are given described West to East.

	Top O' The Finger Lakes Route	
E to W	**Spencerport**	W to E
mi. (km.) Read↓	**to Seneca Falls**	mi. (km.) Read↑

Info.: Finger Lakes Association, 309 Lake St., Penn Yan NY 14527, 800 548-4386/315 536-7488, www.fingerlakes.org

Lodging: The Finger Lakes Bed & Breakfast Association, 309 Lake St., Penn Yan, NY 14527, 800 695-5590; Campground Owners of NY, PO Box 497, Dansville NY 14437, 585 335-2710.

Attractions: The Lakes! Wineries, architecture, historic sites and the scenery.

0.0 (0.0)   Washington St./NY 36   85.8 (138.1)
        @ Erie Canal Tow Path (CTP)
Turn South on to Washington St. which becomes NY 36
as it crosses NY 31/BR 5. Northhampton Park, at the
intersection of NY 31 & NY 36, has group camping. See
Main Erie Canal Route for information. Spencerport/
Adams Basin.

5.5 (8.0)   NY 33 @ NY 36   80.3 (129.2)
Continue riding South on NY 36.
Churchville: restaurants, grocery.

12.8 (20.6)   Rte. 5 @ NY 36   72.9 (117.3)
Continue South on NY 36 to Letchworth State Park.
Border Crossing, Livingston County & Monroe County

Caledonia
Info.: Area code: 585. Zip code: 14423. Caledonia and
Mumford are adjoining villages.
Services: Restaurants, grocery, convenience, hardware
& general merchandise stores.
Lodging: Motels. B&Bs: Roberts-Cameron House, 68
North St., 538-6316; Robertson Clan, 75 North St., 538-
2348; Genesee Country Inn, 948 George St., Mumford
NY 14511, 585 538-2500. Camping: Genesee Country
Cpgd, 40 Flint Hill Rd., Box 100, 538-4200.
Attractions: NYS Fish Hatchery, 16 North St., Genesee
Country Mus., Flint Hill Rd., Mumford 14511, 538-6866.
Genesee Greenway Trail.

25.2 (40.6)   Rts. 39/20A @ NY 36   60.5 (97.4)
Continue traveling South on NY 36.
Leicester: B&B: National Hotel, 2927 Main St. Leicester
14481, 585 382-3130; NY International Raceway Park (hot
rod racing), 2011 New Rd., Leicester 14481, 585 382-3030;
Camping supply stores in Leicester and Perry. Attraction:
Genesee Greenway Trail.

27.0 (43.5)   Letchworth St. Park @ NY 36   58.7 (94.5)
Info.: Letchworth St. Pk., Park Office, 585 439-2611.
Cycling & hiking Info.: Mtb patrol; mtb trails (some very
technical); road biking encouraged. Many hiking trails,
backcountry camping. Mtbers must register at the Park
office.
Hikers will particulary enjoy the less used East side of
the Gorge. Park hiking trails connect with the Finger

Lakes Trail system (limited biking) and the Genesee Greenway (multi-use trail from Rochester, NY to Pennsylvania.

Facilities: camping, tent sites, cabins, hot showers snack bars, restaurant, and camp store.

Attractions: Genesee River gorge extending the length of the Park; dam, museum, and swimming pool.

Lodging: Inn and convention center.

28.0 (45.1)   NY 408 @ NY 36   57.7 (92.9)
Turn East on to NY 408.

Mt. Morris

Info.: Area code: 585. Zip code: 14510.

Cycling & Hiking Info.: Friends of the Genesee Valley Greenway, PO Box 42, Mt. Morris 14510, 658-2569, www.netacc.net/~fogvg; Finger Lakes Trail Conference, PO Box 18048, Rochester 14618. Camping supply stores in Leicester, 1.5 mi. (2.4 km.) North, and Geneseo 5 mi. (8 km. Northeast). Bike shop in Geneseo.

Services: All.

Lodging: B&Bs: Allan's Hill, 2446 Sand Hill Rd., 658-4591; Allegiance, 145 S. Main St., 658-2769; Kathleen's Country Est., 7989 Union Corners Rd., 658-4441. There are additional B&Bs in villages bordering the Park.

Attractions: Letchworth State Park; Mt. Morris Dam.

29.9 (48.1)   NY 63 @ NY 408   55.8 (89.8)
Turn North on to NY 63.

32.5 (52.3)   NY 20A @ NY 63   53.2 (85.6)
Turn East on to NY 20A.

Geneseo

Info.: Area code: 585. Zip code: 14454.

Cycling & Hiking Info.: Bike shop and camping supply store (Swain Ski & Sports) in shopping plaza at the intersection of Rts. 20A & 63.

Services: All. College.

Lodging: Motels. B&Bs: Benton, 5385 Servis Rd., 243-3656; MacPhail House, 5477 Lakeville Rd. (NY 20A), 346-5600; Oak Valley Inn, 4235 Lakeville Rd., 346-6338; Some Place Else, 20 Main St., 243-9440.

Attractions: Livingston County Hist. Mus. 30 Center St., 243-9147; State College. Abbey of the Genesee, 3258 River Rd., Piffard NY 14533, 585 243-0660 (by appointment only; Trappist Monastery, home of Monk's bread).

37.7 (60.7)   NY 15 @ NY 20A   48.0 (77.2)
Continue East on NY 20A
Had enough of the Top O' the Finger Lakes? You
haven't really encountered any of the Lakes yet! You're
about to! If you want to return to the Erie Canal Route,
go North on NY 15 for 7.6 mi (12.2 km) and you'll hit the
Canal Tow Path just South of Rochester.

Lakeville & Conesus Lake

Info.: North end of Conesus Lake. Area code: 585.
Bike Info.: Lots of bicyclists round this small Finger
Lake.   Basically a level circumnavigation route on a
narrow, moderately trafficked, no shouldered, 2 lane
County road. ~20 mi. (32 km.) round trip.
Services: Convenience   stores,   small   grocery,
restaurants, hardware store. Park & Ride weekday bus
to Rochester.
Lodging: Note that Conesus Village is ~5 mi. (8 km.)
South of Lakeville. B&Bs: Blue Stone, 2387 East Lake
Rd., Conesus 14435, 346-6929; Conesus Lake, 2388
East Lake Rd., Conesus 14435, 346-6526.
Camping: Conesus Lake Cpgd., 2202 East Lake Rd.,
Conesus 14435, 346-5472.

40.0 (64.4)   NY 15 @ NY 20A   45.7 (73.5)
Continue East on NY 20A.

Livonia

Info.: Area code: 585. Zip code: 14487.
Services: Grocery, hardware store.
Lodging: B&Bs: Cobblestone House B&B, 2534 East
Lake Rd., 346-2805; Stefano's Countryside B&B, 3915
Pennemite Rd., 346-6338.
Note: NY 15 is the main road (there are County roads
closer to the Lake) closest to the West side of Hemlock
Lake. It is a steep decline to Springwater at the southern
end of this Lake. NY 15A goes along the East side of
Hemlock Lake. A very steep climb up from Springwater.
Round trip: ~30 mi. (48 km.). Definitely not advised if
you are traveling loaded touring.

44.5 (71.7)   NY 15A Jct. NY 20A   41.2 (66.3)
Note: NY 20A goes along the North ends of both
Hemlock and Honeoye Lakes. It is a very steep decline
from this intersection to Hemlock Lake; and then a very

steep incline to Honeoye Lake. The view is magnificent! The road has a wide shoulder.

Continue straight on to Richmond Mills Rd. if you want a more moderate route but you'll miss actually going to both Hemlock and Honeoye Lakes. The total distance is about the same any way you travel.

If you really like long steep hills turn South on to Rtes. 20A/15A. NY 15A goes along the East side of Hemlock Lake beginning about .5 mi (.8 km) South of Hemlock Hamlet. NY 20A turns Northeast just before Hemlock Lake and climbs above Honeoye Lake. It's a wicked up and down from this intersection of Rtes. 20A and 15A. The scenery is worth the effort.

To avoid a this very steep hill (down & up) on NY 15A, travel straight across NY 15A (be careful). You are actually facing North at this point) on to Richmond Mills Rd./County Rd. (CR) 15. Turn East on to Richmond Mills Rd./CR 15 which bcomes Pierpoint Rd. then Tilton Rd. then Cooper Rd. It then meets Rtes. 20A/64 and you can continue reading the directions from W to E at 54.5 mi. (87.8 km.) below. These are lightly trafficked rural roads with a good chip seal surface.

Hemlock Lake

Hemlock Lake is Rochester's reservoir. The Lake is on NY 15A, .5 mi (.8 km) South of the 20A/15A junction to Honeoye. Turn off NY 15A at Lake Rd. (what else!), there will be a small sign. Officially, a permit (free) is needed to even stop here. Fill out the form and keep it as a momento. In 30 years of going to Hemlock Lake no one has ever asked to see my permit. Great fishing. No swimming. Day use park at the northern end of the Lake with H_2O, clean toilets, shelters, picnic grills. Go down the dirt road along the East side of the Lake, round the water plant for a great place to fish and have your lunch. Circumnavigation route: Rough dirt roads and hiking trails, Mt. bikes only. Ideal for the adventurous. ~20 mi. (32 km.); See note under Livonia.

Border! In rural areas such as this there are no County border guards! But the police might ticket you for speeding down the NY 20A hill! What a wonderful momento!
Ontario County & Livingston County.

Round Bales Are Easier to Move

48.6 (78.2)   West Lake Rd. @ NY 20A   37.1 (59.7)
Continue East on NY 20A

Honeoye Lake

E to W Traveler Note: Read the directions in the preceeding entry, "Hemlock Lake" to avoid a steep incline/decline, before continuing on your trek. You can reach County Rd. 15/Richmond Mills Rd. by going North on County Rd. 37 which is just West of the Village.

Honeoye Village

Info.: Area code: 585. Zip code: 14471.
Services & Facilities: Convenience store, restaurants; hardware, general merchandise stores.
Lodging: Aubin's Lodgings in the Pines, 495 West Lake Rd., 346-3774; Greenwoods, 8136 Quayle Rd. 229-2111.
Honeoye Lake: Except for a 2 mi. (3.2 km.) section of good dirt road, Honeoye Lake can be circumnavigated using East Lake & West Lake Rds.   Long inclines/declines. ~20 mi. (36 km.) round trip.

54.5 (87.8)   NY 64 @ NY 20A   31.2 (50.2)
Turn North on to NY 64.
E to W Note: Before continuing on your trek, read the directions in the entry, Hemlock Village and Lake to avoid a steep inclines/declines.

57.7 (92.9)   Rtes. 20A/64 @ Rtes. 5 & 20   28.0 (45.1)
W to E: Turn East on to Rtes. 5 & 20. If you want to return to the Erie Canal Route it will be more efficient to continue onwards to Canandaigua and take a North bound route from there.
E to W: If you want to return to the Erie Canal Route, follow NY 64 North for 13 mi (21 km) to the Canal just South of Rochester.

B&B: Enchanted Rose, 7479 Rtes. 5 &20, East Bloomfield, 14443, 657-5003. Camping: Creekside Cpgd., 2528 Wheeler Station Rd., Holcomb 14469.

62.3 (100.6) NY 21 Jct. Rtes. 20A/5 & 20   23.4 (37.7) Continue traveling East on Rtes. 5 & 20. You are now in Canandaigua. See traveler notes after the Canandaigua information entries.

Canandaigua

Info.: Canandaigua CofC, 113 S. Main St., Canandaigua NY 14424, 585 394-4400, www.canandaigua.com Area code: 585. Zip code: 14424.

Cycling & Hiking Info.: Bike/camping store on Rts. 5 & 20; camping store on Main St. Ontario Pathways Rail Trail, PO Box 996, 394-7968. Lake City Cyclists (informal riding group) ride Tuesday evenings, 6 PM, behind Courthouse. Canandaigua Lake is circumnavigated using asphalt roads which are parallel to the Lake. There are several steep descents/ ascents on both sides of the Lake. Heavily trafficked, on weekends. Many people attempt and succeed at circling Lake Canandaigua. Be cautious. ~45 mi. (72 km.) round trip.

Services: All. Hospital.

Lodging: Motels, hotels, cabin rentals. Over 16 B&Bs, Canandaigua Lake Area B&Bs, PO Box 282.

Attractions: Canandaigua Lake; swimming at Kershaw Pk. North end; and at town & village beaches which dot the shore line; boat and jet ski rentals; good fishing. Sonnenberg Gardens (formal gardens and restored *robber baron* summer *cottage*), 151 Charlotte St., 394-4922; Granger Homestead & Carriage Mus., 295 N. Main St. 394-1472. Finger Lakes Performing Arts Ctr. (country, classical, rock music concerts & other performing arts), Lincoln Hill Road, 222-5000. Canandaigua Speedway, Fairgrounds, 394-0961. Canandaigua Lady Cruise Ship, PO Box 856, 394-5365; Capt. Gray's Boat Tours, 115 Howell St., 394-5270. Ganondagan St. Hist. Site (Seneca Nation), PO Box 239, 1488 Victor Holcomb Rd., Victor 14564, 924-5848, 9 mi. (14 km.) North.

W to E Traveler Notes

To return to the Erie Canal Route, Turn North on to NY 21. One way, 8.6 mi. (13.9 km.) to Palmyra. A more pleasant and interesting ride is to go through Phelps: Turn North on to NY 21. At Chapin Rd., 3.9 mi. (6.2 km.), turn East on to NY 488. At Phelps turn North on to NY 88, to Newark for a total of 23.6 mi. (38 km.) one way.

Phelps

Services: Grocery and general merchandise stores.
Lodging: B&B. Junius Ponds Cpgd., 1475 W. Townline
Rd., Phelps NY 14532, 315 539-9008; Cheerful Valley
Cpgd., NY 14, Phelps NY 14532, 315 781-1222.

68.4 (110.1) County NY 20 @ Rts. 5 & 20   17.3 (27.8)
W to E: Through travellers continue East on Rts. 5/20.
E to W: Turn on to CR 20 (sign will say, to BOCES or
Finger Lakes Ed. Center). CR 20 Jct. with NY 488 to
return to the Main Canal Route via Phelps. See entry
immediately above this one.

74.8 (120.4) NY 14A/ @ Rts. 5 & 20   10.9 (17.5)
Keuka Lake turn off. Although Keuka Lake is not
geologically one of the Finger Lakes it is usually
considered a part of this chain of Lakes. It is a 14 mi.
(22.5 km.) traverse southward on 14A to Penn Yan.
Another 3 mi (4.8 km) to beautiful Keuka Lake St. Pk.
Shouldered State roads which have some severe hills.
Wineries dot the hills surrounding Keuka Lake.

76.0 (122.3) NY 14 @ Rtes. 5 & 20   9.7 (15.6)
Continue East on Rtes. 5 & 20. Almost at Seneca Falls.

Geneva

Info.: Geneva CofC, 35 Lakefront Dr, Geneva NY 14456,
877 543-6382/315 789-1776. AC: 315. Zip: 14456.
Cycling & Hiking Info.: Geneva Bike Ctr., 789-5922
Seneca Lake Circumnavigation: The roads circling
Seneca Lake are major 2 lane State highways with well
defined wide paved shoulders. There are severe
descents/ascents towards the southern end of the Lake.
~85 mi. (136 km.) round trip.
Services & Facilities: All.
Lodging: Motels. B&B: 99 William St., 789-1273.
Camping: 10 mi. (16 km.) South of Geneva on East Lake
Rd. is Sampson St. Pk., Romulus NY, 315 585-6392,
bike trail, and WW II Mus.
Attractions: Terminus of the Seneca & Cayuga Canal.
Actually the Seneca-Cayuga Canal terminates 2 mi. (3.2
km.), South of Watkins Glen (Grand Prix auto racing) at
the southern end of Seneca Lake in Montour Falls.
Prouty-Chew Mus. & Rose Hill Mansion, Geneva Hist.
Soc. 543 S. Main St., 789-5151; Smith Opera House,
restored 19th century theatre. Colleges. Seneca Lake

Wine Trail (21 wineries ring Seneca Lake), 350 Elm St., Penn Yan, NY 14527, 315 536-9996. Sampson WW II Mus., Sampson St. Pk., 10 mi. South on NY 96A. Border Crossing, Seneca County & Ontario County.

82.8 (133.3) Seneca/Cayuga Lock 4 @ Rts. 5 & 20   2.9 (4.7)
Continue traveling East on 5 & 20

Waterloo

Info.: Area code: 315. Zip code: 13165.
Services: Convenience stores, antique and outlet stores.
Lodging: Motels. B&B: Waterloo House, 45 Virginia St., 539-9739. Camping: Oak Orchard Cpgd., PO Box 454, NY 89N, 365-3000; Waterloo Harbor Cpgd,, 1278 Waterloo-Geneva Rd. (Rts. 5 & 20), 539-8848.
Attractions: Waterloo Library & Terwilliger Mus., 31 E. Williams St., 539-0533. Waterloo Memorial Day Mus., 35 E. Main St., 539-9611.

83.9 (135.0) NY 414 @ Rts. 5 & 20   1.9 (3.1)
Continue traveling East on 5 & 20
Main Canal Route *groupies* join us here.

85.8 (138.1) Womens' Rights Nat'l Hist. Pk   00.0 (00.0)
          @ Rts. 5 & 20
Seneca Falls: See Main Erie Canal Route for information. In truth the Seneca-Cayuga Canal terminates at Montour Falls, 1.5 mi. (2.4 km.) south of Watkins Glen. Watkins Glen, noted for its auto race track, is at the southern end of Seneca Lake.

E to W	**Top O' The Finger Lakes Route** **Seneca Falls**	W to E
mi. (km.) Read↓	**to Spencerport**	mi. (km.) Read↑

East to West Traveler Note
The Top O' The Finger Lakes Route is an optional route which runs E—W and South of the Erie Canal Route from Seneca Falls to Spencerport.
The Erie Canal Route directions are continued before the Top O' The Finger Lakes Route.

Seneca Falls to Syracuse

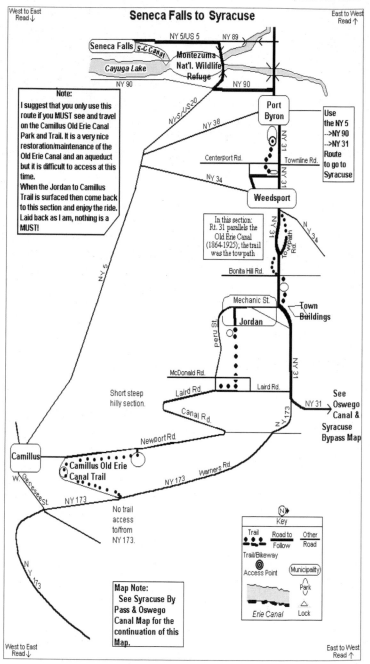

West to East
Read ↓

East to West
Read ↑

NY 5/US 5   NY 89

Seneca Falls S-C Canal

Montezuma Nat'l. Wildlife Refuge

Cayuga Lake

NY 90

NY 90

Port Byron

Note:
I suggest that you only use this route if you MUST see and travel on the Camillus Old Erie Canal Park and Trail. It is a very nice restoration/maintenance of the Old Erie Canal and an aqueduct but it is difficult to access at this time.
When the Jordan to Camillus Trail is surfaced then come back to this section and enjoy the ride. Laid back as I am, nothing is a MUST!

NY 5/US 20

NY 38

Centerport Rd.   Townline Rd.

NY 34

Weedsport

Use the NY 5 -->NY 90 -->NY 31 Route to go to Syracuse

NY 5

NY 31

NY 31

NY 34

In this section:
Rt. 31 parallels the Old Erie Canal (1864-1925); the trail was the towpath

Towpath Rd.

Bonita Hill Rd.

Mechanic St.

Town Buildings

Peru St.

Jordan

McDonald Rd.

Laird Rd.   Laird Rd.

Short steep hilly section.

Canal Rd.

NY 173

NY 31

NY 31

See Oswego Canal & Syracuse Bypass Map

Newport Rd.

Camillus

Camillus Old Erie Canal Trail

W. Genesee St.

NY 173

NY 173   Warners Rd.

No trail access to/from NY 173.

N Y 173

Map Note:
  See Syracuse By Pass & Oswego Canal Map for the continuation of this Map.

Key

Trail

Road to Follow

Other Road

Trail/Bikeway

Access Point

Municipality

Park

Erie Canal   Lock

West to East
Read ↓

East to West
Read ↑

CENTRAL NEW YORK STATE

If you started in Tonawanda then you've traveled approximately 150 mi. (240 km.). Likewise if you've started in Albany you've traveled approximately 130 mi. (210 km.)
What a nice place to be, in the geographical center of the Erie Canal route! Syracuse and environs owes a good deal of its development to its central location. The almost equidistant meeting place of roads going South to Philadelphia, North to the forests and mines of the Adirondacks, the Erie Canal going East to Albany and West to Buffalo. The perfect location for the establishment of industrial enterprises manufacturing machines, tools and other items necessary but lacking in the mid-West during the 19th century.

W to E	**Erie Canal Route**	E to W
mi. (km.) Read↓	**Seneca Falls to Fayetteville**	mi. (km.) Read↑

0.0 (0.0)   Rtes. 5/20 @ NY 414 South   54.1 (87.1)
Ride East on Rtes. 5/20
Seneca Falls, See previous Main Erie Canal Route Chapter for information.

3.1 (5.0)   Rtes. 318/89 @ Rtes. 5/20   51.0 (82.1)
Continue traveling on Rtes. 5 & 20.
Cayuga Lake circumnavigation: St. NY 89 (West side) & NY 90/34B/34 (East side) are wide 2 lane wide shouldered roads. Traffic is usually light during the day. ~95 mi. (153 km.) round trip. Travel clockwise around the Lake. It is dangerous to use NY 34 from Lansing to Ithaca. Camping: On NY 89N, Oak Orchard Cpgd.,

5.2 (8.4)   Montezuma Wildlife Refuge   48.9 (78.7)
@ NY 89 and Rts 5 & 20
Info.: Refuge Manager, Montezuma Nat'l Wildlife Refuge, 3395 Rte 5 & 20 East, Seneca Falls, NY 13148, 315 568-5987, TTD: 800 439-2370. A prime resting place for migratory waterfowl and other birds. Best times to view are just after sunrise or sunset. Toilets, Visitors Ctr. and at some trailheads and viewing platforms. No camping.

5.0 (8.0)   Cayuga Co. & Seneca County Border   48.8 (78.5)

5.8 (9.3)   NY 90 @ Rts. 5 & 20   48.3 (77.7)
Turn North on to NY 90.
You just rode over the Cayuga-Seneca Canal & are

riding parallel to the Canal along the Cayuga River. **Info.**: NY 90 Assoc., PO Box 587, Union Springs, NY 13160, 315 889-5836. **Attraction**: Cayuga-Seneca Canal Lock 1, the *Mud Lock* is 1.5 mi. (2.4 km.) South of this intersection off NY 90.

Lake Cayuga circumnavigation: NY 90/34B/34 are used on the East side for the circumnavigation of Cayuga Lake. NY 89 on the West side. These are wide 2 lane shouldered roads. Traffic is generally light. ~95 mi. (153 km.) round trip. This is not an easy Lake to circumnavigate. Do not use NY 34 south of Lansing.

10.4 (16.7)   NY 31 @ NY 90   43.7 (70.3)
Turn East on to NY 31/BR 5.

14.7 (23.7)   NY 38 @ NY 31/BR 5   39.4 (63.4)
Continue riding East on NY 31/BR 5.
Owasco Lake: Going South on NY 38 will bring you to Auburn, 7mi. (11 km.), which has a number of museums and 19th century homes, including the Harriet Tubman House. Auburn is at the northern end of Lake Owasco. Owasco circumnavigation route: NY 38 (West side) to Moravia and NY 38A (East side) back to Auburn. These roads are lightly trafficked with wide shoulders. ~30 mi. (48 km.) round trip.

Port Byron
Info.: Auburn and Cayuga County CofC, 36 South St., Auburn NY 13021, 315 252-7291.
Services: Grocery, convenience store, & restaurant.
Lodging: Lillebo Camp B&B, Hard Point Rd., Port Byron NY 315 776-8506.

Cayuga County Erie Canal (CCT) Trail/Jordan-Camillus Erie Canal (ECP) Parkway/NY 31
Port Byron to Jordan

Route Notes
Road cyclotourists who do not like stone dust/cinder/grass bikeways should follow NY 31/BR 5 to Jordan and then all the way to Baldwinsville. NY 31 has a wide paved shoulder.
Hikers should use the CCT and ECP.
2004 Trail Conditions: Both the CCT and ECP have been surveyed and marked with brown and yellow square *blazes* with a *5B* route indicator. The Trail surfaces have either not been significantly improved or have degenerated since the 1st & 2nd editions of this Tour Guide were published.

Road bicyclists should not use either of these Trails or the hilly route leading from Jordan to Camillus to Syracuse. Road cyclists should follow NY 31 to Baldwinsville and then use either NY 370 along the northeastern side of Onondaga Lake; or Syracuse St. to Van Buren St. to St. Fair Blvd. along the southwestern side of Onondaga Lake.

With the exception of a short section through Weedsport, the Cayuga County Erie Canal Trail (CCT) is entirely on a graded unimproved cinder/grass 10 ft. (3 m.), surface which parallels NY 31/BR 5. It took me a full day to simply determine where the trail access points from NY 31 existed.

The map contained in this book is the only map of the trail in existence at this time. Essentially the CCT follows the enlarged *Old* (1847) Erie Canal's traverse through 19th century America's *bread basket.*

The CCT connects with the Jordan-Camillus Erie Canal Parkway (ECP) at Jordan. The first 12 mi. (19 km.) of the ECP is on a well defined and maintained off road trail. After that it degenerates into a single track trail and then a goes on a dirt road paralleling the old Canal. The final 8 mi. (13 km.), in Camillus, is on a smooth well maintained stone dust surface.

Both trails are relatively straight lines (the Canal was too!) which are easy to follow. Notations are made in this route description & on the map where the trails are impassible, the surface changes or where the trail traveler must exit the trail and go on NY 31 or on to another road.

Possibilities for guerilla camping here are endless, but bring H_2O and toilet paper (as well as a shovel to bury your remains)

W to E	**Cayuga Canal Trail or NY 31**	E to W
mi. (km.) Read↓	**Port Byron to Camillus**	mi. (km.) Read↑

14.7 (23.7)   NY 38 @ NY 31   37.9 (61.0)
Continue traveling on NY 31 through Port Byron.
Note that during the 2004 summer NY 31 might be closed to traffic due to construction. Use the CCT Trail to avoid a roadway long detour.

14.9 (24.0)   Cayuga County Canal Trail (CCT)   37.7 (60.7)
                    @ NY 31 PORT BYRON
An official Erie Canal Trail round sign and a tiny brown sign mark the entrance to a small park with a 3 sided shelter & playground. The CCT begins at the eastern end of this Park. Rough gravel, stone dust grass Trail surface.
NY 31 parallels the CCT and if you have trouble traveling on the CCT then return to NY 31 and take it to

Weedsport. Then read the directions from Weedsport.

16.7 (26.9)   Centerport Rd. @ CCT or NY 31   35.9 (57.8)
Trail surface degenerates to a grass single track trail.
Too much for you? Turn South on to Centerport Rd.
Travel to Hamilton St. (<.1 mi, <.1 km).
Turn East on Hamilton St. Hamilton St. goes directly into
Weedsport. Turn North on to S. Seneca St./NY 34 to
return to NY 31.
Or continue on the CCT for another mile (1.6 km.)

17.7 (28.5)   Hawley St. @ CCT & NY 31   34.9 (56.2)
The CCT ends just after a small parking area on NY 31.
Turn either on to NY 31 or on to Hawley St. then East on
Hamilton St. to S. Seneca St./NY 34.
Turn North on S. Seneca St./NY 34 & go into Weedsport
to encounter NY 31/BR 5.

18.7 (30.1)   NY 34 @ NY 31/BR 5   33.9 (54.6)
Continue East on NY 31/BR 5.
Note that during the 2004 summer NY 31 might be
closed to traffic due to construction. Use the CCT Trail to
avoid a roadway long detour.

Weedsport

Info.: Town Clerk, Town of Brutus, Weedsport NY
13166. Area code: 315. Zip code: 13166.
Services: Grocery, restaurants, & other stores.
Lodging: Motels. B&B: Mansard on the Lake, 8755
South Seneca St., 834-2262. Camping: Riverforest Pk.
Rec. Area, NY 38, 1 mi. (1.6 km.) N., 834-9458.
Attractions: Weedsport Speedway; Motorsports Hall of
Fame, Fairgrounds, 834-6606. Erie Canal Centerport
Aqueduct, 1 mi. (1.6 km.), West of Weedsport.

19.1 (30.7)   NY 34 @ NY 31   33.5 (52.3)
          East end of Weedsport
Road cyclotourists should use NY 31. The CCT is very
rough. The Trail directions are given because the old
locks on the Trail are particularly interesting.
The CCT trail picks up on the Southeast side of the NY
34 bridge. There is a sign.

20.1 (32.3)   CCT @ Towpath Rd.   32.5 (52.3)
The CCT from downtown Weedsport abruptly ends at
Towpath Rd. The Brutus Town Highway Dep't. & County
Fairgrounds are in front of you. Turning North you will
see Towpath Rd. Travel on Towpath Rd. The trail

disappears behind the Highway Department & Fairgrounds. Doing the research for this section, I stepped into the Highway Department office. A new *Towpath Rd.* sign sat on the desk waiting to be placed on a pole for hikers & bikers.

Along Towpath Rd., behind the fairgrounds & opposite a truck parking lot, is a small sign denoting a snowmobile route. That's the CCT! The snowmobile trail might be overgrown so travel on Towpath Rd. to NY 31.

21.0 (33.8)   Towpath Rd. @ NY 31.   31.6 (50.8)

W to E Travelers: Pedestrian crossing signs! Cross NY 31. A small brown sign denotes the CCT, it is near the pedestrian crossing sign on the eastbound (South) side of NY 31.

E to W Travelers: Go past the Y jct. of NY 31 & Towpath Rd., just past this intersection is a second Pedestrian crossing sign on the westbound (North) side of NY 31. You will see a CCT sign. This section of the CCT might be overgrown, use Towpath Rd.

Havin' Fun on the Trail

21.8 (35.1)   NY 31 @ CCT   30.8 (50.0)
CCT crosses to the South side (westbound) of NY 31.

23.9 (38.5)   NY 31 @ CCT   28.7 (46.2)
CCT exits on to NY 31. Hikers will cross NY 31 to the trail. Bicyclists will cross NY 31 to bicycle with traffic and travel to Bonita Hill Rd.

24.1 (38.8)   Bonita Hill Rd. CCT @ NY 31   28.5 (45.9)

Turn North on to Bonita Hill Rd. You will pass a Lock and ride on a smooth gravel to Jordan. After the Old Erie Canal Lock, bear South when the trail divides. Not on to the driveway to NY 31, but on the CCT parallel to NY 31. Border. No passports, visas or id cards are necessary! Onondaga County & Cayuga County.

25.7 (41.3)   NY 31 @ CCT   26.9 (43.3)
You will exit the CCT on to NY 31. Be very, very careful at this curve and this intersection! If necessary walk across the lawn in front of the Jordan Community Center and cross at the driveway.
Alternatively, Cross NY 31, at the curve, to McLaughlin St. McLaughlin St. is directly opposite the Community Center. Travel straight on McLaughlin on to Clinton St. Turn North on to Clinton St. to go into downtown Jordan.

ROAD Cyclists should continue to follow NY 31 to Baldwinsville. Hikers and mtb cyclists can use the CCT Trail going West or the Jordan-Camillus Erie Canal Parkway (BR 5B) going East.

25.9 (41.7)   Main St. @ Clinton Ave./Mechanic St.   26.7 (43.0)
Cross Main St. and ride straight on to Mechanic St.
That's many lines of directions for about a .2 mi. (.3 km.) of travel!

Jordan Village

Info.: Elbridge Town Clerk, Elbridge Town Hall, Jordan NY 13080; Jordan Village Clerk, Village Hall, Jordan, NY.
Services: Grocery, restaurants, other stores.
Attraction: Erie Canal Parkway, PO Box 397, Jordan, NY 13080. This is a 7 mi. (11 km.), cleared and maintained towpath trail along the Old Erie Canal from the Cayuga County line to Camillus.

26.1 (42.0)   Beaver St. @ Mechanic St.   26.5 (42.6)
Turn North on to Beaver St.
The entrance to the Jordan-Camillus Erie Canal Parkway (ECP) is near Auburn Wire Works plant on Beaver St.

Rural Road Route Note
This Rural Road Route is very hilly and not really appropriate for loaded cyclotourists (I have no idea what I was thinking 10 years ago when I cycled & then included this route in the Guide.).
If you would rather use rural roads than the Jordan-Camillus Erie Canal Parkway (ECP) continue East on

Mechanic St. Mechanic St. becomes Peru Rd. which ends at Laird Rd. Turn South on to Laird. Then read from W to E 14.8 mi. (23.8 km.), below.
Hikers should use the ECP.

26.2 (42.2)   Beaver St. @ ECP Entrance   26.4 (42.5)
Enter the Erie Canal Parkway. No H_2O, a small shelter.

28.6 (46.0)   South McDonald Rd. @ ECP   26.0 (41.8)
Turn South on to South McDonald Rd.
You can go another .9 mi. (1.4 km.) further on a very rudimentary single track trail which exits on to Laird Rd.

28.8 (46.3)   Peru Rd. @ South McDonald Rd.   25.8 (41.5)
Turn East on to Peru Rd.

29.9 (48.1)   Laird Rd. @ Peru Rd.   24.7 (39.7)
Turn South on to Laird Rd.

Route Note
Travelers wantng to use the Syracuse By Pass Routes or go to Lake Ontario via the Oswego Canal Route should turn North on to Laird Rd. and then turn East on to NY 31. At the intersection of Rts. 31 and 173 follow the directions in the Syracuse By Pass & Oswego Canal Route chapters. Using NY 31 & the South of Lake Oneida By Pass Route is the most rapid way to go East.

31.2 (50.2)   Whiting Rd. @ Peru Rd.   23.4 (37.6)
Turn East and then, very quickly (<.1 mi./<.1 km.) North. This intersection is not marked well. You want to go to Memphis! (*Graceland* is in Tennessee.)

33.0 (53.1)   Canal Rd.   21.6 (34.7)
          @ Whiting Rd./Bennetts Rd.
You've travelled through Memphis and saw Elvis! Turn on to Canal Rd.

Route Note
Travelers wantng to use the Syracuse By Pass Routes or go to Lake Ontario via the Oswego Canal Route should turn North on to Bennetts Rd. and then turn West on to NY 173. At the intersection of Rts. 31 and 173 follow the directions in the Syracuse By Pass & Oswego Canal Route sections.

34.2 (55.0)   Newport Rd. @ Canal Rd.   20.4 (32.8)
Turn North on to Newport Rd.

34.4 (55.4)   Camillus Erie Canal Pk.   20.2 (35.5)

@ Newport Rd.
Enter the Camillus Canal Park, 5750 Devoe Rd., Camillus NY 13031, 315 672-5110 & ride on the Camillus Erie Canal Trail (CECT).

Route Note
Travelers going to Lake Ontario via the Oswego Canal Route or using the Syracuse By Pass Routes via Lake Oneida should continue North on Newport Rd. to the intersection of NY 173. Then turn West on to NY 173. At the intersection of Rts. 173 and 31 the Oswego Canal Route and Lake Oneida Syracuse By Pass Routes begin.

34.7 (55.0)　Devoe Rd. @ CECT　　　　　19.9 (32.0)
Continue traveling on the Camillus Erie Canal Trail.

Camillus
Services: Grocery, convenience and hardware store.
Lodging: Re Family B&B, 4166 Split Rock Rd., Camillus NY 13031, 315 468-2039.
Attractions: Camillus Canal Park, 315 672-5110.

35.2 (56.6)　Three Arch Aqueduct @ CECT　　18.9 (30.4)
The Aqueduct is a masterpiece of Canal stonework.

39.1 (62.9)　Camillus Canal Park @ NY 173　　15.0 (24.1)
You can no longer access the Camillus Erie Canal Trail (CECT) from NY 173.

Route Notes
W to E: Following very hilly NY 173 southward will bring the traveller through Syracuse and to the Old Erie Canal State Park tow path. A 40 mi. (64 km.), stone dust path from DeWitt/Fayetteville to Rome.
Options for traveling through or around Syracuse:
　Oswego Canal to Lake Ontario
　Syracuse By Pass via Oneida Lake North to Rome
　Syracuse By Pass via Oneida Lake South to Rome
　Main Route: Camillus through Syracuse to Fayetteville
E to W Travelers going to Lake Ontario via the Oswego Canal Route turn North on Newport Rd. to the intersection of NY 173. Then turn West on to NY 173. At the intersection of Rts. 173 and 31 the Oswego Canal Route begins.

40.7 (65.5)　NY 5 (limited access highway)　　13.4 (21.6)
　　　　　　@ NY 173
Continue traveling on NY 173. NY 173 changes its name

from Warners Rd. to Onondaga Rd. South of NY 5.

41.3 (66.5)   West Genesee St. @ NY 173   12.8 (20.6)
Turn East on to West Genesee St.

41.9 (67.4)   NY 5 Jct. W Genesee St.   12.2 (19.6)
Continue traveling East on NY 5/W. Genesee St.

44.2 (71.1)   Erie Blvd. W @ NY 5/W. Genesee St.   9.9 (15.9)
Follow the NY 5 signs on to Erie Blvd. W. Both W.
Genesee St. and Erie Blvd. W./NY 5 will end up at the
same point in downtown Syracuse.

45.7 (73.5)   West St. @ NY 5/Water St./Erie Blvd.   8.4 (13.5)
Continue traveling East on NY 5/Water St./Erie Blvd.

Syracuse

Info.: Greater Syracuse CVB, 572 S. Salina St., Syracuse NY
13202, 800 234-4797/315 470-1910. AC: 315. Zip: various.

Cycling & Hiking Info.: Onondaga Cycling Club, Inc., PO Box
6307, Teall Station, Syracuse NY 13217, regular weekend
and Wednesday night rides throughout the season.

Services: All. Hospitals.

Lodging: Motels galore! B&Bs: See listings for Baldwinsville and
Camillus (eastern suburbs) and Fayetteville (western suburb).
B&B Wellington, 707 Danforth St., 13208, 471-2433; Benedict
House, 1402 James St., 13203, 476-6541; Dickenson House
on James, 1504 James St., 13203, 423-4777; Russell-
Farrnkoph House, 209 Green St., 13203, 472-8001;
Lakeview, 204 Brow St., Liverpool 13088, 457-5269. Hostel:
Downing HI/AYH Hostel, 535 Oak St., 13203, 472-5788.
Camping: See Fayetteville, below.

Attractions: Canal: Erie Canal Mus., 318 Erie Blvd. East, 13202,
471-0593.

New York State Fair, State Fair Blvd., Syracuse NY 13209.

Sports: Skates soccer, Chiefs baseball, Crunch hockey; Syracuse
University sports.

Neighborhood festivals throughout the summer.

Culture: Music & Drama: Jazz Festival, 475-7979; Syracuse
Sympony Orchestra, 411 Montgomery St., 13202, 800 724-
0113; Syracuse Opera, PO Box 6904, 13217, 475-5915;
Rock/Country concerts are held at the Carrier Dome,
Syracuse University, 13244, 443-4534; SummerFest Drama
Festival, Mulroy Civic Ctr. 411 Montgomery St., 13202, 435-
2121.

Museums: Everson Mus. of Art, 401 Harrison St., 13202;
Onondaga Historical Mus., 321 Montgomery St., 13202, 428-
1864; Mus. of Science & Technology, 500 S. Franklin St.,

13202, 425-0747; Burnet Park Zoo, 1 Conservation Place, 435-8511; Oakwood Cemetery, PO Box 65, 13215. The Salt Mus., Onondaga Lake Pkwy, Liverpool, 453-6715; Sainte Marie Among the Indians, NY 370, Liverpool, 453-6767.

Public Transportation: All public ground transportation (bus, Amtrak, light rail) facilities emanate from the Transportation Center at the Carousel Mall.

Bus: Local: CNY Centro, 200 Cortland Ave., PO Box 820, 13205, 442-3400, has an extensive system of routes including Camillus and Fayetteville routes from downtown Syracuse. Alas, some buses have bike racks.

Intercity: Syracuse is served by Greyhound; Adirondack and New York Trailways; Cortland Transportation.

Amtrak: Baggage service.

Airport: Hancock Airport is in North Syracuse. Airport to Downtown Syracuse: Turn South on to South Bay Rd. from the Airport Blvd. access road. In .5 mi. (.8 km.), South Bay Rd. junctions with NY 11/Brewerton Rd. Continue riding South on NY 11/Brewerton Rd. [Turning North on to NY 11 will take you to the Syracuse By Pass Routes around Lake Oneida.] In 2.9 mi. (4.6 km.), Brewerton Rd./NY 11 changes its name to N. Salina St./NY 11. Continue traveling on NY 11. At the intersection of N. Salina St./NY 11 and N. State St., NY 11 becomes N. State St. Continue following NY 11 and in 1.6 mi. (2.8 km.), you will be in downtown Syracuse at the intersection of Erie Blvd./NY 5 and the Erie Canal Mus.

46.1 (74.2)   Salina St. @ NY 5/Erie Blvd E   8.0 (12.9)
Continue on NY 5/Erie Blvd. E.
During rush hours this is a busy street and you will have to use caution or the sidewalk. Off hours it isn't too bad. Erie Blvd. widens and becomes a divided roadway as it goes East from downtown. NY 5 is basically a level road, alternative routes such as NY 92 are very hilly.

50.2 (80.8)   Kinne Rd. @ NY 5/Erie Blvd. E   3.9 (6.3)
Turn North on to Kinne Rd. Landmark: Shopping Mall.

51.0 (82.1)   Butternut Dr. @ Kinne Rd.   3.1 (5.0)
Landmark: Bridge over Interstate highway.
Turn North on to Butternut Drive.
To choose the correct ramp to go down to Butternut Dr., first look for the Ryder Park access on the Southeast corner of the bridge. At the base of the ramp is the entrance to Old Erie Canal State Park @ Ryder Park.
Old Erie Canal State Park, 687-7821. Locks, bridges, and other *works* of the Old (1847) Erie Canal will be seen

along this trail. It is a 37 mi. (60 km.), stone dust trail between DeWitt/Fayetteville (Syracuse) and Rome. The trail is not necessarily very smooth and you might prefer to use parallel roads. Green Lakes St. Pk. (camping) and numerous villages with lodging and services are along the way. You will be able to pick up a map of the Park at almost every cross road.

51.1 (82.23) Trail Entrance @ Butternut Drive   3.0 (4.8)
This is called Ryder County Park but it is really the beginning of the Old Erie Canal St. Pk. (OECSP) Trail.

51.9 (83.5)   Cedar Bay Picnic Area   2.2 (3.5)
@ (OECSP) Trail

54.1 (87.1)   Manlius Center Rd./   0.0 (0.0)
Shepps Corners Rd./Minoa Rd.
@ OECSP Trail
Travelers who tired of NY 31/BR 5 on the South Shore of Oneida Lake join the main Erie Canal Route here.
Crossing the Canal here and riding Southwest on NY 257 will bring you into the heart of Fayetteville. Return to the Canal Path via NY 257 rather than via NY 5 through Green Lakes St. Pk. The hill on NY 5 is steep and you'll have to go extra miles through Green Lakes to get to the Path.

Fayetteville

Info.: Area code: 315. Zip code: 13066
Services: All. Stores, restaurants abound in and around Fayetteville on NY 5. A large shopping mall is at the intersection of NY 5 and Kinne Rd.
Lodging: Motels. Hostel: Downing HI/AYH Hostel, 535 Oak St., Syracuse NY 13203, 472-5788. B&Bs: Collin House, 7860 E. Genesee St., 637-4671; Beard Morgan House, 126 E. Genesee St., 637-4234/800 775-4234

1.2 (1.8)   Green Lakes St. Pk.   0.0 (0.0)
@ OECSP Trail
Cross the pedestrian bridge and enter the Park.
Green Lakes St. Pk., 637-6111 Facilities: Camping.

W to E	**Fayetteville to**	E to W
mi. (km.) Read↓	**Seneca Falls**	mi. (km.) Read↑

Weedsport to Syracuse/Fayetteville Direct Route

S to N mi. (km.) Read↓	**Jordan to Syracuse** **Direct Road Route**	N to S mi. (km.) Read↑

0.0 (0.0)   Jordan Community Ctr.   30.2 (48.3)
          @ NY 31/BR 5
Continue traveling East on NY 31/BR 5. Hikers should use
the JCECParkway Trail.
Hikers can take a commuter bus from Jordan to Syracuse.

5.0 (8.0)   Laird Rd. @ NY 31   25.2 (40.3)
Continue traveling on NY 31. Turn South on to Laird Rd.
to go to Camillus Canal Park.

6.6 (10.6)   NY 173/Warners Rd. @ NY 31   23.6 (37.8)
Continue traveling on NY 31. Use NY 173 to sweep along
the southern edge of Syracuse, a hillier route.

10.6 (17.0)   NY 31 Jct. Downer St./NY 31   19.6 (31.4)
Continue traveling East on NY 31/Downer St. You are on
the East side of the Seneca River.

11.6 (18.6)   I 690 @ NY 31/Downer St.   18.6 (29.8)
Continue traveling straight on Downer St. You can not
use the I 690/NY 31 bridge going over the Seneca River.
NY 31 disappears but Downer St. remains.

12.8 (20.5)   Syracuse St./NY 48 @ Downer St.   17.4 (27.8)
Turn East on to Syracuse St. to go to Syracuse. Turn
West on to Syracuse St. to go into Baldwinsville & use
the Oneida Lake Routes & Oswego Canal Routes.

13.4 (21.4)   Van Buren St./Maple Ave./NY 48   16.8 (26.9)
          @ Syracuse St./NY 48
Turn Southeast on to Van Buren St. You could follow Maple Ave./NY 48 to State Fair Blvd. but there are a few
turns which will only confuse you. 2004 construction and
other factors (highways) make Van Buren a better choice.
Van Buren does have some rolling hills and goes through
industrial areas.

16.8 (26.9)   Walters Rd. @ Van Buren Rd.   13.4 (21.4)
Either continue traveling East on Van Buren Rd. or turn
northwards on to Walters Rd. which ends at St. Fair Blvd.

18.5 (29.6)   Armstrong Rd. @ Van Buren Rd.   11.7 (18.7)
Turn Northeast on to Armstrong Rd.

19.7 (31.5)   State Fair Blvd. @ Armstrong Rd.   10.5 (16.8)

Turn East on to State Fair Blvd. The signs will state "to NYS Fair."

21.1 (33.8)   Bridge St./NY 297 @ St. Fair Blvd.   9.1 (14.6)
Continue traveling on St. Fair Blvd.

22.0 (35.2)   Willis Ave. Jct St. Fair Blvd.   8.2 (13.1)
Continue traveling on Willis Ave.

22.5 (36.0)   Erie Blvd. W. @ Willis Ave.   7.7 (12.3)
Turn East on to Erie Blvd. W.

23.2 (37.1)   Hiawatha Blvd. W. @ Erie Blvd W.   7.0 (11.2)
Continue traveling on Erie Blvd. W. Use Hiawatha Blvd. N. to go to the Transportation Ctr., Carousel Ctr. & the northern route around Onondaga Lake. Weird, both streets are labeled "West!"

24.9 (39.8)   Clinton Ave. @ Erie Blvd. W.   5.3 (8.5)
Strange intersection due to highways and one way streets. I suggest you turn South on to Clinton Ave. travel 1 block to Water St. and then turn East on Water St.

25.0 (40.0)   Water St. @ Clinton Ave.   5.2 (8.3)
Turn East on Water St.

25.2 (40.3)   State St. @ Water St.   5.0 (8.0)
Erie Canal Museum. Turn North on State St.

25.3 (40.5)   State St. @ Erie Blvd. E./NY 5   4.9 (7.8)
Turn East on to Erie Blvd. E. Somewhere in this vicinity Erie Blvd. E. adds the NY 5 route sign to its name.

26.5 (42.4)   Erie Blvd. E. widens.   3.7 (5.9)
At this point Erie Blvd. E. widens and becomes less bicycle friendly. There is a sidewalk use it if traffic becomes very heavy.

29.5 (47.2)   Kinne Rd. @ Erie Blvd. E.   0.7 (1.1)
Turn North on to Kinne Rd.

30.2 (48.3)   Butternut Dr. @ Kinne Rd.   0.0 (0.0)
After cycling over the over pass turn North on to Butternut Dr. and enter Old Erie Canal St. Pk./ Ryder Pk.

S to N	**Syracuse to Jordan**	N to S
mi. (km.) Read↓	**Direct Road Route**	mi. (km.) Read↑

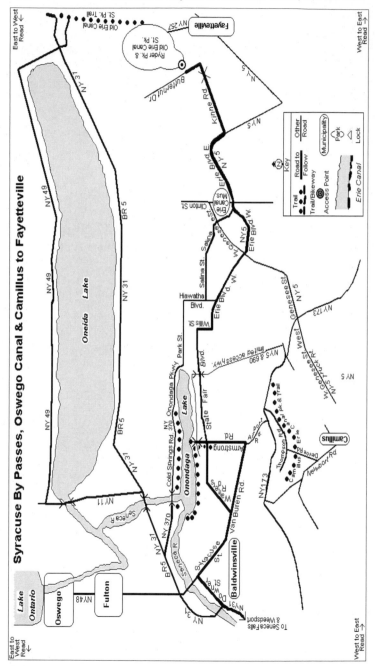

Syracuse By Passes, Oswego Canal & Camillus to Fayetteville

OSWEGO CANAL ROUTE

S to N mi. (km.) Read↓	Oswego Canal Route	N to S mi. (km.) Read↑

0.0 (0.0)　　NY 173 @ NY 31/BR 5　　　　**32.1 (51.7)**
Travel East on NY 31.

5.0 (8.0)　　I 690 @ NY 31/Downer St.　　**27.1 (43.6)**
Continue East on Downer St.. Sorry you can not bicycle
or walk on an Interstate! Write your Congressperson!

6.4 (10.3)　　NY 48/Syracuse St. @ Downer St.　　**25.7 (41.3)**
Turn North on Syracuse St./NY 48 to go to the Oswego
Canal and Lake Ontario. Travel East on Syracuse St. to
go into downtown Syracuse.

6.7 (10.8)　　Lock 24 @ NY 48　　　　**25.4 (40.9)**

Baldwinsville

Services: Restaurants, stores.
Bike Info.: Bike shop.
Lodging: Motels. Pandora's Getaway, 83 Oswego St.,
Baldwinsville 13027, 315 635-9571.
Attractions: Erie Canal Lock.

6.9 (11.1)　　NY 48 @ NY 31/BR 5　　　　**25.2 (40.6)**
Continue traveling North on NY 48 to go to Oswego.
　　Uh, Oh! Second thoughts about riding North to
Oswego and Lake Ontario! You can change your mind
here several different ways. Go through Syracuse to the
Old Erie Canal State Park Path or by pass Syracuse by
going North or South around Lake Oneida.
　　I. To go to Syracuse & the Old Canal Path: Travel
South on NY 48/Syracuse St./Maple Rd./State Fair Blvd.
(NY 48 changes names several times). At Farrel St. it
becomes John Glenn Blvd. Turn East on to John Glenn
Blvd. Turn South on to Van Vleck Rd. Turn East on Long
Branch Rd.　Enter Onondaga Lake Park. Follow the
stone dust path on the South shore of Onondaga Lake.
At the end of the path is a pedestrian bridge over I 690.
Cross over I 690 to Pleasant Beach Rd.. Ride up
Pleasant Beach Rd. (not a pleasant hill) to State Fair
Blvd. Turn Southeast on to State Fair Blvd. Just past the
Fairgrounds, turn Southwest on to Willis Ave. and then
East on to Erie Blvd. Where Erie Blvd becomes NY 5/
Erie Blvd turn East on to Genesee St. Genesee St. leads

you directly to downtown Syracuse. See Main Canal
Route W to E 41.9 mi. (67.4 km.)
  II & III. See Syracuse By Pass Routes to continue
East on Rtes. 31 and 49 via Lake Oneida.

12.8 (20.6)   County Border   19.3 (31.1)
Oswego County & Onondaga County.

20.0 (32.2)   NY 3 @ NY 48   12.1 (19.5)

Fulton
Info.: Greater Fulton CofC, PO Box 148, Fulton NY
13069, 315 598-4231. Area code: 315. Zip code: 13069.
Bike Info.: Bike shop.
Services: All. Hospital.
Lodging: Motels. B&Bs: Aunt T's, RD 1, NY 48, Box 28,
592-2425, Battle Island Inn, RD 1, Box 101, NY 48N,
593-3699; Doney's, RR 2, NY 176E, 593-7419.
Camping: North Bay Cpgd., Philip St., 592-2256.
Attractions: Oswego Canal Locks 2 & 3; Hist. Soc., 177
South First St., 598-4616.

23.0 (37.0)   Battle Island St. Pk. @ NY 48   9.1 (14.5)
Day use only park.

26.3 (42.3)   Oswego Canal Lock 5 @ NY 48   5.8 (9.3)

32.1 (51.7)   NY 48 @ NY 104   0.0 (0.0)

Oswego
Info.: Oswego Co. TO, 46 Bridge St., Oswego NY
13126, 800 248-4386/315 349-8322. AC: 315.
Bike Information: Bike shop.
Services & Facilities: All. Hospital.
Lodging: Motels. B&Bs:
Attractions: Lake Ontario; Fort Ontario St. Hist. Site
(military demonstrations, WWII refugee internment camp
museum), E. 7th St. at Lake Ontario, 342-4117; H. Lee
White Marine Mus., W. First St. Pier at Lake Ontario 343-
0480; Rice Creek Biological Field Station, SUNY Oswego
Coll. 342-0961; Oswego Speedway (NASCAR), E.
Albany St., 342-0646. State College.

S to N	**Oswego Canal**	N to S
mi. (km.) Read↓	**Route**	mi. (km.) Read↑

SYRACUSE BY PASS ROUTES

Lake Oneida is part of the New York State Canal System.

W to E mi. (km.) Read↓	South of Lake Oneida By Pass	E to W mi. (km.) Read↑
0.0 (0.0)	NY 48 @ NY 31/BR 5 Continue traveling on NY 31/BR 5. **Baldwinsville:**	32.9 (52.9)
12.2 (19.6)	NY 11 @ NY 31/BR 5 Continue East on NY 31/BR 5. Turn off for the **North of Lake Oneida** Route.	20.7 (33.3)
19.3 (31.1)	NY 298 @ NY 31/BR 5 Continue traveling on NY 31/BR 5. Tired of NY 31? Turn South on NY 298/Minoa Rd. and travel for 7.5 mi. (12.2 km.), to rejoin the Main Erie Canal Route on the Old Erie Canal State Park Tow Path.	13.6 (21.9)
20.2 (32.5)	Chittenango Creek @ NY 31/BR 5 County border: Madison County & Onondaga County.	12.7 (20.4)
24.2 (38.9)	Lakeport Rd. @ NY 31 **Lodging:** Thrall's Lakeport Marina, 2025 NY 31, Lakeport, 315 633-8153.	5.6 (9.0)
31.3 (50.4)	NY 13 @ NY 31/BR 5 Through travellers continue on NY 31/BR 5 **Lodging:** Camping: 1.5 mi. (2.4 km.), North on NY 13 is Verona Beach St. Pk., NY 13, Verona Beach, Sylvan Beach 13157, 315 762-4463 (reserve at least one day in advance). There are b&bs, motels in Sylvan Beach.	1.6 (2.6)
32.5 (52.3)	NY 316 @ NY 31/BR 5 Border! Watch out! Border guards are looking for speeding cyclists! Oneida County& Madison County.	.4 (.6)
32.9 (52.9)	Old Erie Canal St. Pk. Trail @ NY 31 Enter the path! You have rejoined the main route!	0.0 (0.0)

W to E mi. (km.) Read↓	South of Lake Oneida By Pass	E to W mi (km) Read↑

W to E	North of Lake Oneida	E to W
mi. (km.) Read↓	By Pass	mi. (km.) Read↑

0.0 (0.0)   NY 31/BR 5 @ NY 11   **45.4 (73.1)**
Turn North on to NY 11.

4.6 (7.4)   Oneida River/Erie Canal @ NY 11   **40.8 (65.7)**
Oswego County & Onondaga County.
NY 49 Information: Ft. Brewerton CofC, PO Box 655,
Brewerton NY 13029, 315 668-3408.

8.9 (14.3)   NY 49 @ NY 11   **36.5 (58.7)**
Turn East on to NY 49.
Central Square: Grocery, convenience store, motel.

20.7 (33.3)   Constantia Hamlet @ NY 49   **24.7 (39.7)**
Constantia: Lodging: Constantia Cove Cpgd., NY 49,
Box 304, Constantia NY 13044, 315 623-7405.
Attraction: State Fish Hatchery, 315 668-7311.

28.8 (46.3)   Cleveland @ NY 49   **16.6 (26.7)**
No, you're not in Ohio! County border.
Cleveland Hamlet: Grocery, motel.

36.3 (58.4)   NY 13 @ NY 49   **9.1 (14.6)**
Through travelers continue East on NY 49.
Lodging: Camping: 3.6 mi (5.8 km) South on NY 13 is
Verona Beach St. Pk., NY 13, Sylvan Beach NY 13157,
315 762-4463 (reseve at least one day in advance).

45.4 (73.1)   Old Erie Canal St. Pk. Trail @NY 49   **0.0 (0.0)**
Enter the Trail and ride East towards Rome. Have your
chariot ready!

W to E	North of Lake Oneida	E to W
mi. (km.) Read↓	By Pass	mi. (km.) Read↑

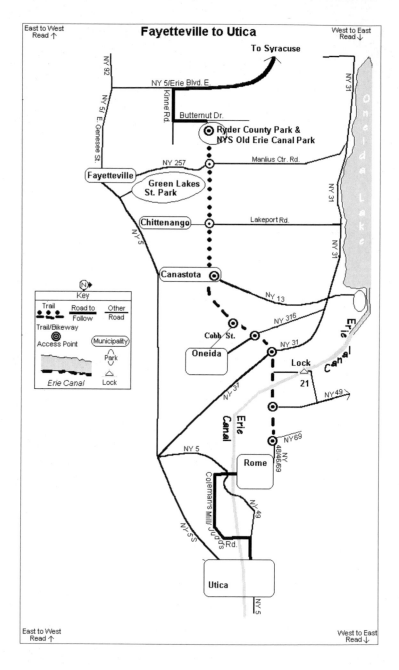

Fayetteville to Utica

East to West
Read ↑

West to East
Read ↓

To Syracuse

NY 92

NY 5/Erie Blvd. E.

Kinne Rd.

NY 31

Oneida Lake

NY 5/ E. Genesee St.

Butternut Dr.

Ryder County Park &
NYS Old Erie Canal Park

NY 257

Manlius Ctr. Rd.

Fayetteville

Green Lakes
St. Park

NY 31

Chittenango

Lakeport Rd.

NY 5

NY 31

Canastota

NY 13

Key

Trail ●●●

Road to
Follow

Other
Road

Trail/Bikeway

Access Point

Municipality

Park

Erie Canal

Lock

NY 316

Cobb St.

NY 31

Oneida

Erie Canal

Lock

21

NY 49

NY 37

NY 69

Erie Canal

NY 48 46 69

NY 5

Rome

Coleman's Mill Rd.

Judd's Rd.

NY 49

NY 5 S

Utica

NY 5

East to West
Read ↑

West to East
Read ↓

OLD CANAL AND THE ADIRONDACKS

The first forty miles of this section are along the *Old* Erie Canal. This is the longest remaining continuous section of the major mid-19th century expansion of the original Canal.

Begun in 1842, the expansion was necessitated by the increased demand for food, industrial raw materials and building supplies from cities along the eastern seaboard. The increased immigration of Europeans to eastern seaboard cities, primarily in the Philadelphia to Boston corridor, demanded an expansion of the food supply. The area's rich farmland could easily produce sufficient food for the exploding population of these cities. The problem was transporting this agricultural largess from farm to city.

The industrial revolution with its need for industrial raw materials along with the construction of housing and commercial buildings led to the development of mines and lumber sources in the Adirondack Mountains, western New York and the mid-west. The burgeoning factories of the Atlantic coast provided a ready market for these raw materials.

The road system was definitely incapable of handling the transport of bulk commodities. The original Erie Canal was overcrowded with barges due to its shallow draft, narrow width and short locks. The logistics of sending the food and industrial raw materials to the cities was hampered by the original Erie Canal's limited tonnage capacity.

With all this economic development and shipping of goods both East and West, the Canal with its 8 and 10 foot width locks was incapable of handling the traffic. Remember that this was just prior to the development of an extensive railroad network and prior to the Civil War when Canals served as America's primary long distance shipping network. To meet the demand for goods, the State began to enlarge the Canal in 1842. Like the original canal it was an immediate success. Even with increased tolls the Erie Canal became the logistical choice of shippers. The increased tonnage passing through the Canal quickly made it a profitable venture for the State.

There was a sociological and economic change for the villages bypassed by the *Old* Canal which foreshadowed what would happen to villages which were by passed by the Interstate Highway System in the mid-20th century. The villages which developed along the *Original* Canal simply became smaller and in some cases ceased to exist. Their economic raison d'être having disappeared.

The politics and lobbying to set the *Old* Erie Canal's right of way was just as vicious, scandal ridden and intense as highway routing projects in the mid 20th century. Original documents, newspaper articles and New York State Legislature records all attest to the fierce competition among communities to have the Canal right of way go through their towns. Local museums from Fayetteville to Utica celebrate the success of the political process and economic importance of expanded Erie Canal.

The *Old* Erie Canal's route contributed to the development of a vast parcel of land, the Adirondack Mountains. This area was rich with the natural resources needed for 19th industrial development. This vast tract of land supplied lumber, iron, copper, and garnet to fuel the factories of the seaboard.

Individuals who saw a greater benefit in moving from the crowded cities of the Atlantic seaboard to the mid-West and beyond used the *Old* Erie Canal as their transportation mode. Compared to freight tonnage and number of freight barges, passenger traffic was a relatively small factor in the success of expanding the *Original* Canal.

W to E	**Fayetteville to**	E to W
mi. (km.) Read↓	**Utica**	mi. (km.) Read↑

0.0 (0.0)   Manlius Center Rd./   47.4 (76.3)
              Shepps Corners Rd./Minoa Rd.
              @ Old Erie Canal St. Pk. (OECSP) Trail
Continue traveling East on the Trail.
Travelers who tired of NY 31/BR 5 on the South shore of Oneida Lake join the Main Erie Route here.
Crossing the Old Erie Canal here and riding Southwest on NY 257, will bring you into the heart of Fayetteville. Return to the Canal Path via NY 257, rather than via NY 5, through Green Lakes St. Pk. The hill on NY 5, is steep and you'll have to go extra miles through Green Lakes to return to the Trail.
Fayetteville: See last page of the Central NY chapter.

1.2 (1.8)   Green Lakes St. Pk. @ Trail   45.2 (74.4)
Cross the bike/ped. bridge and enter the Park.
Green Lakes St. Pk. (camping), 315 637-6111.

6.9 (11.1)   County Border Crossing   40.5 (65.2)
Madison County & Onondaga County.

7.9 (12.7)   Chittenango-Lakeport Rd. @ Trail   39.5 (63.6)

Chittenango

Info.: Area code: 315. Zip code: 13037.

Services: Grocery, convenience stores, restaurants, general merchandise & hardware stores.

Lodging: B&Bs: Greyrock Farm, 6065 E. Lake Rd., 687-9866; The Old Rectory, 418 Genesee St., 687-9749.

Camping: Chittenango Falls St. Pk., 5 mi., (8 km.), South of Chittenango on NY 13, Cazenovia 13035, 655-9620.

Attractions: Chittenango Landing Canal Boat Mus., 7010 Lakeport Rd., 687-3801. Original and restored Old Erie Canal dry dock, lock, & boats. Chittenango Falls St. Pk., amazing falls at the northern end of the Allegheny Plateau. Formed due to glaciation and erosion.

13.4 (21.6)   Canastota @ Trail   34.0 (54.7)

Canastota

Info.: Greater Canastota CofC, PO Box 206, Canastota NY 13032. Area code: 315. Zip code: 13032.

Services: Grocery, convenience stores, restaurants, general merchandise & hardware stores.

Lodging: Motels.

Attractions: Canal Town Mus., 122 Canal St., 697-3451. Interesting exhibition of Erie Canal and Chenango Canal memorabilia. International Boxing Hall of Fame, 1 Hall of Fame Dr., 697-7095,

18.3 (29.4)   Cobb St. @ Trail   29.1 (46.8)

Oneida

Info.: Greater Oneida CofC, 154 Main St., Oneida NY 13421. Area code: 315. Zip code: 13421.

Cycling & hiking Info.: Bike shop.

Services: All. Hospital.

Lodging: Motels. B&Bs: Oneida Community Mansion House, 170 Kenwood Ave., 361-3671; The Pollyanna, 302 Main St., 363-0524; Governor's House, 80 Seneca Ave., 363-5643.

Attractions: Oneida Nation Shako:wi Cultural Center, NY 46 2 mi. (3.6 km.), South of Oneida. 363-1424; Oneida Community Mansion House, 170 Kenwood Ave., 363-0745. The Oneida Community was a 19th century utopian *socialist* community which among other things produced silverware. Oneida Indian Bingo, Rts 5 & 46, 3 mi. (4.8 km.), South of Oneida), 800 782-1938.

18.9 (30.4)   NY 31B @ OECSP Trail   28.5 (45.9)
Continue East on the Trail.
Info.:   Leatherstocking Country, 327 North Main St.,
Herkimer 13350, 800 233-8778.
Lodging: Towering Maples B&B, 3239 Foster Corners
Rd., Durhamville (on trail), 315 363-9007.
Madison - Oneida County Border. Watch out for wildlife!

19.4 (31.2)   NY 31 @ OECSP Trail   28.0 (45.1)
Continue East on the Trail.
Travelers taking the Lake Oneida Routes join the Main
Erie Canal Route/Old Erie Canal Trail here.
Disregard the St. Pk. map which states that there is no
path between NY 31 and Durhamville.
Use NY 46, which parallels the Trail at this point if the
Trail surface is too rough.
To Go to Verona State Beach St. Pk. (camping) exit the
Path here and travel North on NY 46 to Pappleton Rd.
Turn West on to Pappleton Rd. and travel 4 mi. (6.5 km.),
to the Verona St. Beach Pk. on NY 13.
To go to the Oneida Nation Mus. and Casino use NY 31
S to 365 West. The signs on 31 & 365 will direct you.

24.1 (38.8)   Lock Rd. @ OECSP Trail   23.3 (37.5)
Continue traveling on the Trail or NY 46.
It's a half mile ride to Lock 21 on the *new* Erie Canal. If
you go to Lock 21, you can return to the Trail by using
the Path along the New Canal to Old NY 46 @ Glur Rd.
and rejoin the main route there. Signs will direct you on
this 2.1 mi (3.4 km), side trip.

30.3 (48.7)   Erie Canal Village   17.1 (27.5)
          @ OECSP Trail & Rtes. 46/49
Turn East on to Rtes. 46/49.
Attraction: Erie Canal Village, 5789 New London Rd.,
Rome 13440, 315 337-3999, restaurant, museum, mule
drawn canal boat excusions; very accommodating to
bicyclists; possible emergency camping.

31.2 (80.2)   Rtes. 46/49 @ NY 69/Erie Blvd. W   16.2 (26.1)
Turn Southeast on to NY 69/Erie Blvd. W.
Erie Blvd./Rtes. 46/69 can be a busy *main street.* Try not
to use it during rush hours. There is a sidewalk on both
sides of the street. There really is no way of avoiding this
street without adding many excess miles.

33.2 (53.4)   Black River Blvd./NY 46   14.2 (22.9)
          @ Rtes. 49/69/Erie Blvd. W.

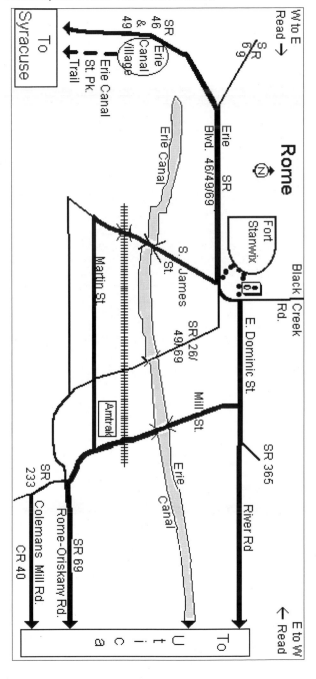

in front of Fort Stanwix
See *Route Notes* after the Rome entries.

Rome

Info.: Rome CofC, 200 Liberty Plaza, Rome NY 13440, 315 337-1700. Area code: 315. Zip code: 13440.
Cycling & hiking Info.: Bike shop.
Services: All. Amtrak baggage service.
Bus: Local: Rome VIP Transit, Liberty-George Parking Garage, 13440, 336-5310. Intercity bus: Greyhound & Trailways.
Lodging: Motels. B&Bs: Maplecrest B&B, 6480 Williams Rd., 337-0070; Wright Settlement, 7966 Wright Settlement Ln., 337-2417. Camping: Delta Lake St. Pk., 6 mi. (9.6 km.) North of Rome, 8797 St. NY 46, 337-4670.
Attractions: Ft. Stanwix Nat'l. Monument, 112 East Park St., 336-2090. 18th century Fort built by the British to defend the frontier! Period customs and demonstrations. Capital Theatre (restored 1928 vaudeville theatre with summer stock plays), 218 Liberty Plz., 337-6277. Rome Hist. Soc., 200 Church St., 336-5870; Ft. Rickey Discovery Zoo, Rts. 46 & 49, 336-1930. Peterpaul Recreation Park (go kart track), NY 49W, 339-2666.

Route Note

Four routes are provided between Rome & Utica:
Bike Route 5/NY 5/NY 49
South of Canal, NY 69 Route, the preferred route.
North of Canal Route.
This is due to the ridiculous routing of BR 5 on to NY 49/NY 5, which is a limited access highway for 15 mi. (24 km.) between these two cities.
Unfortunately, NY 49/BR 5, is the flattest route since it runs almost directly along the Canal.
The other routes between Rome & Utica may not be as flat as BR 5, but they are more scenic and certainly safer.
The Colemans Mill Road Route has a few rolling hills, nothing severe. The Colemans Mill Route joins NY 69 at Oriskany.

Note

The most direct route between Rome and Utica is to use BR5/NY 5/NY 49 or a trail along the Canal. Ask around. I have not been to this area to confirm these reports of a trail extension.

W to E	**Rome to Utica**	E to W
mi. (km.) Read↓	**South of the Canal Route**	mi. (km.) Read↑

Gettin' to the Routes South of the Canal

Route Note

There are three ways of going to the Routes South of the Canal: James St. Route, Mill St. Route and BR 5/NY 49 Route. All start and end the same point,

33.2 (53.4)   S. James St.   14.2 (22.9)
              @ Erie Blvd. Rtes. 46/49/69
Landmark: Fort Stanwix St. Hist. Site.
This is a complicated intersection and you have a choice of roads to continue your trek along the Canal, James St. Route or the Mill St. Route. Both will lead to to the same intersection South of the NY 233 @ NY 69.

James St. Route

Turn South on to S. James St.
    Travel .9 mi. (1.4 km.) to Martin St. (Immediately after going under the railroad trestle.
Turn East on to Martin St.
    Travel 1.1 mi. (1.8 km.) to Mill St./NY 233; just past the Amtrak Station.
Turn South on to NY 233.
    Travel to NY 69/Oriskany Rd.

39.3 (63.2)   NY 233 @ Oriskany Rd./NY 69.   7.8 (12.6)
Turn East on to NY 69/Oriskany Rd. to go to Utica.
OR continue on NY 233 to Colemans Mill Rd.

Mill St. Route

Cross Erie Blvd. to the sidewalk bordering Ft. Stanwix.
    Walk along the sidewalk on the East side of Ft. Stanwix to the traffic light at Dominic St. E. @ Black Creek Rd./NY 46. This bit of sidewalk allows you to avoid using the NY 46 underpass at this intersection. If you do use the underpass then Dominic St. E. is the first traffic light after emerging from the underpass.
Cross Black Creek Rd./NY 46 at the traffic light.
    Travel East on Dominic St. E. for ~.3 mi. (.5 km.) to Mill St.
Turn South on to Mill St.
Travel .5 mi. (.8 km.) to Martin Rd. @ Mill St./NY 233.
    The Amtrak Station is just West of this intersection.

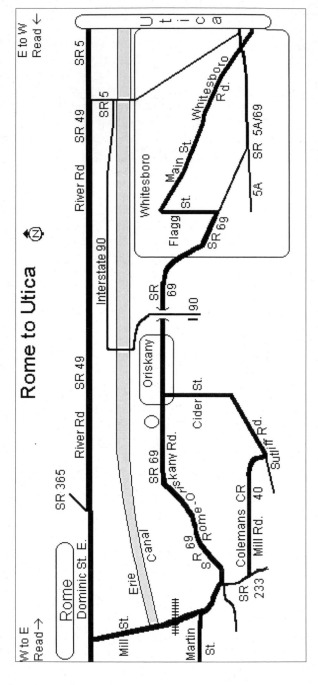

Rome to Utica

W to E Read →

E to W Read ←

Continue traveling South on NY 233 for .8 mi. (1.3 km.) to NY 69/Oriskany Rd.

37.7 (60.8)   NY 233 @ Oriskany Rd./NY 69.   9.7 (15.6)
Turn East on to NY 69/Oriskany Rd. to go to Utica.
OR Continue South on NY 233 to Colemans Mill Rd.

Routes 5 & 49/ Bike Route 5 Route

Route Note

This is the least attractive of the the three routes leading to the South side of the Canal. It is included because someone will follow BR 5/Rtes. 5 & 49 signs & then become a bit confused.

34.3 (55.2)   NY 233/Stanwix Exit   13.1 (21.1)
              @ NY 49/Bike Route 5
Exit NY 49/Bike Route 5.
Travel the direction you are going, East, as you exit NY 49. You will be on Lamphear Rd., the access road paralleling the South Side of NY 49 at this point.
Bike Route 5 continues East as part of NY 49, a limited access highway.

35.2 (56.6)   NY 233/Mill St. @ Lamphear Rd.   12.2 (19.6)
Turn South on to NY 233.

35.3 (56.8)   Martin Rd./NY 69 @ NY 233/Mill St.   12.1 (19.4)
Turn East on to NY 69/Oriskany Rd.
Follow the NY69/Oriskany Road Route from this point.
OR continue South on NY 233 to Colemans Mill Rd.

36.0 (57.9)   Colemans Mill Rd. @ NY 233   12.8 (20.6)
Turn East on to Colemans Mill Rd.
Follow the Colemans Mill Road Route from this point.

W to E	**Rome to Utica**	E to W
mi. (km.) Read↓	**South of the Canal Route**	mi. (km.) Read↑
	Gettin' to Rome from South of the Canal	

W to E	Rome to Utica	E to W
mi. (km.) Read↓	**South of the Canal Route**	mi. (km.) Read↑
	NY 69/Oriskany Road Route	

37.7 (60.8)   NY 233 @ Oriskany Rd./NY 69.   9.7 (15.6)
Turn East on to NY 69/Oriskany Rd. to go to Utica.
OR Continue South on NY 233 to Colemans Mill Rd.

41.5 (66.8)   Oriskany Battle Monument @ NY 69   9.1 (14.6)
Continue traveling on NY 69.

43.5 (70.1)   Cider St. @ NY 69/Main St.   7.1 (11.4)
Continue traveling on NY 69/Main St.
ORISKANY

56.1 (90.2)   I 90 overpass @ NY 69   3.8 (6.1)
Continue traveling on NY 69. NY 69 becomes a typical
suburban commercial strip from this point to Utica.

56.4 (90.7)   Flagg St. @ NY 69   3.5 (5.6)
Turn North on to Flagg St.
If you miss Flagg St. turn at the next light.

56.6 (91.1)   Main St./Whitesboro St. @ Flagg St.   3.3 (5.3)
Turn East on to Main St./Whitesboro St.
WHITESBORO

58.4 (93.9)   NY 5A/Oriskany St. W   1.5 (2.4)
              @ Whitesboro St./Main St.
Continue traveling on Whitesboro St. by crossing NY 5A
at the traffic light.

59.4 (95.6)   Columbia St. @ Whitesboro St.   .5 (.8)
East bound travelers, bear left on Whitesboro St.
If you go on Columbia St. you'll go up a steep hill.
Westbound travelers you'll come to this intersection if
you turned West on Columbia St. @ Genesee St.
Bike Info: Welch's Bike Shop.

59.9 (96.4)   Whitesboro St./Oriskany St.   0.0 (0.0)
              @ Genesee St.
   UTICA

W to E	Rome to Utica	E to W
mi. (km.) Read↓	**South of the Canal Route**	mi. (km.) Read↑
	NY 69/Oriskany Road Route	

W to E	**Rome to Utica**	E to W
mi. (km.) Read↓	**North of the Canal Route**	mi. (km.) Read↑

33.2 (53.4)   Black River Blvd./NY 46/S. James St.   14.2 (22.9)
            @ Erie Blvd. SR 46/49/69
      Landmark: Fort Stanwix St. Hist. Site.
      This is a complicated intersection.
      Cross Erie Blvd. to the sidewalk bordering Ft. Stanwix.

33.3 (53.5)   Sidewalk Bordering Ft. Stanwix.   14.1 (22.7)
      Walk along the sidewalk on the East side of Ft. Stanwix
      to the traffic light at Dominic St. E. @ Black Creek Rd./
      SR 46.
      This bit of sidewalk allows you to avoid using the SR 46
      underpass at this intersection. Dominic St. E. is the first
      traffic light after emerging from the underpass.

33.4 (53.8)   Black Creek Rd./SR 46 @ Dominic St.   14.0 (22.5)
      Cross Black Creek Rd./SR 46 at the traffic light.
      Travel East on Dominic St. E. for .3 mi. (.5 km.) to Mill St

33.7 (54.2)   Dominic St. E. @ Mill St.   13.7 (22.0)
      Continue traveling East on Dominic St. E.
      Mind change? Want to use the South of the Canal Rtes?
      Turn South on to Mill St. & follow the Mill St. NY

36.6 (58.9)   NY 365/Dominic St. E.@ River Rd.   10.8 (17.4)
      Eastbound: Travel East on River Rd. to go to Utica.
      Westbound: Travel West on Dominic St. E. to Rome.

42.7 (68.7)   Hayes Rd. @ River Rd.   4.7 (7.5)
      Turn South on to Hayes Rd.

42.9 (69.0)   Hayes Rd. @ Rtes. 49/5   4.9 (7.9)
      Turn East on to NY 49/River Rd.
      Lock 20 park.

46.0 (74.0)   NY 12/I 790 @ Rtes. 49/5   1.8 (2.9)
      Continue traveling on Rtes. 49/5.

47.8 (76.9)   Genesee St./Coventry Rd.   0.0 (0.0)
            @ Rtes. 49/5
      UTICA

W to E	**Utica to Rome**	E to W
mi. (km.) Read↓	**North of the Canal Route**	mi. (km.) Read↑

47.4 (76.3)   NY Genesee St. @ NY 5   0.0 (0.0)

Utica

Info.: Utica Area CofC, 258 Genesee St., Utica NY 13502, 315 724-3151.

Area code: 315. Zip code: 13502.

Cycling & hiking Info.: There is only one bike shop, Welch's, Columbia St.

Services: All. Hospitals. Amtrak (baggage service) & intercity buses are all in one terminal, the Amtrak station. The station has been restored to it's original brilliant condition.

Lodging: Motels & hotels. B&Bs: Leatherstocking B&B Assoc., PO Box 53, Herkimer 13350, 800 941-2337; Adam Bowman Manor, 197 Riverside Dr., 738-0276; Herbs & Hospitality, 2806 Ogden Place, 797-0079; The Iris Stonehouse, 16 Derbyshire Place, 732-6720.

Camping: Elmtree Cpgd., NY 5, 6 mi. (9.6 km.), East of Utica, Box 33C, Frankfort 13340, 315 724-6678.

Attractions: Amtrak terminal, a restored masterpiece. F. X. Matt Brewery (tours), Court & Varick Sts., 733-6976; Munson-Williams-Proctor Institute (art mus.) 310 Genesee St., 797-0000. Italian Cultural Ctr. & Mus., 668 Catherine St., 735-0960.

W to E	**Utica to**	E to W
mi. (km.) Read↓	**Fayetteville**	mi. (km.) Read↑

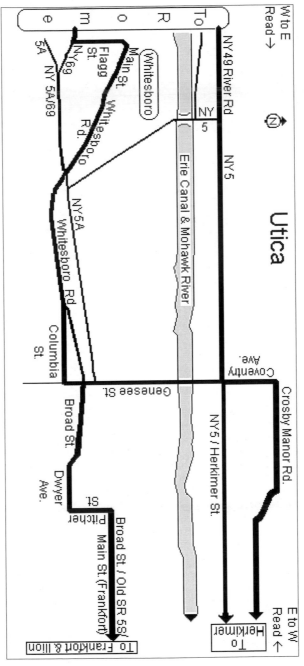

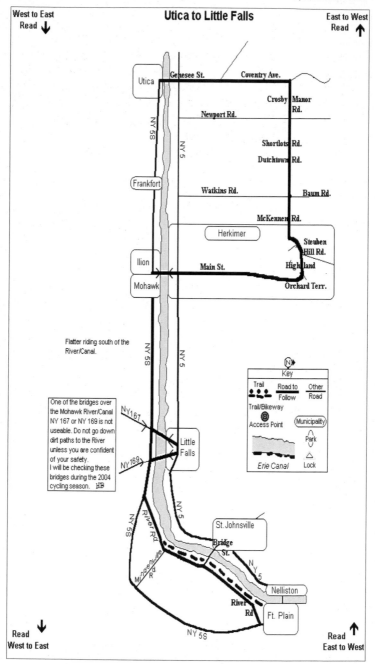

Utica to Little Falls

West to East
Read ↓

East to West
Read ↑

Read ↓
West to East

Read ↑
East to West

Flatter riding south of the River/Canal.

One of the bridges over the Mohawk River/Canal NY 167 or NY 169 is not useable. Do not go down dirt paths to the River unless you are confident of your safety.
I will be checking these bridges during the 2004 cycling season. HB

Key

Trail   Road to Follow   Other Road

Trail/Bikeway

Access Point   Municipality

Erie Canal   Park   Lock

Utica · Genesee St. · Coventry Ave. · Crosby Manor Rd. · Newport Rd. · Shortlots Rd. · Dutchtown Rd. · Frankfort · Watkins Rd. · Baum Rd. · McKennen Rd. · Herkimer · Steuben Hill Rd. · Ilion · Main St. · Highland · Mohawk · Orchard Terr.

NY 5S · NY 5 · NY 167 · NY 169 · Little Falls

River Rd. · St. Johnsville · Bridge St. · NY 5 · Nelliston · Minden ville Rd. · River Rd · Ft. Plain · NY 5S

RIVER AND CANAL

The Mohawk River flows like a lake shore line from its source near Utica to its mouth at Cohoes near Albany. It flows along a wide river plain which was the southern most boundary of great Lake Iroquois of the glacial epoch. The languid flow which you see during the summer is due to catch basin dams and other controls which allow numerous small hydroelectric plants to supply the power for this industrial corridor.

The Canal and its locks play a vital part in preventing destructive flooding of the Mohawk River's flood plain. The water control function of the Erie Canal is rarely publicized. As one lockmaster told me, *If they* [politicians and administrators] *let the Canal degenerate, the entire Mohawk Valley will be subject to more flood damage than coastal North Carolina ever experiences after a powerful hurricane.*

Control of this Valley was crucial for the British in their successful quest for North America during the French and Indian War. The Mohawks, brilliant military strategists in their own right, played the British off the French and the French off the British. Finally settling on supporting the British. Their support and knowledge of what, today, we term *guerilla* warfare allowed the British to garner this area from the French and thus control all of North America.

W to E	**Utica to Fort Plain**	E to W
mi. (km.) Read↓	**Utica to Herkimer**	mi. (km.) Read↑

North of the Canal High Road Route

Route Note

Refer to Utica Map at the end of the Old Canal and Adirondacks chapter.

It is possible to use NY 5, on the North side of the Canal as a possible route to go all the way to Herkimer. It is neither as interesting as the North of the Canal High Road Route nor the South of the Canal Route. NY 5, has a wide shoulder and the traffic is moderate to light. It does have a few hills.

The South of the Canal Route is a much leveler route.

0.0 (0.0)   NY 5 @ Genesee St.   **41.8 (67.2)**
Travel North on Genesee St.
North of the Canal.
Utica information is at the end of the previous chapter.

<.1 (<.1)   Coventry Ave. @ Genesee St.   **<41.8 (<67.2)**
Continue traveling North. Genesee St. simply changes its name to Coventry Ave.

1.9 (3.1)   Crosby Manor Rd. @ Coventry Ave.   **39.9 (64.2)**
Turn East on to Crosby Manor Rd., look carefully the sign is small and may be obscured. If you find yourself on a narrow winding steep hill you passed it! Crosby Manor Rd. is a level road with superb views of the Mohawk Valley.

4.4 (7.1)   County Border @ Crosby Manor Rd.   **37.4 (60.2)**
Continue traveling on Crosby Manor Rd.
Nice View! Herkimer County & Oneida County border.

5.4 (8.7)   Newport Rd. @ Crosby Manor Rd.   **36.4 (58.6)**
Tired of the view? Crosby Manor Rd. becomes a bit *rolling hills* from here to Herkimer. If you would prefer a leveler route, turn South to NY 5, 1 mi. (1.6 km.); or cross the Canal to NY 5S [an additional 1 mi. (1.6 km.)] and then ride East to Herkimer. Personally, NY 5S is a much nicer ride than NY 5.

6.0 (9.7)   Windfall Rd.   **35.8 (57.6)**
          @ Crosby Manor Rd./Shortlots Rd.
Continue straight on Shortlots Rd./Crosby Manor Rd..
You'll have to make a wierd ½ turn to continue on Shortlots Rd.

The name of the road changes the direction is the same to confuse travelers!

7.9 (12.7)   Mowers Rd. @ Shortlots Rd.   33.9 (54.6)
Name change, again! Shortlots becomes Dutchtown Rd.

10.0 (16.1)   Millers Grove Rd. @ Dutchtown Rd.   31.8 (51.2)
And again a name change! This time to Baum Rd..

13.5 (21.7)   Stevens Hill Rd. @ Baum Rd.   28.3 (45.5)
And again! To Stevens (Hill) Rd. What a pain these road name changes are. A better way might designate this route as Herkimer-Oneida Bike Route 4. Then clearly numbering and signing at regular intervals this bike route. Write the Chamber of Commerce in both Counties!

16.5 (26.5)   German St. @ Stevens Rd.   25.3 (40.7)
Turn South on to German St.

16.7 (26.9)   Main St. @ German St.   25.1 (40.4)
Turn South on to Main St.

17.2 (27.7)   Main St. @ NY 5/BR 5/State St.   24.6 (39.6)
Turn East on to State St./NY 5, for 1 block to Washington St.
Westbound Traveler Note: The ride up Main St. and German St. to Steuben St/Stevens Hill Rd. is very steep. The view is worth the effort! If you want a more level route, return to NY 5S and ride West through Mohawk, Illon and Frankfort to Utica.

Herkimer & Ilion

Info.: Leatherstocking Country Tourism, 327 North Main St., Herkimer NY 13350, 800 233-8778.
Area Code: 315. Zip code: Herkimer: 13350; Ilion: 13357.
Cycling & Hiking Info.: Just North of Herkimer (and Little Falls as well as encompassing most of Herkimer County) is Adirondack St. Pk. Many residents will refer to this area as above the *Blue Line* or Park boundary. The Adirondacks is the largest state park in the lower 48 States. Most trails are for hiking only. However a number have recently been opened for Mt. Biking. For information on the Adirondack Mts. area, contact: Tourist Info. Ctr., Old Forge NY 13420, 315 369-6983. If you plan on hiking or Mt. Biking in the Adirondacks it would help if you belonged to and purchased the guide books published by the Adirondack Mt. Club.
Services: All. Hospital.

Lodging: Motels. B&Bs: Leatherstocking B&B Assoc., PO Box 53, Herkimer, 800 941-2337; Chesham Place, Ilion, 894-3552. Camping: Ace of Diamonds Cpgd. 7 mi. (11 km.), North of Herkimer, NY 28, Middleville NY 13406, 891-3855/866-3900; Herkimer Diamond KOA, PO Box 510, Herkimer, 891-7355. Ilion Marina has a camping area.

Attractions: Herkimer Diamond Mines, 800 Mohawk St., 800 562-0897/315 891-7355; Ace of Diamonds Mine 7 mi. (11 km.), North of Herkimer), NY 28, Middleville NY 13406, 891-3855; Remington Firearms Mus., NY 5S, 3 mi. (4.8 km.), East of Ilion, Ilion, 895-3301.

W to E	**Utica to Fort Plain**	E to W
mi. (km.) Read↓	**Herkimer to Utica**	mi. (km.) Read↑
	North of the Canal High Road Route	

Route Note
Refer to Utica Map at the end of the Old Canal and Adirondacks chapter.

W to E	**Utica to Fort Plain**	E to W
mi. (km.) Read↓	**Utica to Ilion**	mi. (km.) Read↑
	South of the Canal Route	

Route Notes

The North of the Canal Route and using NY 5, to go between Utica & Herkimer/Ilion are alternatives to the South of the Canal Route.

North of the Canal High Road Route

Refer to Utica Map at the end of the Old Canal and Adirondacks chapter.

0.0 (0.0)   Genesee St. @ Liberty St./Jay St.   14.1 (22.7)
Travel East on Jay St.
Jay St./Liberty St. is the multilane street just before the bridge over the Canal & River at the base of Genesee St. Look East before you begin biking. You'll see that the road branches and you'll have to make a left hand turn. Use care.

0.3 (0.4)   2nd St. @ Jay St.   13.8 (22.2)
Bear left on to Broad St.
Broad St. is a wide industrial street.
Watch for trucks. Traffic is relatively light.

1.6 (2.6)   Dwyer Ave. @ Broad St.   12.5 (20.1)
Continue traveling East on Dwyer St.

2.3 (3.7)   Pitcher Rd. @ Dwyer Ave.   11.8 (19.0)
Turn North on to Pitcher Rd.

2.5 (4.0)   Broad St./Old NY 5S @ Pitcher Rd.   11.6 (18.6)
Turn East on to Broad St./Old NY 5S.
Landmark: Post Office. Only way to go!
As you travel East Broad St., changes its name to Old NY 5S and then to Main St. in Frankfort Village.

9.2 (14.8)   Old NY 5S/Main St. @ Railroad St.   4.9 (7.9)
Continue traveling East on Main St./Old SR5S.
OR Cross the River & Canal and travel East on SR 5.
Frankfort

11.7 (18.8)   Old NY 5S/Main St. @ Clark St.   2.4 (3.9)
Turn East on to Clark St.

11.9 (19.2)   Clark St./W. Main St.   2.2 (3.5)
               @ NY 51/Central Ave.
Continue East on Clark St.
As you travel East Clark St. becomes W. Main St.
Or Turn North on NY 51/Central Ave. & cross the Canal.
Ilion

13.5 (21.7)   W. Main St./Clark St. Jct. NY 28   .6 (1.0)
Continue traveling East on W. Main St./NY 28.
As you travel West W. Main St. becomes Clark St.
Mohawk

14.1 (22.7)   E. Main St./SR 28 @ SR 5S   0.0 (0.0)
To go to Herkimer, continue traveling N. on SR28.
To go East, South of the Canal Turn East on SR5S.

W to E	**Fort Plain to Utica**	E to W
mi. (km.) Read ↓	**Ilion to Utica**	mi. (km.) Read ↑
	South of the Canal Route	

Route Notes
The North of the Canal Route and using NY 5, to go
between Utica & Herkimer/Ilion are alternatives to this
South of the Canal Route.
Refer to Utica Map at the end of the Old Canal and
Adirondacks chapter.
Information on Herkimer, Ilion and Frankfort is in the
North of the Canal Route.

W to E	**Utica to Fort Plain**	E to W
mi. (km.) Read↓	**Herkimer/Ilion to Ft. Plain**	mi. (km.) Read↑

Westbound Traveler Route Note

Refer to Utica Map at the end of the Old Canal and Adirondacks chapter.

There are two routes between Herkimer/Ilion and Utica:
  South of the Canal
  North of the Canal High Road Route
  NY 5 can also be used as an alternative route

27.8 (44.7)   Washington St./NY 922B @ State St.   24.5 (39.4)
Turn South on to Washington St./NY 922B.
Cross to the South side of the Canal.

28.4 (45.7)   Washington St. @ NY 5S   23.9 (38.5)
Turn East on to NY 5S.

34.0 (54.7)   NY 167 @ NY 5S   18.3 (29.5)
Through travelers continue straight on NY 5S.
Turn North on to NY 167 to go to Little Falls.
Through traveler mileage to NY 169 @ NY 5S=3.8 mi. (6.1 km.) if you decide to by pass Little Falls. If you suddenly change your mind, simply use NY 169 to go to Little Falls.

36.2 (58.3)   Albany St./NY 5S @ NY 167   16.1 (25.9)

36.5 (58.7)   NY 169 @ Albany St./NY 5S   15.8 (25.4)
Eastbound travelers use NY 169 to continue your route eastbound.
Westbound travelers use NY 167 to continue your route westward.

Little Falls

Bike Info.: Bike Shop.
Services & Facilities: All. Hospital.
Lodging: Motels. B&Bs: Gansevoort House, 42 W. Gansevoort St., Little Falls NY 13365, 315 823-3969.
Attractions: Canal Path from Canal Park on William St. to Lock 17. It goes over the hydroelectric plant. Herkimer House, restored home of Revolutionary General Herkimer, NY 169, Little Falls NY 13365, 315 823-0398.

37.0 (58.7)   NY 169 @ NY 5S   15.3 (24.6)
Through travelers continue straight on NY 5S.
If you went to Little Falls then:
Westbound Cyclotourists, turn North on to NY 169.
Eastbound Cyclotourists, turn East on to NY 5S.

42.4 (68.2)   River Rd. @ NY 5S   9.9 (15.9)
Turn on to River Rd. We will be following Montgomery
County's Bike route and path. It is marked, sometimes
clearly, sometimes not. Essentially it follows the Mohawk
River/Erie Canal. If you prefer to use NY 5S do so. In
Fort Plain, the Bike Route and NY 5S, touch each other.

44.9 (72.2)   Another County to write home about.   7.4 (11.9)
Montgomery County & Herkimer County.

45.0 (72.4)   Beginning of Bike Route @ River Rd.   7.3 (11.7)
Follow the signs. If you miss the entrance to the Bike
Path simply keep riding on River Rd., another entrance
will appear soon.

46.3 (74.5)   Mindenville Rd. @ Bike Route.   6.0 (9.6)
Mindenville Rd. is a connecting Rd. between NY 5S and
the Bike Route.

47.0 (75.6)   Bridge St. @ Bike Route   5.3 (8.5)
Through travelers continue riding on the Bike Route.
Turn North to go to St. Johnsville.

St. Johnsville

Info.: St. Johnsville CofC, PO Box 144, St. Johnsville,
NY 13452, 518 842-8200. I received a very friendly letter
from the C. of C. President.
Area code: 518. Zip code: 13452.
Services: Grocery, restaurants, & other stores.
Lodging: B&B: Inn by The Old Mill, 1679 Mill Rd., 568-
2388. Camping: St. Johnsville Cpgd. & Municipal
Marina, South Bridge St., 568-7406; Crystal Grove
Diamond Mine Cpgd., 161 County Highway 114, 568-
2914.
Attractions: Crystal Grove Diamond Mine, 161 County
Highway 114, 568-2914. Margaret Reaney Lib. & Mus.
(Civil War artifacts), 19 Kingsbury Ave., 568-7822. Fort
Klock (1750 trading post restoration & gardens), NY 5.

52.3 (84.2)   River St. @ Bike Route   0.0 (0.0)

Fort Plain & Nelliston

Info.: Fort Plain- Nelliston CofC, Ft. Plain NY 13339, 888 762-0438/518 993-4731. Area code: 518.
Zip codes: Ft. Plain: 13339; Nelliston: 13410.
Services: Grocery, restaurants. & other stores.
Lodging: B&Bs: Palantine House, Old 141 Mill Rd. (NY 5), Ft. Plain 993-3539; Historian 6487 St. NY 5, Box 224, Nelliston (Nelliston is directly across the Canal from Ft. Plain), 993-2233.
Attractions: Ft. Plain Mus. (extensive 19th century material from the Erie Canal expansion & industrialization of the Mohawk Valley), Upper Canal St., NY 5S, 993-2527.

W to E	**Forth Plain to Utica**	E to W
mi. (km.) Read↓	**Ft. Plain to Herkimer/Ilion**	mi. (km.) Read↑

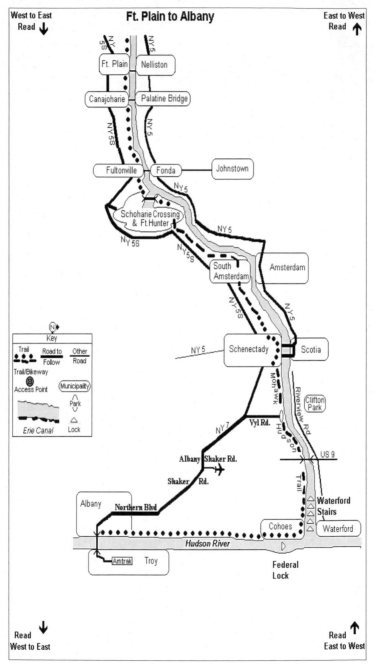

Ft. Plain to Albany

West to East
Read ↓

East to West
Read ↑

Read ↓
West to East

Read ↑
East to West

TRANSPORTATION INTERSECTION

The Mohawk River flows into the Hudson River linking the Great Lakes with the Atlantic Ocean. At Waterford, the *Stairs*, raise recreational boats and commercial barges to bypass Cohoes Falls. Between Lock 2, at the Hudson River in Waterford and Lock 6, just 2 mi. (3.2 km.), upstream, the Canal rises 32 ft. (10 m.)

The rich history of this area is evidenced by the numerous Native American and Dutch village names. Henry Hudson, was the first European to make the journey up the Hudson from the Atlantic Ocean to the Mohawk River.

The Dutch established a *patroon* system of farming the Hudson and lower Mohawk valleys. Many of the manor houses have been restored to their original grandeur with period furnishings.

All types of industrial enterprises were established along the banks of the Canal during the 19th and 20th centuries. The key ingredient for this industrial expansion, electrical generators, were manufactured in Schenectady. Heavy industry, *e. g.*, locomotive manufacturing, and more prosaic industries such as carpet and glove manufacture made their home in the industrial corridor along the Mohawk River and the Canal.

It was the ease of transporting products via the Canal to any place in America and for that matter the world which made this area a vital economic force.

W to E	**Fort Plain to**	E to W
mi. (km.) Read↓	**Albany**	mi. (km.) Read↑

0.0 (0.0)   River St. @ Bike Route   69.0 (111.0)
W to E: Enter bike Trail in Fort Plain.
E to W: Fort Plain, See last entry in previous chapter for info., services, lodging, and attractions.

2.4 (3.9)   End of Bike Path   66.0 (106.2)
Turn East on to NY 5S/BR 5.

3.0 (4.8)   Rock St./Church St.   65.4 (105.3)
@ NY 5S/BR 5
Continue traveling on NY 5S.

Canajoharie & Palatine Bridge

Info.: Canajoharie-Palatine Bridge CofC, PO Box 38, Canajoharie NY 13317. Canajoharie is on the South side of the Canal, Palatine Bridge on the North side. Area code: 518. Zip code: 13317.
Services: Grocery, restaurants,retail stores.
Lodging: Motel.
Attractions: Canajoharie Library & Art Gallery (American artists), 2 Erie Blvd. (NY 5S), 673-2314; Arkell Hall (victorian home), 55 Montgomery St., 673-4408.

14.4 (23.1)   Main St. @ Bike Path/NY 5S/BR 5   54.6 (87.8)
Continue traveling on NY 5S.

Fultonville & Fonda

Info.: Area code: 518.   Zip code: Fultonville: 12072 Fonda: 12068. Fonda is on the North side of the Canal; Fultonville on the South side.
Services: Grocery, restaurants, retail stores.
Lodging: Motels.
Attractions: Fonda Speedway (stock car), Fairgrounds, 853-3151. Montgomery County Dep't. of Archives, Old Court House, 853-8187.   Popular Mist Boat Tours, Mohawk River, Fultonville 853-4511   Charleston St. Forest, 7 mi. (11 km.), South of Fultonville on NY 30A. Fonda National Kateri Tekakwitha Shrine & Mus. (complete excavated Iroquois (Mohawk) Village of Caughnawaga) NY 5, Fonda NY 12068, 518 853-3646. Johnson Hall St. Hist. Site (pre-Revolutionary *manor* house), Hall Avenue, Johnstown NY 12095, 518 762-8712, 3.5 mi. (5.6 km.), North of Fonda..

Schoharie Crossing

19.4 (31.2)   Schoharie Crossing Hist. Site/   49.6 (79.8)
Fort Hunter Hist. Site
@ SSBPath/NY 5S/BR 5
Turn North at the entrance to Schoharie Crossing St.
Hist. Site or Ft. Hunter Hist. Site.
Fort Hunter St. Hist. Site, 129 Schoharie St., PO Box
140, Ft. Hunter NY 12069, 518 829-7510. The Hist. Site
begins on the West bank of the Schoharie River. A MH
Bikeway bridge allows you to cross over the River. The
Pk. Mgr. has a wonderful cut out booklet of the
Aqueduct.

Mohawk-Hudson Bikeway

The magnificent Mohawk Hudson Bikeway (MHBikeway)
begins here. It will take you all the way to the Hudson!
Although I've broken the MHBikeway into parts ranging
from 12 mi. (19 km.), to .1 mi. (.1 km.), it has longer
stretches of unrestricted/unbroken trail. All of it is asphalt
paved! Only in, Amsterdam, Schenectady and Cohoes
do you have to leave the actual Bikeway.

21.9 (35.2)   Putman's Store Exhibit   47.1 (75.8)
@ MHBikeway
An original Erie Canal double lock set.

24.1 (38.8)   MHBikeway/SSBPath @ NY 30   44.9 (72.3)
Through travelers continue straight on the South Shore
Bike Path (SSBPath)/Cleveland Ave. in South
Amsterdam. The South Shore Bike Path is also named
the Mohawk Hudson Bikeway. NY 5S/BR 5 is one mile

South of this point. Stay with the (MHBikeway).
Crossing the NY 30 Bridge takes you into Amsterdam.

Amsterdam

Information: Amsterdam CofC, PO Box 309, 366 W.
Main St., Amsterdam NY 12010, 518 842-8200.
Area code: 518. Zip code: 12010.
Bike Information: Bike shop.
Services: All. Hospital.
Lodging: Motels. B&Bs: Brown House Inn, NY 30S,
South Amsterdam, 843-5662.
Attractions: Guy Park St. Hist. Site, Lock 11; 366 W.
Main St., 842-7550. Fort Johnson Nat'l. Hist. Site, Ft.
Johnson 12070 (NY 5), 518 843-0300.

30.6 (49.2) Border!   38.4 (61.8)
Schenectady County & Montgomery County
Fulton County is not directly on our route; several listed
attractions are in the County.

31.1 (50.1) NY 5S @ MHBikeway   37.9 (60.9)
Ride East on NY 5S.

31.3 (50.4) Bridge St./NY 103   37.7 (60.7)
             @ NY 5S/MHBikeway
Continue riding on NY 5S.
Rotterdam Junction

31.6 (50.9) Stafford St. @ NY 5S/BR 5   37.4 (60.2)
Turn South on to Stafford St. Then East on to the
Mohawk Hudson Bikeway (MHBikeway).

33.0 (53.1) NY 5S/BR 5 @ MHBikeway   36.0 (57.9)
This is a dangerous intersection. Use extreme caution
crossing NY 5S.

36.2 (58.3) Lock 8 @ MHBikeway   32.8 (52.8)
Visit the Lock

38.6 (62.1) NY 5 @ MHBikeway   30.4 (48.9)
             Really, behind Schenectady Community Coll.
The maximum distance between the entrances to the
MHBikeway going through Schenectady is ~1.5 mi.
Distance indicators are not shown on the routes
connecting the two sections of the Mohawk-Hudson
Bikeway in Schenectady. Two routes are provided:
    Direct with Bakeries
    Thru the Stockade Historic Area

W to E	**Fort Plain to Albany**	E to W
mi. (km.) Read↓	**MHBikeway Connection**	mi. (km.) Read↑

Direct Thru Schenectady with Bakeries

Western Bikeway Entrance
@ Schenectady Comm. Coll. Athletic Fields.
Travel South, counterclockwise, around the parking lot roadway circle.

SCC Roadway Circle @ Parking Lots
Travel East, away from the Schenectady Comm. College (SCC) building. Travel through the parking lots towards the front of the SCC building.

Washington St. @ SCC Parking Lot Entrance
Turn North on to the sidewalk in front of the College.

State St./NY 5 @ Washington St.
Cross State St./NY 5, at the traffic signal and travel North on Washington St. All the streets in the Stockade Hist. Dist. are narrow.

Union St. @ Washington St.
Turn East on to Union St.

Erie Blvd. @ Union St.
Turn East on to Union St.

N. Jay St. @ Union St.
Turn North on to N. Jay St.

South St. @ N. Jay St.
Continue traveling North on N. Jay St. to reach the bikeway entrance. The Bikeway entrance is just after the dip in the road where a railroad trestle used to be. Using the East side sidewalk along N. Jay St. going North from South St. is the best way to reach the MHBikeway.
Stop & shop along N. Jay St. on the block before South St. Excellent real Italian bakery & deli, pastry shop & on South St. the neighborhood luncheonette. Real treats!

Eastern Bikeway Entrance @ N. Jay St.
Enter the Mohawk-Hudson Bikeway and travel East towards Albany, only way to go on the Bikeway!

W to E	**Albany to Fort Plain**	E to W
mi. (km.) Read↓	**MHBikeway Connection**	mi. (km.) Read↑

Direct Thru Schenectady with Bakeries

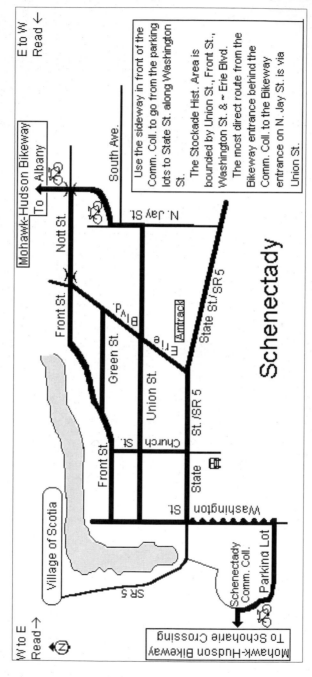

E to W
Read ←

Mohawk-Hudson Bikeway
To Albany

Use the sideway in front of the Comm. Coll. to go from the parking lots to State St. along Washington St.

The Stockade Hist. Area is bounded by Union St., Front St., Washington St. & ~ Erie Blvd. The most direct route from the Bikeway entrance behind the Comm. Coll. to the Bikeway entrance on N. Jay St. is via Union St.

South Ave.

N. Jay St.

Nott St.

Front St.

Green St.

Erie Blvd.

Amtrack

State St./SR 5

Schenectady

Union St.

Front St.

Church St.

State St./SR 5

State St.

Washington St.

Village of Scotia

SR 5

Schenectady Comm. Coll.

Parking Lot

Mohawk-Hudson Bikeway
To Schoharie Crossing

W to E
Read →

W to E	**Fort Plain to Albany**	E to W
mi. (km.) Read↓	**MH Bikeway Connection**	mi. (km.) Read↑
	Thru the Historic Stockade District	

Western Bikeway Entrance
@ Schenectady Comm. Coll. Athletic Fields.
Travel South, counterclockwise, around the parking lot roadway circle.

SCC Roadway Circle @ Parking Lots
Bike East, away from the SCC building, and travel through the parking lots towards the front of the SCC building.

Washington St. @ SCC Parking Lot Entrance
Turn North on to the sidewalk in front of the College.

State St./SR 5 @ Washington St.
Cross State St./SR 5 at the traffic signal, and travel North on Washington St.
All the streets in the Stockade Hist. Dist. are narrow.
If you continue going North on Washington St. you'll come to Riverside Pk. on the Mohawk R.

Front St. @ Washington St.
Turn East on to Front Street.

N. Ferry St. & Green St. @ Front St.
Front St. becomes one way, going East to West for a block or two at this point. Although its against the Rules of the Road, use care & continue traveling on Front St.

Erie Blvd. @ Front St./Nott St.
Traffic Light! Stop!
Cross Erie Blvd. to the road under the highway overpass, Nott St.

Eastern Bikeway Entrance @ Nott St.
Just past the railroad trestle, on the North side of Nott St. and before Union College is a parking lot & apartment building. Go into the apartment building parking lot & look back at the trestle! Bikeway entrance.

W to E	**Albany to Fort Plain**	E to W
mi. (km.) Read↓	**MH Bikeway in Schenectady**	mi. (km.) Read↑
	Thru the Historic Stockade District	

Schenectady

Info.: Schenectady CofC, 306 State St., Schenectady NY 12305, 800 962-8007. Schenectady Visitors Center, Nott Terrace Heights, Schenectady NY 12308, 518 382-7896. Area code: 518. Zip code: various

Cycling & Hiking Info.: Mohawk Hudson Cycling Club, PO Box 12575, Albany NY 12212, 518 437-9579, www.albany.net/~kormisto/index.htm

Services: All. Hospital.

Lodging: Motels & Hotels. B&B: American Collection Res. Serv., 1353 Union St., 370-4948.

Attractions: Museums: Center for the Hist. of the Electrical Industry, 1 River Rd., Bldg. 28-310, 12305, 385-1104; Schenectady Mus. & Planetarium, Nott Terrace Hts., 12305, 382-7890; Empire State Aerosciences Mus., 130 Saratoga Rd. (NY50), Scotia NY 12302, 518 377-2191 (just over the Mohawk River/Canal). History: Hist. Stockade, self guided walking tours, 382-5147. Schenectady Co. Hist. Soc., 32 Washington Ave., 12305, 374-0263.

Gardens: Central Park Rose Garden, Central Parkway at Wright Ave., 12305, 382-5152; Jackson's Garden, Union College Campus, 12305, 388-6000.

Arts: Proctor's Theatre (restored vaudeville/movie theatre with concerts on the Mighty Wurlizter), 12 South Church St., 12305, 346-6204. Outdoor concerts in summer.

Public Transportation: Local: Capital Distr. Trans. Auth. (CDTA), 110 Watervliet Ave., Albany NY 12206, 518 482-3371. Provides public transit service in & from Schenectady to Albany, Saratoga, and Rensselaer Counties. Amtrak: (baggage service), 346-8651.

41.5 (66.8)   Jay St. @ MHBikeway   27.5 (44.2)
MHBikeway ends.

Westbound Traveler Note
The Mohawk Hudson Bikeway suddenly ends at Jay St. in Schenectady. Two routes and a map through Schenectady are provided:
Thru the Historic Stockade area and
Direct Through Schenectady with Bakeries.

43.9 (70.6)   NY 146 @ MHBikeway   25.1 (40.4)
Continue traveling on the MHBikeway
OR for a change from the Bikeway travel on the North Side of the Canal. Turn North on to NY 146 and then West on to Riverview Rd. Follow Riverview Rd. to River

Rd. Then turn South on to Calm Steam Rd. which junctions with Towpath Rd. and leads directly to Lock 2, and Cohoes. All on the North side of the Canal.
Clifton Park: Info.: Twn. Hall, Vischers Ferry Rd., Clifton Pk. 12065, 518 371-3763.Southern Saratoga CofC, 15 Park Ave., Clifton Park NY 12065, 518 695-4159, www.southernsaratogachamber.com

46.6 (75.0)   Blatnick Park @ MHBikeway   22.4 (36.0)
Continue Traveling on the MHBikeway
Toilets, phones, picnic tables.
Niskayuna

48.1 (77.4)   Lock 7 @ MHBikeway   20.9 (33.6)

49.1 (79.0)   Border   19.9 (32.0)
Albany County & Schenectady County.

50.0 (80.5)   Vly Rd./Rosendale Rd.   19.0 (30.5)
                @ MHBikeway
Continue East on Bikeway to Champlain Canal Route and Albany. Landmark: Old Railway station, phones, portable toilets, marsh, nice view.
Albany direct travelers use the Street Route.

Route Notes
The most direct route ($a^2+b^2=c^2$) to downtown Albany is exiting the MHBikeway here and using heavily trafficked Rtes. 7 & 2. The Bikeway is more scenic and nicer riding but longer in distance and time.
Bikeway = 15 mi (24 km).
Albany-Niskayuna St. Route = 8.5 mi (13.7).
Cyclotourists directly (not stopping in Albany) on their way to the Montréal via the Champlain and Chambry Canals should continue on the MHBikeway.

W to E	**Main Erie Canal Route**	E to W
	via the Mohawk-Hudson Bikeway	
mi. (km.) Read↓	**Albany to Niskayuna**	mi. (km.) Read↑

W to E	**Street Route**	E to W
mi. (km.) Read↓	**Niskayuna to Albany**	mi. (km.) Read↑

Albany Niskayuna Street Route

00.0 (00.0)   MH Bikeway @ Old Railroad Station   8.5 (13.7)
               @ Vyl Rd./Rosendale Ave.
Turn on to Vyl Rd./Rosendale Ave. from the Bikeway and
go South on Vly Rd., up the hill.
Clifton Park: Across the Canal but no method to do so.

.2 (.3)   NY 7/Troy Schenectady Rd. @ Vyl Rd.   8.3 (13.4)
Turn East on to NY 7.
Use caution, NY 7 is a heavily trafficked road.

.8 (1.3)   Albany-Shaker Rd. @ NY 7   7.7 (12.4)
Turn South on to Albany-Shaker Rd..

2.4 (3.9)   Francis Rd. @ Albany Shaker Rd.   6.1 (9.8)
Access Rd. for Albany Airport.

2.7 (4.3)   Shaker Rd. Jct. with Albany Shaker Rd.   5.8 (8.9)
Continue Southeast on Albany Shaker Rd.

6.6 (10.6)   Albany-Shaker Rd.   1.9 (3.1)
                 @ Northern Blvd.
Turn South on to Northern Blvd.   Northern Blvd makes
a ⌐|_ turn in about .5 mi. (.8 km.) Continue traveling on
Northern Blvd. Northern Blvd. also changes its name to
Henry Johnson Blvd.

7.9 (10.7)   Central Ave.   .6 (.9)
                 @ Northern Blvd./Henry Johnson Blvd.
Turn South on to Central Ave.

8.0 (12.9)   Washington Ave. @ Central Ave.   .5 (.8)
Turn South on to Washington Ave.

8.5 (13.7)   Washington Ave. @ State St.   0.0 (0.0)
Capital Building.
See Route notes after the Main Route arrives at the
Capital.

W to E	**Street Route**	E to W
mi. (km.) Read↓	**Albany to Niskayuna**	mi. (km.) Read↑

Mohawk River Flood Plain

W to E	**Main Erie Canal Route**	E to W
	via the Mohawk-Hudson Bikeway	
mi. (km.) Read↓	**Niskayuna to Albany**	mi. (km.) Read↑

54.1 (87.1)   Island View Rd. @ MHBikeway   14.9 (23.9)
Turn East on to Island View Rd..

54.5 (87.7)   Dunsbach Ferry Rd. @ Island View Rd. 14.5 (23.3)
Turn South on to Dunsbach Ferry Rd.
Or turn South on to Dunsbach Ferry Rd. and then East
on Schaefer Rd. which becomes Schmerhorn Rd. just
before it meets with the MHBikeway again.   The
Schaefer Rd. route goes along Colonie Twn. Pk.

54.6 (87.9)   MHBikeway @ Dunsbach Ferry Rd.   14.4 (23.2)
Turn on to Bikeway.

57.3 (92.2)   Vliet Blvd./St. @ MHBikeway   17.7 (18.8)
Through travelers to Albany continue on MHBikeway
Cut off for Champlain Canal Route.
Cyclotourists who really want to see Lock 1, should
continue on the riding on the Main MHBikeway route, see
75.6 mi. (121.6 km.), on the Main MHBikeway route.

W to E	**Main Erie Canal Route**	E to W
	via the Mohawk-Hudson Bikeway	
mi. (km.) Read↓	**Albany to Niskayuna**	mi. (km.) Read↑

W to E	**Champlain Canal Route Connector**	E to W
	Mohawk-Hudson Bikeway to Champlain Canal Route	
mi. (km.) Read↓	**Vliet Blvd. to NY 32**	mi. (km.) Read↑

Vliet Blvd. to Champlain Canal Route

0.0 (0.0)   Vliet St. @ MHBikeway   .7 (1.1)
Exit Bikeway West on to Vliet St.

.2 (.4)   Mohawk St. @ Vliet St.   .5 (.8)
Turn Southwest (facing the Mohawk River, towards your
right) on to Mohawk St..

.7 (1.1)   Saratoga St./NY 32 @ Mohawk St.   0.0 (0.0)
Turn North on to Saratoga St.
Route continued
Waterford: Waterford Visitors Center, 1 Tugboat Alley,
Waterford   NY   12188,   518   233-9123,   www.
champlaincanal.org Attractions: 5 Erie Canal Locks in a
row, the *Waterford Stairs*. Original Champlain Canal lock.

W to E	**Champlain Canal Route Connector**	E to W
	Mohawk-Hudson Bikeway to Champlain Canal Route	
mi. (km.) Read↓	**NY 32 to Vliet Blvd.**	mi. (km.) Read↑

W to E	**Main Erie Canal Route**	E to W
	via the Mohawk-Hudson Bikeway	
mi. (km.) Read↓	**Niskayuna to Albany**	mi. (km.) Read↑

57.8 (93.0)   High St. @ MHBikeway   11.2 (18.0)
Through travelers continue on on MHBikeway.
Diversion to Peebles Island State Park, day use only, no other reason to exit the MHBikeway here. Some good picture spots at the Park.
This is a really tiny access point to the MHBikeway which if you blink your eye you will miss.
To go to Peebles State Park: Turn East on to High St.; quick North turn on to Bedford St. which becomes Ontario St. as it rounds a bend; Ontario St. ends at Delaware St. on Green Island. Turn North on Delaware St. to Peebles Island State Park. Total Distance: 2 mi (3.2 km).
Of course if you suddenly change your mind and want to go to Lake Champlain and Montréal instead of Albany you can exit here and turn North at Saratoga St./NY 32 [.5 mi (.8 km)] and follow the Champlain Canal Route in the next chapter.

58.5 (94.1)   Alexander St. @ MHBikeway   <10.5 (<16.8)
MHBikeway goes into city streets for a bit here. As an added bonus you'll see (from a distance) Lock 1.
Turn East on to Alexander St..

58.6 (94.3)   Lincoln Ave. @ Alexander St.   <10.4 (<16.7)
Turn North on to Lincoln Ave.

<58.7 (<94.5)   Spring St. @ Lincoln Ave.   <10.3 (<16.6)
Turn East on to Spring St..

<58.7 (<94.5)   Saratoga St./NY 32   <10.3 (<16.6)
**   @ Spring St.**
To Albany: Look! A bit to the South and across Saratoga St. is Dyke Ave. Cross Saratoga St. and enter Dyke Ave.
To Champlain Canal: Forget the Bikeway if you're going to the Champlain Canal! Simply turn North on Saratoga St./NY 32 to the Mohawk River/Saratoga St. Bridge. Saratoga St./NY 32 is trafficked and not great riding but its only 1.1 mi (1.7 km) to the Bridge.

58.8 (94.6)   Dyke Ave. @ Saratoga St.   10.2 (16.4)
Ride East/Southeast on Dyke St..

59.8 (96.2)   Tibbets Ave. @ Dyke Ave.   9.2 (14.8)
Turn East on to Tibbets Ave.

60.2 (96.9)   George St./Hudson Ave   8.8 (14.2)
               @ Tibbets Ave.
Albany bound travelers turn South on to George St.
West and North bound cyclotourists use Hudson Ave.
Ah! Lock 1, *the* Federal Lock. Yes, travellers there is a
Lock 1 but it is not actually part of the New York State
Barge Canal System. It is owned and operated by the
United States of America! The Federal compound is at
this point on your tour. Lock 1 is a Customs and
Immigration check point. The INS and Customs officers
may let you in to to take a picture, it never hurts to ask.
Do not enter the compound without permission. Federal
Prisons do not have a bike paths!

60.9 (98.0)   George St./Hudson Ave.   8.1 (13.0)
               @ Lower Hudson Ave.
George St and Hudson Ave. junction/spit to form Lower
Hudson Ave..

61.4 (98.8)   Lower Hudson Ave. @ Broadway   7.6 (12.2)
Lower Hudson Ave. turns and goes under I 787.
Turn South on to Broadway.

63.2 (101.7) 4th St./MH Bikeway @ Broadway   5.8 (9.3)
Turn East (towards the Hudson River) and enter the
MHBikeway.

68.4 (109.9) MH Bikeway @ Dunn Bridge/Quay St.   .7 (1.3)
Turn West (away from the River). You will be behind a
beautiful gothic structure. Travel to the front of this
building and you will be at State St.

68.4 (110.1) Bottom of State St.   .6 (.9)
Look up State St.! See the Capital! Yes, you have to
climb the hill to the State Mus. and the Capital!

69.0 (111.0) NY State Capital @ State St.   0.0 (0.0)
If you're going West, simply use the Albany-Niskayuna
City Street Route to go to the Mohawk Hudson Bikeway
and Niagara Falls/Buffalo.

W to E	**Main Erie Canal Route**	E to W
	via the Mohawk-Hudson Bikeway	
mi. (km.) Read↓	**Albany to Niskayuna**	mi. (km.) Read↑

Route Notes

Travelers beginning in Albany and going North to Montréal via the Champlain and Chambry Canals should follow the Main Erie Canal Route via the Mohawk-Hudson Bikeway North along the Hudson. They should exit at Vliet Blvd. and use the Champlain Canal Connector Route from there. Read directly above this paragraph.

Travelers beginning in Albany and going West to Niagara Falls/Buffalo can use either the Main Canal Route via the Mohawk-Hudson Bikeway, reading directly above this paragraph; or the Albany-Niskayuna Street Route. The Street Route is shorter but has much more traffic.

Albany

Info.: Albany County CVB, 25 Quackenbush Sq., Albany NY 12207, 800 258-3582/518 434-1217; NYS Capital Visitors Office, Rm 106, Concourse, Empire State Plz., Albany NY 12242, 474-2418. AV: 518. ZipC: various.

Cycling and Hiking Info.: *Bike Club*: Mohawk Hudson Cycling Club, PO Box 12575, Albany 12212, 437-9579.

Bike shops & hiking equipment stores are scattered about the Capital District. Klarsfeld and others are on NY 7/State St. Check the phone book for others.

Bikeway Map: The CVB will send you one upon request.

Services & Facilities: All. Hospital.

Public Transportation: Local: Capital Dist. Trans. Auth. (CDTA), 110 Watervliet Ave., 12206, 482-3371. Provides public transit service in & from Albany to Schenectady, Saratoga, and Rensselaer Counties. The CDTA has a booklet and map of its bus system. No bike racks

Intercity: The bus terminal is hidden under the access ramps to the Dunn Bridge. One block from the base of State St. Trailways: 436-9651; Greyhound: 434-8095; Yankee Trails (Bennington, VT & Albany), 286-2400; Upstate Transit (Saratoga & Albany), 584-5252.

Amtrak: The Albany Amtrak station is across the Hudson River in Rensselaer! It's called Albany-Rensselaer, East St., Rensselaer NY 12144, 462-5763. Directions to the Amtrak station are in the next chapter. Trains from Albany go South to New York City; North to Montréal; West to Chicago; East to Boston.

Airport: See Albany Niskayuna Street Route.

Lodging: Motels & Hotels. Mansion Hill Inn, 115 Philip St., 12202, 465-2038; State St. Mansion, 281 State St., 12210, 462-6780; The State House, 393 State St., 12210, 465-

Albany-Rensselear Amtrak Station to Albany & the Mohawk-Hudson Bikeway

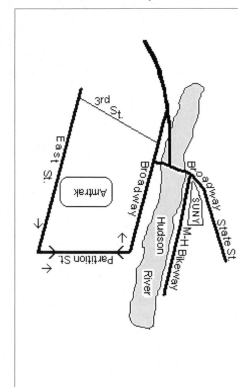

Directions

Exit the Amtrak Station and turn North on to East St.

At Partition St., turn West and go over the railroad tracks using the bridge/trestle.

Turn South on to Broadway.

Ride until you see the ramp to the Bridge over the Hudson River.

West bank of the Hudson River:

Turn on to the Mohawk-Hudson Trail. The Trail head is at the base of the West bank bike-ped access ramp behind the SUNY Admin. Building (Gothic style building). Dist.= 1 mi.

8079; Appel Inn, PO Box 18, RD 3 NY 146, Altamont, NY 12009, 518 861-6557.

Attractions: Museums: New York State Mus., Empire State Plz., 474-5877, geology, flora & fauna, history, sociology and economics of NY; Albany Inst. of Hist. and Art, 125 Washington Ave., 12210, 463-4478, Hudson Valley exhibits. Dutch Apple Cruises, 137 Broadway, 12202, 463-0220.

Architecture: Empire State Plaza, you can't miss this, it's those tall buildings & the egg!; Executive Mansion, 138 Eagle St., 12202, art graces all areas of the Mansion, reservations necessary; Ten Broeck Mansion, 9 Ten Broeck Place, 12210, 436-9626, Albany Historical Assoc. Mus.

Performing Arts: Outdoor concerts. Most of the performing arts activities during the summer take place at the Saratoga Performing Arts Center.

E to W	**Albany to**	W to E
mi. (km.) Read↓	**Little Falls**	mi. (km.) Read↑

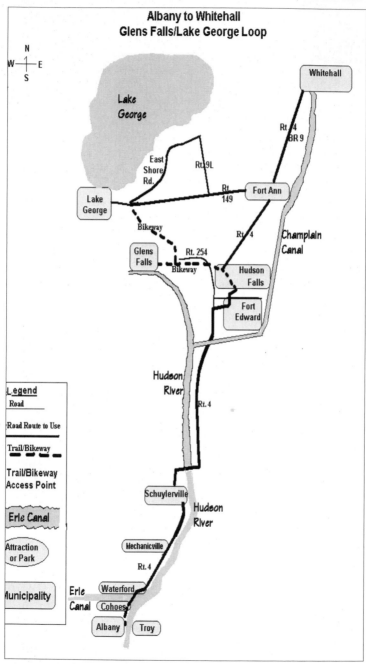

UPPER HUDSON VALLEY

Congratulations! You've bicycled the Erie Canal! You have a few choices now. South to New York City; North to Montréal.

Those of you who have been travelling South from Montréal or North from New York City will most likely turn West and shuffle off to Buffalo along the Erie Canal!

Northbound travelers should stop at the *Waterford stairs* with its four adjacent locks; then pass the Waterford Arsenal where armaments for the United States have been manufactured since the early 19th century. This rich historic area, has mansions which attest to the Dutch patroon system of land ownership; and the Saratoga National Historic Site which commemorates a turning point battle of the American Revolution.

Your progress North along the Hudson River will be unhindered by either traffic or industrial development.

Crossing the Hudson as Canal boats and barges do, we travel inland along the ancient glacial Lake Vermont to its modern vestige, Lake Champlain.

A side trip via the Champlain Feeder Canal and the greatly diminished, in width and flow, Hudson River to Glens Falls bring you to beautiful Lake George. Lake George itself is a *graben* or fallen block of land rather than a glacially carved or erosion formed lake.

The importance of the Champlain Canal becomes readily apparent at Whitehall. The Canal served as medium to transport the riches of timber and minerals ensconced in the Adirondack and Vermont mountains to the markets of the Atlantic coastal cities.

S to N	**Champlain Canal Main Route**	N to S
mi. (km.) Read↓	**Albany to Whitehall**	mi. (km.) Read↑

0.0 (0.0)   Mohawk St.   67.2 (108.1)
              @ Saratoga St./NY 32
The MHBikeway has taken you to this point.
Turn North on to NY 32/Saratoga St.

Cohoes

Info.: Cohoes RiverSpark Visitor Center, 58 Remsen St.,
Cohoes, NY 12047, 518 237-7999.
Services: All. Hospital.
Lodging: Motels.
Attractions: Peebles Island State Park; Federal Lock.

.1 (.1)   Bridge @ NY 32   67.1 (107.9)
Continue traveling North on NY 32.
Saratoga County & Albany County.

1.5 (2.4)   NY32 @ Broad St.   65.7 (105.7)
Turn West on to NY 32/Broad St.

Waterford

Info.: Waterford Visitors' Ctr. 1 Tugboat Alley, Waterford
NY 12188, 518 233-9123, www.champlaincanal.org
Services: Grocery, restaurants and local retail stores.
Attractions: Erie Canal Locks 2-6, The *Waterford Stairs!*
The *old* Lake Champlain Canal. Cresecent Cruise Lines,
NY 9, Halfmoon NY 12065, 518 373-1070.

1.6 (2.5)   6th St./NY 96 @ Broad St./NY 32   65.6 (105.6)
Through Travelers Continue on NY 32.
Tourists go to see Lock 2 & the Waterford Stack.

Waterford Stairs
This is a series of Locks (4, 5 & 6) in a stair arrangement.
Turn on to NY 96/6th St.. Ride 2 blocks on 6th St. to
Division St./NY 97. Division St. jct. with Washington Ave./
NY 97. Turn on to Eighth Rd., where you will see Lock 4.
Total one way mileage: 1 mi. (1.6 km.)
Lock 2 & the Old Champlain Canal
Return from the Waterford Stairs the same way you went
there. Just <u>after</u> you turn West from 6th St. on to Broad
St./NY 32, you will see an almost invisible bridge and
then 5th St.. Turn South on to 5th St.. It ends at Lock 2
and the Old Champlain Canal. Return to Broad St./NY
32 via 5th St..

The Old Champlain Canal at Waterford

1.8 (2.9)   NY 32/Broad St. @ 3rd St./NY 32   65.4 (105.3)
Turn North and continue riding on NY 32.
BR 9 junctions here.

2.3 (3.7)   NY 32/BR 9 Jct. NY 4   64.9 (104.4)
Junction Rtes. 32 & 4. This street is also called Hudson
River Rd. We'll use Rtes. 4/32/BR 9 for clarity

3.7 (6.0)   Champlain Lock 1 @ Rtes 4/32   63.5 (102.2)
Take a look!

7.7 (12.4)   Champlain Lock 2   59.5 (95.8)
              @ Rtes 4/32/BR 9
Take a look!

8.7 (14.0)   Central Ave. Jct. Rtes 4/32/BR 9   58.5 (94.1)
Rtes 4/32/BR 9 is renamed Central Ave.

9.6 (15.4)   2nd St./Terrace Ave. @ Rtes 4/32   57.6 (92.7)
Continue North on Rtes. 4/32.
Turn East on to 2nd St. to go to the River.

9.9 (15.9)   Howland Ave./NY 67 @ Main St.   57.3 (92.2)
Continue North on NY 67/Howland Ave.
Diversion: We're going to Champlain Lock 3! A pleasant
spot. This is a short diversion primarily for the benefit of
guerilla campers. Directions:
   Cross the Howland Ave. Bridge. Turn North on Linden
St. [.6 (1.0 km.) from the Bridge @ Main St.] The Lock
is .5 mi. (.8 km.) North on Linden St. One way distance:
1.2 mi. (1.9 km.)

Mechanicville

Services: Grocery and local retail stores.
Lodging: Motels.
Attractions: Champlain Canal Lock 3.

10.1 (16.3)   Main St./NY 67 @ Rtes 4/32/BR 9   57.1 (91.9)
Back on track! Turn North on to Rtes 4/32/BR 9.

12.8 (20.6)   NY 125 @ Rtes 4/32/BR 9   54.4 (87.5)
Continue traveling on Rtes. 4/32/BR 9.

Stillwater

Info.: Area code: 518. Zip code: 12170
Lodging: B&Bs: Cottage on the Hudson, 93 S. Hudson
Ave., 664-8780; Lee's Deer Run, 411 County Rd. 71,
584-7722; River's Edge, 90 Wrights Loop, 518 664-3276.
Attractions: Saratoga National Hist. Pk., Rts. 4 & 32,
664-9821. Site of the Revolutionary War battles which
turned the tide for the Americans.

26.1 (42.0)   NY 29 @ Rtes 4/32/BR 9   41.1 (66.1)
Continue traveling on Rtes. 4/32/BR 9.

Schuylerville

Info.: Area code: 518. Zip code: 12871.
Services: Grocery, other stores. Friendly people.
Lodging: Motel. B&B: Kings Ransom Farm, 178 King
Rd., 695-6876. Camping: Schuyler Yacht Basin, NY 29,
1 Ferry St., 695-3193;
Attractions: General Philip Schuyler House, NY 4, 664-
9821. Period home and furnishings.

28.4 (45.7)   NY 32 @ Rte. 4/BR 9   38.8 (62.4)
Continue on NY 4/BR 9. You are now traveling on the
East side of the Hudson River.

39.4 (63.4)   NY 197 @ NY 4/BR 9   27.8 (44.7)
Continue riding North on NY 4/BR 9.

Fort Edward

Services: Restaurants, grocery, & retail stores.
Lodging: Motel.
Attractions: Old Fort House Mus. (local history), 518
632-5237; Ft. Edward Arts Center, 518 747-3090.

39.9 (64.2)   Case St. @ NY 4/BR 9   27.3 (43.9)
Turn East on to Case St.

40.6 (65.3)   McIntyre St. @ Case St.   26.6 (42.8)

Turn South on to McIntyre St.

40.7 (65.5)   Parking Lot at End of McIntyre Rd.   26.5 (42.6)
Beginning of Glens Falls Feeder Canal Trail. Enter the
Trail riding Northeast.

42.5 (68.4)   Trail turns Northeast   24.7 (39.8)
You have passed Champlain Lock 8.
Entering the historic Canal Lock area.

43.3 (69.7)   Burgoyne Ave. @ Trail   23.9 (38.5)
Continue traveling on the Trail.

43.8 (70.5)   Maple Ave./NY 196 @ Trail   23.4 (37.7)
Continue traveling on the Trail.

Hudson Falls

Services: Grocery, restaurants, antique, & retail stores.
Cycling & Hiking Info.: Bike shop.
Lodging: B&B on the Green, RR 2, Box 538 (Notre
Dame St. Ext.), Hudson Falls NY 12839, 518 747-2462.

44.2 (71.1)   NY 4/Main St. @ Trail   23.0 (37.0)
Through travelers to Lake Champlain and Montréal turn
North on to NY 4/Main St.

Travelers Note
The Main Champlain Canal Route continues after the
Glens Falls Feeder Canal Trail & Glens Falls/Lake
George/Ft. Ann Loop.

Travelers taking the diversionary path to Lake George
should follow the **Glens Falls Feeder Canal Trail** and
Glens Falls/Lake George/Ft. Ann Loop.

S to N	**Champlain Canal Main Route**	N to S
mi. (km.) Read↓	**Whitehall to Albany**	mi. (km.) Read↑

Glens Falls Feeder Canal to
Glens Falls/Lake George/Ft. Ann Loop

Before you start out on this Loop you should be aware of a few roadway and general tourist factors.

1. One way distance, **Hudson Falls/Glens Falls/Lake George/ Ft. Ann Loop** = 31.2 mi. (50.0 km.)
2. You will be entering a prime tourist area. You must book lodging at least one day in advance. This includes campgrounds.
3. The roadways tend to be crowded, not overly crowded, but with some traffic. Many drivers are not used to bicyclists and may be distracted by children, the beauty of the terrain, looking for groceries, attractions, etc. Use extreme caution.
4. Now for the good stuff! There is a wonderful bikeway from Glens Falls to Lake George.
5. And a caveat! NY 9N going North from Lake George to Ticonderoga is a magnificent scenic road paralleling Lake George. Unfortunately it is <u>not</u> suitable for cyclotourists no less hikers. NY 9N (on the West side of Lake George) is a well paved but narrow road with almost no shoulder. During the season it is heavily trafficked with cars, RVs and local truck traffic. Additionally NY 9N has a number of severe hills on which any diversion from a pace line parallel to the road edge will put you in danger of being killed.
6. There is no continuous road close to and parallelling the East side of Lake George to the Village to Ticonderoga. To safely continue northward to Ticonderoga and Lake Champlain you will have to either:

    a. Return to NY 4 and continue riding on the Main Canal Route;

    b. Take a *cruise* from Lake George to Ticonderoga.
7. Having said all this, I know there will be some adventurous cyclotourist who says, "damn the drivers, I want the super scenic route!" and will use NY 9N to go to Ticonderoga. The distance, using NY 9N, between Lake George Village (Fort Henry) and Ticonderoga (Fort Ticonderoga) = 37 mi. (60 km.)

E to W	**Glens Falls Feeder Canal to**	W to E
	Glens Falls/Lake George/Ft Ann Loop	
mi. (km.) Read↓		mi. (km.) Read↑

0.0 (0.0)   NY 4/Main St. @ Feeder Canal Trail   31.2 (50.2)
Trail continues on South side of the Feeder Canal.

.7 (1.5)   County Border @ Warren St.   30.5 (49.1)
Continue traveling West on the Trail.
Washington County & Warren County.

1.4 (2.3)   NY 254/Quaker Hill Rd. @ Trail   29.8 (48.0)
To go to Lake George: Turn on to NY 254. NY 254 has a
local road name, Quaker Hill Rd.
To go to downtown Glens Falls: Continue on the Trail to
Shermantown Rd. Exit the Trail on to Shermantown Rd.
Turn West on to Warren St. Just beyone the Hyde Art
Museum turn South on to Oakland Ave. Follow Oakland
Ave. to Glen St./NY 9. At the Glen St. Bridge, cross over
to the South side of the Feeder Canal. The Trail
continues to Richardson St. on the Southwestern edge of
Glens Falls.

Glens Falls/Queensbury & S. Glens Falls

Info.: Glens Falls CofC, PO Box 327, Glens Falls, NY 12801,
518 743-1506.

Area code: 518. Zip codes: Glens Falls, 12801; Queensbury,
12804; Lake George, 12845.

Cycling & Hiking Info.: Bikeway map: Warren County Tourism,
Municipal Center, Lake George NY 12845, 800 958-4748.

Mt. Biking: Warren Co. Mt. Bike Trail System, $10.00 fee payable
at most Town and Village offices and selected organizations
(ADK), bike shops and camping outfitters, 668-4447. Gore
Mt. Cross Country Trails (Gore Mt. is well off our route),
Olympic Regional Development Authority, 251-2411.
Adirondack North Country Assn. Trails, Adirondack
Mountain Club (ADK), Luzerne Rd., Lake George, 668-4447.

Bike Shops/Outdoors Stores: In and around Glens Falls and
South Glens Falls.

Hiking: Adirondack Mountain Club, Luzerne Rd., Lake George,
668-4447. Department of Environmental Conservation,
Hudson Ave., Warrensburg NY 12885, 623-3671.

Outfitters: Outfitters, guide services and equipment stores make
their base in or around Glens Falls.

Services: All. Hospital.

Lodging: Motels galore!. B&Bs: Berry Farm, 623 Bay Rd.,

Queensbury, 792-0341; Crisp's, 693 Ridge Rd., RD 1, Box 57, Queensbury, 793-6889; Sanford's Ridge, 749 Ridge Rd., RR 1, Box 70, Queensbury, 793-4923. Camping: Lake George Cpgd., Queensbury, 798-6218.

Attractions: Glens Falls is a primary gateway to the southern Adirondacks. Contact the CofC, DEC and ADK for additional information on attractions in this area. Hyde Art Mus. (old masters), 161 Warren St., Glens Falls, 792-1761.

4.4 (7.1)   Bay Rd. @ NY 254/Quaker Hill Rd.   26.8 (43.1)
Turn North on to Bay Rd.

4.5 (7.2)   Bikeway Entrance @ Bay Rd.   26.7 (43.0)
Turn West on to the Warren County Bikeway (WCBikeway). It will parallel Glenwood Ave. The WCBikeway is well signed and well maintained. It's terminus in Glens Falls is about a 1.5 mi. (2.4 km.) North of this point on Bay St. at Adirondack Community Coll.

12.0 (19.3)   Beach Rd. @ WC Bikeway   19.2 (30.9)
You are now at Lake George. You've gone through Battleground Public Cpgd. and are facing Lake George Beach St. Pk.

Lake George

Info.: Lake George Reg. CofC, 2176 St. Rte. 9, Lake George NY 12845, 800 705-0059/518 668-5755, AC: 518. Zip: 12845. www.lakegeorgechamber.com.

Cycling & Hiking Info.: See Glens Falls for basic cycling & hiking information sources. Bike & camping shops.

Hiking Trails: Prospect Mt. trailhead on Montcalm St. in the Village, modest climb to 2030 ft. (619 m.), great views of Adirondack High Peaks, Green & White Mts.

Services: All. Hospital.

Lodging: Note: Book at least one day in advance. Lodging along NY 9N going towards Ticonderoga are not listed. Consult the Warren County Travel Guide.

Motels, hotels, resorts and cottage rentals ad infinitem.

B&Bs: Adirondack B&B Assn., PO Box 801; Corner Birches, 86 Montcalm, 668-2837; Pine Knoll, 35 Dieskau St., 668-3905;

Camping: Call and ask how far the cpgd. is from the Village. Adirondack Camping Village, NY 9, 668-5228; Hearthstone Point St. Cpgd., NY 9N, 668-5183, 2 mi. (3.2 km.) N. of Village; King Phillips Cpgd., 668-5763; Lake George Battleground Cpgd., NY 9, 668-3348. Lake George Cpgd., 798-6218; Lake George KOA, 696-2615; Mohawk Camping on Lake George, 668-2760; Rainbow View, 623-9444; Swiss

Trail, 696-3591; Whipporwill, 668-5565.   Lake George
Islands Public Cpgds., accessible <u>only</u> by boat from various
villages along the Lake, primitive sites; H_2O, vault toilets - 3
islands, Glen Island (Bolton Landing), 644-9696; Long Island
(Cleverdale), 656-9426; Narrow Island (Hulett's Landing),
499-1288.
Attractions: Lake George.   Local historical museums.   Many
commercial theme parks.   Fourth of July celebration.   Lake
George Shoreline Cruises, Kurosaka Lane, 668-4644; Lake
George Steamship Cruises, Beach Rd., 668-5777.   Ft.
William Henry Beach Rd. at Canada St., 668-5471.

[12.6 (20.3)   NY 9N @ Beach Rd.   19.8 (31.9)]
Turn West on to Beach Rd. to go to NY 9N & the Village
of Lake George.
You can use NY 9N, to go Ticonderoga.

12.0 (19.3)   Beach Rd. @ WCBikeway   19.2 (30.9)
Turn East on to Beach Rd.

12.5 (20.1)   US 9L/East Shore Rd. @ Beach Rd.   18.7 (30.1)
Turn Northeast on to US 9L/East Shore Road

16.3 (26.2)   Bay Rd. @ US 9L/East Shore Rd.   14.9 (24.0)
Continue traveling Northeast on NY 9L/East Shore Rd.
If you want to shorten the trip by about 2 mi. (4 km.) then
turn South on to Bay Rd.; travel 3.8 mi. (6.1 km.) to NY
149; turn East on to NY 149 and travel 1.5 mi. (2.4 km.)
to NY 9L. A total distance of 5.3 mi. (8.5 km.) vs 7.1 mi.
(11.4 km.) using 9L all the way.

23.4 (37.7)   NY 149 @ US 9L/Ridge Rd.   7.8 (12.6)
Turn East on to NY 149.
Warren County & Washington County.

31.2 (50.2)   US 4/BR 9 @ NY 149   0.0 (0.0)
Fort Ann

E to W	Ft. Ann/Lake George Glens Falls/	W to E
mi. (km.) Read↓	Hudson Falls Loop	mi. (km.) Read↑

Route Notes
Main Champlain Canal Route is continued after the
Glens Falls Hudson Falls Loop.
Before you start out on this Loop you should read the
information at the beginning of the loop.

Whitehall

S to N	**Champlain Canal Main Route**	N to S
mi. (km.) Read↓	**Albany to Whitehall**	mi. (km.) Read↑

54.5 (87.7)   NY 149 @ US 4/BR 9   12.7 (20.4)
   S to N: Continue traveling on NY 4/BR 9
   N to S: The Main Champlain Canal Route continues after
   the Glens Falls Feeder Canal & Loop Routes.

Fort Ann

Services: Convenience & antique stores; restaurant.
Lodging: Motel, 518 639-4411. Camping: Fort Ann
Cpgd., on a dirt road and up a hill but very nice sites &
owners, 518 637-8840.

58.8 (94.6)   NY 22 @ Rte. 4/BR 9   8.4 (13.5)
   Champlain Lock 11, Take a look!

66.7 (107.3) NY 4 @ NY 22/BR 9   .5 (.8)
   NY 4 Junctions with Rt. 22.

67.2 (108.1) Champlain Lock 12 @ NY 22/BR 9   0.0 (0.0)

Whitehall

Info.: Whitehall CofC, 259 Broadway/US 4, Whitehall NY 12887, 518 499-2292.

Area code: 518. Zip code: 12887.

Cycling & Hiking Info.: Bike Shop, The General's Bike Shop, 6 N. William St., 499-2686; owner can lead you to Mt. Biking areas. Camping supply store on Rt. 22, owner can point you to hiking areas.

Services: All. Amtrak stop (no baggage service). Local bus: Greater Glens Falls Transit, 792-1086

Lodging: Motel. Apple Orchard Inn, RD 2, Box 85, 518 499-0180; Finch & Chubb Inn, 82 N. Williams St., 499-2049. Camping: Indian Hill Campsite, US 4, 499-2690.

Attractions: Skenesborough Museum & Visitor Center, Skenesborough Dr., 499-0716. Lock 12. Village architecture. Outdoor concerts (classical, rock & country), Saturday nights in July & August.

S to N	**Champlain Canal Main Route**	N to S
mi. (km.) Read↓	**Whitehall to Albany**	mi. (km.) Read↑

Whitehall to Westport

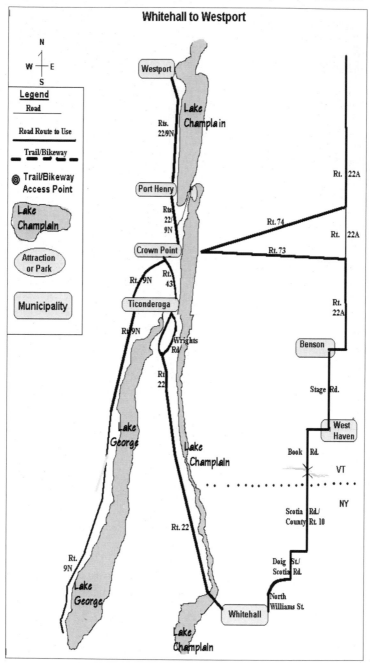

LAKE CHAMPLAIN

Residents of the southern end of New York State, the New York City area don't realize that many of the 19th century skyscrapers, of which they are so proud, were built with iron ore shipped from Adirondack mines via the Champlain Canal. Timber which allowed the metropolis to house its growing population was also derived from the lands bordering both sides of Lake Champlain.

In 1892, the New York State Constitution was amended to reserve six million acres of land for the Adirondack Park. This land was to remain *forever wild*. Warren and Essex Counties are actually entirely within the *Blue Line*, as the Park's border is called. Hiking, canoeing and mt. biking in the Adirondacks is an ultimate adventure.

The importance of the Lake Champlain region to the United States' independence and early economic development can not be under estimated. The rich forests provided lumber as well as animals for hunting and trapping. The mines, raw materials for building and manufacturing. With the development of the Champlain Canal an economical way of transporting these products was achieved.

The capture of Fort Ticonderoga by Ethan Allen and Benedict Arnold in May, 1775, represents the first significant victory of Continental forces over the British.

After crossing the southern lobe of Lake Champlain along a dropped *graben* or fault line with its exposed rock its clear sailing to Ticonderoga with views of the Lake.

S to N mi. (km.) Read↓	**Champlain Canal Route** **Whitehall to Westport**	N to S mi. (km.) Read↑
00.0 (00.0)	Champlain Lock 12 @ Clinton St. Travel West on Clinton St. to NY 22/BR 9. **Whitehall:** For information see Upper Hudson chapter.	55.5 (89.3)
.1 (.1)	NY 22/BR 9 @ Clinton St. Turn North on to NY 22. NY 22 has a well defined shoulder. It is not heavily trafficked.	55.4 (89.2)
2.4 (3.8)	South Bay Bridge @ NY 22/BR 9 Boat Launch at the southern end of Lake Champlain.	53.1 (85.5)

17.8 (28.6)   Putnam Center @ NY 22   37.7 (60.7)

Route Alternatives

Scenic Route: Turn East here (small convenience/
grocery) on to Lower Rd./Wrights Ferry Rd. There are
several steep inclines/declines. At Wrights do <u>NOT</u>
turn down Wrights Ferry Rd., it has a steep decline to
the Lake. Continue riding on Lower Rd. Lower Rd. is
called Wrights Ferry Rd. in Essex County.   Very
confusing! But essentially stay on the main roadway
rather than making any turn offs towards the Lake.

Not so Scenic Route: Continue North on NY 22.

Lodging: Lake Champlain Inn, Lake Road, Box 105,
Putnam Station, NY 12861, 518 547-9942.

22.8 (36.7)   Border   32.7 (52.6)

Washington & Essex Counties.

23.8 (37.9)   Lower Rd./Wrights Ferry Rd.   31.7 51.0)
               @ NY 22

Turn North on to NY 22.

Not so Scenic Route for **S to N** travelers: Continue South
on NY 22

Scenic Route: **S to N** travelers, see N to S mi. 37.7 (km.
60.7), before turning on to Wrights Ferry Rd./Lower Rd.
for the scenic route. Turn on to Wrights Ferry Rd./Lower
Rd.

27.3 (43.90) NY 74 @ NY 22/BR 9   28.2 (45.3)

Turn West on to Montcalm St. to go to Ticonderoga.

A bit of mileage/kilometage information:

1.6 mi (2.6 km) East on NY 74 to Ferry.

1.9 mi (3.1 km) East on NY 74 to Ft. Ticonderoga
entrance & the Fort. This is total mileage to the fort.
The entrance is about 1.3 mi (2.1 km) from this
intersection.

S to N	**Champlain Canal**	N to S
mi. (km.) Read↓	**Ticonderoga By Pass**	mi. (km.) Read↑

Route Note

To by pass Ticonderoga continue North on Rts. 22/74.
NY 74 splits off to go West and NY 22 continues North,
junctioning with NY 9N. Personally, go into Ticonderoga
and have lunch, see the museum and wander about
town.   But I've also provided the following scenic
alternative recommended by Lake Champlain Bikeways/
Voles Cyclables Du Lac Champlain:

Scenic but slightly hilly alternative to Rts. 22/74
27.8 (44.7) Shore-Airport Rd.@ NY 22
Turn on to Shore-Airport Rd.
29.5 (47.5) NY 22/9N
Turn North on to NY 22/9N

S to N	Champlain Canal	N to S
mi. (km.) Read↓	Ticonderoga By Pass	mi. (km.) Read↑

28.7 (46.2)   Montcalm St. @ NY 9N   26.8 (43.1)
Turn North on to 9

Ticonderoga

Info.: Ticonderoga & Crown Point CofC, PO Box 70, Ticonderoga NY 12883, 518 585-6619.
Area code: 518. Zip code: 12883.
Cycling & Hiking Info.: Bike shop. Camping supply stores. La Chute River Interpretive Trail.
Services: All. Hospital. Ticonderoga, NY-Shoreham, VT Ferry, 802 897-7999. Amtrak station. Adirondack Trailways bus. Professional Guide Services for exploring the Adirondacks.
Lodging: Motels. B&Bs: Stone Wells Farm, 331 Montcalm St., 585-6324, Ranchouse at Baldwin, Baldwin Rd., 585-6596. Camping: BrookWood, NY 9N, 585-7113; Putnam Pond St. Forest Cpgd., 9 mi. (15 km.) West on NY 74—>Putts Pond Rd., 595-7280.
Attractions: Fort Ticonderoga, PO Box 390B, 585-2821 (reinactments & description of crucial Revolutionary War battle). Ticonderoga Herit. Mus., Moses Circle, 585-2696.

29.5 (47.5)   NY 22/BR 9 @ NY 9N   26.0 (41.8)
Continue traveling North on Rts. 9N/22/BR 9

37.4 (60.2)   Crown Point Center @ NY 9N/22   18.1 (29.1)
Continue North.

Crown Point

Info.: See Ticonderoga. Area code: 518. Zip code: 12928.
Services & Facilities: Convenience store, restaurants. Ferry to Vermont.
Lodging: Motel. B&Bs: Crown Point, Box 474, Main St., 597-3651. Camping: Crown Point Reservation (see next entry); La-Ku Cpgd., c/o Oscar Kugler, Bridge Rd., 597-3495; Monitor Bay Cpgd., 597-3235.
Attractions: State Hist. Site (see next entry). Essex County Fish Hatchery, PO Box 501, 597-3844.

Lake Champlain from Ft. Ticonderoga's Rampart.

41.1 (66.1)   NY 903 @ NY 9N/22/BR 9   14.4 (23.2)
Through travelers continue North on Rts. 9N/22/BR 9.
Tourists can turn East on to NY 903 for 4.6 mi. (7.4 km.)
and visit Crown Point St. Hist. Site & Forest Preserve
Cpgd.
You can cross to Vermont using NY 903.

44.8 (72.1)   Broad St./Port Henry @ NY 9N/22   10.7 (17.2)
Through travelers continue northward.

Port Henry

Info.: Moriah & Port Henry C of C, 518 546 7261.
Area code: 518. Zip code: 12974.
Services: Amtrak stop.   Grocery, convenience store,
restaurants, and antique stores.
Lodging: Motels & cabins. B&Bs: Elk Inn, HCR 1 Box
87, 546-7024; King's Inn, 109 Broad St., 546-7633.
Camping: Bulwagga Bay Beach & Campsite, 14 Park Pl.,
546-9981; Port Henry Municipal Beach & Campsite, 25
S. Main St., 546-9981/518 546-9933; Craig Harbor
Canyon, Rts 9/22, 546-3500.

55.5 (89.3)   NY 22 Jct. with NY 9N   0.0 (0.0)

Westport

Info.: Westport C of C, 518 962-8383.
Area code: 518. Zip code: 12993.
Services: Grocery, restaurants, antique and Adirondack crafts shops. Amtrak stop.
Lodging: Motels & cabins. B&Bs: All Tucked Inn, Main St., 962-4400; Victorian Lady, S. Main St.,; Grey Goose, 42 Main St.; Inn on the Library Lawn, Washington St., 962-8666.
Attractions: Train Depot Theatre, Box 414, 962-4449. Essex County fair.

S to N	**Champlain Canal Route**	N to S
mi. (km.) Read↓	**Westport to Whitehall**	mi. (km.) Read↑

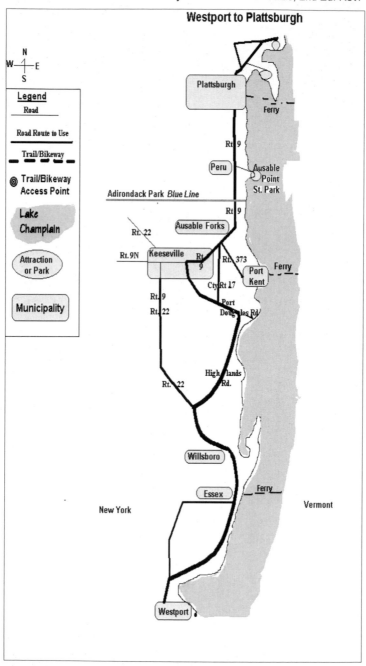

Westport to Plattsburgh

N W—E S

Legend

Road

Road Route to Use

Trail/Bikeway

Trail/Bikeway Access Point

Lake Champlain

Attraction or Park

Municipality

Plattsburgh

Ferry

Rt. 9

Peru

Ausable Point St. Park

Adirondack Park *Blue Line*

Rt. 9

Ausable Forks

Rt. 22

Rt. 9N   Keeseville   Rt. 9   Rt. 373   Ferry

Port Kent

Cty Rt 17

Rt. 9   Port Douglas Rd.

Rt. 22

Rt. 22   Highlands Rd.

Willsboro

Essex   Ferry

New York   Vermont

Westport

NORTH COUNTRY

With the Adirondack Park on its western shore and the mountains of Vermont on its eastern shore, Lake Champlain presents an idyllic setting for continuing your journey. Route 22 will not be crowded with cars and RVs since most motorists use the Interstate.

The French, British and Americans constructed forts and bridges on Lake Champlain's shore. The forts are now historic sites and the bridges are of more modern construction. Ferries ply the Lake to connect New York and Vermont.

Vermont is noted for being a prime bicycling destination. New York has reconstructed most of its major and County roadways to inculde a well defined shoulder. Making New York prime cyclotouring country.

Hikers can easily find their way into the Adirondacks and on to Vermont's Lake Champlain Islands.

S to N mi. (km.) Read↓	Westport to Plattsburgh	N to S mi. (km.) Read↑
00.0 (00.0) NY 22 Jct. with NY 9N Travel North on NY 22.		48.0 (77.2)

Westport: See previous chapter for information, services, acommodations and attractions.

.5 (.8) Lakeshore Rd. @ NY 22 Turn Northeast on to Lakeshore Rd.		47.5 (76.4)
11.7 (18.8) NY 22 Jct. with Lakeshore Rd. Travel North on NY 22.		36.3 (58.4)

Essex

Info.: Area code: 518. Zip code: 12936.
Services: Essex, NY-Charlotte, VT Ferry, Lake Champlain Trans., Co., King St. Dock, Burlington VT 05401, 802 864-9804 (passenger fare + $1.00 for bike.)
Lodging: cabins. B&Bs: Essex House, Lakeshore Rd., 963-7739; Essex Inn, 16 Main St., 963-8821

16.5 (26.6) Mountainview Rd. @ NY 22 Continue traveling on NY 22		31.5 (50.7)

Willsboro

Info.: Area code: 518. Zip code: 12996.
Services: Grocery & restaurants. Amtrak stop.
Lodging: Motels and cabins. B&Bs: Champlain Vistas, Lakeshore Rd., 963-8029; 1852 Inn, 277 Lake Shore Rd., 963-4075. Camping: Gusberti's, NY 22, 963-4522.

21.1 (33.9)   Highlands Rd. @ NY 22   26.9 (43.3)
Turn on to Highland Rd. Highland road is a solid surface dirt road for the first 1.5 mi (2.4 km).
If you do not want to ride on Highland Rd. continue riding on NY 22. In 4.0 mi. (6.4 km.) it junctions with NY 9. Travel North for an additional 4.2 mi. (6.7 km.) to Keeseville where the Main Route travelers will meet you! The distance is about the same either way you go.

28.6 (46.0)   Port Douglas Rd. @ Highlands Rd.   19.4 (31.2)
Turn West on to Port Douglas Rd.

30.0 (48.2)   Mace Chasm Rd.   18.0 (29.0)
              @ Port Douglas Rd.
Tourists & hungry travelers continue riding West on Port Douglas Rd. Keeseville is 1.9 mi. (3.0 km.) West of this point. Instead of returning to Mace Chasm Rd., travel through Keeseville to NY 9 and take NY 9 North to NY 373 in Ausable Chasm where the Highland Rd. travelers will meet you.
Through travelers turn North on to Mace Chasm Rd. At Soper Rd., 1.4 mi. (2.3 km.) turn East and travel for .7 mi. (1.2 km.) to NY 373. Turn West on to NY 373 and travel 1 mi. (1.6 km.) to NY 9 in Ausable Chasm where you will meet the hunger satisfied travelers who stopped in Keeseville.

31.9 (51.3)   NY 9 @ Port Douglas Rd.   16.1 (25.9)
Turn North on to NY 9.

Keeseville

Info.: Area code: 518. Zip code: 12944.
Services: Grocery, convenience stores, restaurants.
Lodging: Motels. B&Bs: Ausable Meadows Farm, 834-7660. Camping: Pok-O-Moonshine St. Campsite, 834-9045; Yogi Bear's Jellystone Pk., NY 373, 834-9011. Ausable River Campsite, 367 NY 9, 834-9379.

33.8 (54.4)   NY 373 @ NY 9   14.2 (22.8)

Ausable Chasm & Ausable Forks

Info.: Area code: 518. Zip code: 12912.
Services: Convenince store.
Lodging: Camping: Taylor Pond Cpgd., 647-5250; Douglas Beach Cpgd., 7 Douglas Lane, 647-8061; McIntyre's Cpgd, 611 Union Falls Rd., 647-8083; Ausable Chasm KOA, Jct. Rts. 9 & 373, 834-9990; Ausable Point St. Forest Cpgd., NY 9, 561-7080.
Attractions: Ausable Chasm.

Turning East on to NY 373 will bring you to

Port Kent

Services: Port Kent, NY-Burlington, VT Ferry, Lake Champlain Trans., King St. Dock, Burlington VT, 05401, 802 864-9804 (bikes $1.00.) Amtrak stop.
Lodging: Bolton Acres Cpgd., Port Kent Rd., Keeseville, NY, 518 834-6000; Holiday Trailer Pk., Port Kent Rd., Keeseville, NY, 518 834-9261; Port Kent Cpgd., 2nd & Lumber St., Port Kent, NY 12975, 518 834-9011.

34.3 (55.2)   Border   13.7 (22.0)
Essex and Clinton County border.

35.3 (56.8)   Border   12.7 (20.4)
You have crossed the *Blue Line*! No, not a land of no return but a land of infinite beauty - Adirondack State Park. The *Blue Line* signifies borders of the Park.

Town of Peru

Info.: Centered near NY 442 at NY 9.
Area code: 518. Zip code: 12972.
Lodging: Camping: Ausable Pines, Lake Shore Rd., NY 9 South, 561-1188; Ausable Point St. Cpgd., NY 9 South, 561-7080; Snug Harbor Cpgd., NY 9 South, 563-5140; Birchwood Cpgd., 5 mi. (8 km.) inland, 47 Cayea Rd., 643-8894.

48.0 (77.2)   Cornelia St./NY 3   0.0 (0.0)
              @ NY 9/Margaret St.

Plattsburgh

Info.: Plattsburgh/Clinton County CofC, 7061 NY 9, Plattsburgh NY 12901, 518 563-1000, www. northcountrychamber.com. AC: 518. Zip: 12901.

Cycling & Hiking Info.: Bike & camping shops: Wooden Ski & Wheel, 561-2790; Maui North, 563-7245; Viking Ski, 561-5539.

Services: All. Hospital. Plattsburgh, NY-Grand Isle, VT ferry, 802, 864-9804. Amtrak stop.

Lodging: Motels. B&Bs: Marshall House B&B, 115 Court St., 563-5299; Roswell House, 28 Macomb St., 561-2568; Captain's Cove B&B, 563-7184; C&L's Greystone Manor B&B, 561-7111; Point Au Roche Lodge, 463 Point Au Roche Rd., 563-8714. Camping: Carpenter's Travel Park, Point Au Roche Rd., 563-4365; Cumberland St. Pk., 3 mi. (4.8 km.) North on NY 9 to NY 314; Oak Knoll, Moffitt Rd., 562-0561; Plattsburgh RV Park, NY 9N, 563-3915; Snug Harbor Cpgd., NY 9 South, 563-5140.

Attractions: Kent-Delord House Mus. (18th century home & furnishings), 561-1035. Clinton County Hist. Mus., 48 Court St., 561-0340. Plattsburgh is a gateway to the northern Adirondacks. College.

S to N	**Plattsburgh**	N to S
mi. (km.) Read↓	**to Westport**	mi. (km.) Read↑

Adirondack Lake

Plattsburgh to Saint Jean Sur Richelieu

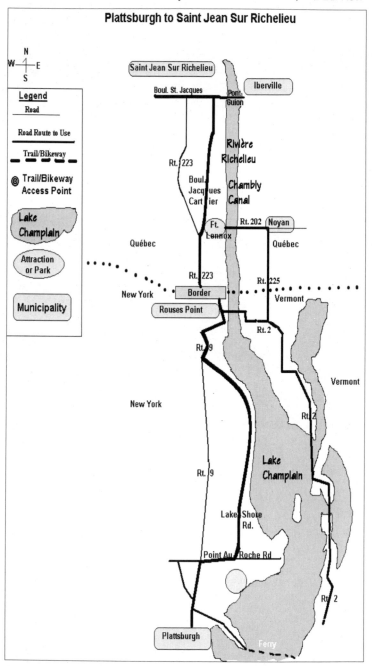

CHAMBLY CANAL

Fearful of an American invasion of Canada during the Revolutionary War, the British constructed a series of forts and blockhouses in the Richelieu River Valley. After the War of 1812, commerce rather than potential warfare became the dominant raison d'etre for the importance of the Valley. The Chambly Canal was completed in 1843 to facilitate commerce between the United States and Canada. Using the Richelieu River as its course, the Chambly Canal physically links the St. Lawrence River with Lake Champlain. Thus a seamless river of commerce flows from the lower Hudson Valley and western New York to Montréal and Toronto via the Saint Lawrence River as well as northeast to the Atlantic.

These days it is rare to see commercial traffic on the Chambly Canal. Like the Erie Canal, the Canal de Chambly is used primarily for recreational craft. A bicycle/pedestrian path along the Canal bank links Saint-Jean-Sur-Richelieu with Chambly.

The Valley is a rich agricultural area thanks to glaciers and layers of sediment. A number of vineyards and orchards produce delicious wines and ciders (apple and pear).

For travelers who want to simply circle Lake Champlain, Saint-Paul-de-l'Île-aux-Noix provides a convenient turn around point.

S to N mi. (km.) Read↓	Plattsburgh, NY to Saint Jean-Sur Richelieu, QC	N to S mi. (km.) Read↑
00.0 (00.0)	Cornelia St. @ US 9	50.9 (81.9)

Turn East (towards the Lake) on to Cornelia St.

Plattsburgh: See the North Country chapter for info.

.1 (.1)	City Hall Pl./Cumberland St. @ Cornelia St.	50.8 (81.7)

Turn North on to Cumberland St.

1.1 (1.1)	Cumberland St. @ US 9/BR 9	49.8 (80.1)

Turn North on to NY 9/N. Margaret St./BR 9

2.5 (4.0)	NY 314 @ US 9/BR 9	48.4 (77.9)

Through travelers continue North on NY 9/BR 9.

Travelers wishing to go to Vermont, turn East on to NY 314; Plattsburgh, NY-Grand Isle, VT Ferry, 802 864-9804; The ferry is at the end of NY 314, 3.7 mi. (5.9 km.). Cumberland St. Pk.

6.0 (9.7)   Point Au Roche Rd. @ NY 9   44.9 (72.2)
Turn East on to Point Au Roche Rd. St. Armand Beach
Co. Pk.

7.7 (12.4)   Lake Shore Rd.   43.2 (69.5)
               @ Point Au Roche Rd.
Turn North on to Lake Shore Rd.
Point Au Roche St. Pk. entrance.

21.0 (33.8)   NY 9B @ Lake Shore Rd.   29.9 (48.1)
Turn North on to NY 9B.

Chazy

Info.: The Village is slightly inland.
Area code: 518. Zip code: 12921.
Lodging: B&Bs: Country, 9677 NY 9, 846-8844; Grand
Vue, 2237 Lake Shore Rd., 298-5700/518 846-7857;
Morningside B&B, 1305 Fisk Rd., 846-8804.

26.2 (42.2)   Platt St./NY 276 @ NY 9B   24.7 (39.7)
Continue North on NY 9B.

Rouses Point

Services & Facilities: Grocery, convenience store, and
restaurants.
Lodging: Motels. Camping: Kings Bay Campsite, NY
9B, Rouses Point NY 518 297-3432.

26.7 (42.9)   US 2 @ NY 9B   24.2 (38.9)
Through travelers continue North on NY 9B.
Travelers to Vermont, turn on to NY 2.

26.9 (42.3)   Border @ NY 9B/QC 223   24.0 (38.6)
US Customs & Immigration.
Canadian Customs & Immigration.
    The general rule is to be polite. Unlike the British
Columbia/Washington State border, a loaded touring
bicyclist or hiker is still a rare sight to Customs and
Immigration officers in the East. You must have proof of
citizenship. A passport is not necessary for citizens of
Canada or the United States. A voter's registration card
plus a picture driver's license is the bare minimum. A
certified copy, not the original, of your birth certificate is
excellent. Simply have a Notary copy and then certify its
authenticity. Almost any bank in the United States or
Canada has a Notary on staff.
    You should have a list of the contents of your panniers
or pack. Simply use the *Equipment Lists* in this book,

check the items contained in your panniers/pack, place your name and address on top of the *Lists*, and copy the *Lists*. In general, Customs and Immigration officers can differentiate between serious cyclotourists/hikers and individuals doing something illegal. I doubt if they will even ask you to open your panniers/pack. They may question you a bit more than other cyclists/pedestrians. But this is probably out of curiosity - to find out about your adventure.

Money: The first thing I do when I cross an international border is find an ATM and get local currency. Banks usually give the best rate of exchange. The second thing I do is forget about making the mental calculations involved in currency exchange. Simply think of the new currency as your regular currency. This is particularly easy between Canada and the United States since both nations use decimal currency with the same name, dollars. US citizens will have to adjust to the $1.00 coin, the *Loony*! Other than that, just think dollars and cents.

Region Montérégie, QC and Clinton County, NY border.

32.5 (52.3)	Rt. 202 @ Rt. 223	18.4 (29.6)

Continue traveling on Rt. 223.

Saint-Paul-de-l'Île-aux-Noix

Info.: Blockhaus de Lacolle, 1, rue Principale, Saint-Paul-de-l'Île-aux-Noix QC J0J 1G0, 450 246-3227.

Bike Information: Bike shop.

Services: Convenience store, and restaurants.

Lodging: Hotel. Cpgds. on the East bank of the Rivière Richelieu. Turn East on to Rt. 202, cross the Rivère and turn South on to Ch. du Bord de l'Eau S.

Attractions: Lieu historique national du Fort-Lennox, 1, 61e Av., Saint-Paul-de- l'Île-aux-Noix QC J0J 1G0, 450 291-5700; Blockhaus de Lacolle. Beaches, swimming.

37.9 (61.0)	Ft. Lennox Entrance @ Rt. 223	13.0 (20.9)

48.4 (77.9)	Boul. Jacques Cartier @ Rt. 223	2.5 (4.0)

Turn East on to Jacques Cartier Blvd. Ride in the reserved bike lane.

50.9 (81.9)   St. Jacques Blvd.   0.0 (0.0)
              @ Jacques Cartier Blvd.

Saint Jean sur Richelieu & Iberville

Info.: Office du tourisme et des congrés du Haut-Richelieu, 31, rue Frontenac, Saint-Jean-sur-Richelieu QC, J3B 7X2, 888 736-0395/450 536-0395. Iberville is directly across the Canal. Area code: 450.

Bike Information: Bike shop

Services: Grocery, convenience stores; restaurants; retail and hardware stores.

Lodging: Motels and hotels. B&B: Auberge Les Trois Rives, 297, rue Richeliu, Saint Jean sur Richelieu QC J3B 6Y3, 358-8077

Attractions: Hot air balloon festival (early August), 346-6000; Théâtre des Deux Rives, 30, av. du Séminaire Nord, Saint-Jean-sur-Richelieu, J3B 7K2, 358-3849. Théâtre de l'Écluse, 190, rue Laurier, CP 223, Saint-Jean-sur-Richelieu, J3B 7K2, 348-5312. Musée régional du Haut-Richelieu (Musée québécois de la céramique) 182, rue Jacques-Cartier Nord, Saint-Jean-sur-Richelieu, J3B 7W3, 347-0649. Musée du fort Saint-Jean, Campus du Fort de Saint Jean, rue Jacques-Cartier Sud, Saint-Jean-sur-Richelieu, J0J 1R0, 346-4945.

S to N	**Saint-Jean-Sur-Richelieu, QC**	N to S
mi. (km.) Read↓	**to Plattsburgh, NY**	mi. (km.) Read↑

Montréal to Saint-Jean-Sur-Richelieu

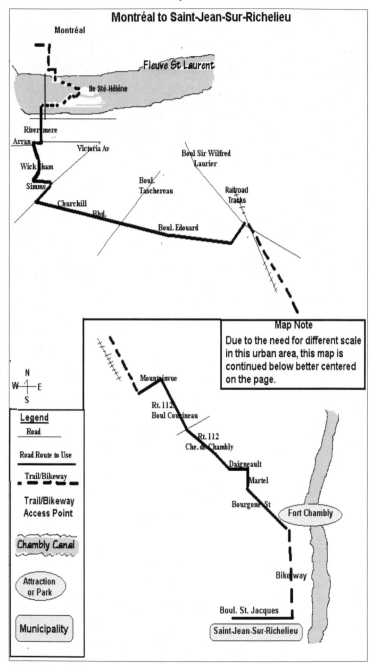

Montréal

Fleuve St Laurent

Ile Sté-Hélène

Rivermere

Arran

Wickham

Victoria Av

Simms

Churchill Blvd.

Boul Sir Wilfred Laurier

Boul. Taschereau

Railroad Tracks

Boul. Edouard

Map Note

Due to the need for different scale in this urban area, this map is continued below better centered on the page.

N
W — E
S

Legend

Road

Road Route to Use

Trail/Bikeway

Trail/Bikeway Access Point

Chambly Canal

Attraction or Park

Municipality

Mountainvue

Rt. 112 Boul Cousineau

Rt. 112 Che. de Chambly

Daigneault

Martel

Bourgone St

Fort Chambly

Bikeway

Boul. St. Jacques

Saint-Jean-Sur-Richelieu

THE ST. LAWRENCE RIVER

As you cross the River into Montréal beneath you is water which theoretically orginated at the continental divide. Great Lakes water which cascaded over Niagara Falls passes through the St. Lawrence River to the Atlantic Ocean.

Montréal with its cosmopolitan atmosphere is one of the great cities of North America. For United States residents who are not used to hearing a language other than English, Montréal becomes a true *foreign* experience. Enjoy it!

More than two thirds of this section's ride is along bikeways. This helps to alievate the rigors of riding through suburbs.

S to N mi. (km.) Read↓	Saint-Jean sur Richelieu to Montréal	N to S mi, (km.) Read↑
00.0 (00.0)	Boul. St. Jacques @ Bikeway	35.1 (56.5)

Saint-Jean-sur Richelieu: Information, etc. is on last page of previous chapter.

12.2 (19.6)	Ft. Chambly @ Bikeway	22.1 (35.6)

Chambly

Info.: 1900, rue Bourgogne, Chambly, QC J3L 2B9, 514 658-1585. Area code: 450. Postal code: various.

Cycling & Hiking Info.: Bike shop.

Services & Facilities: Grocery, convenience store, hardware and retail stores, restaurants.

Accommodations: Motels. B&B: Le Riche Lieu, 4, rue Saint-Jacques, Chambly J3L 3L1.

Attractions: Lieu historique national du Fort-Chambly, 2, rue Richelieu J3L 2B9, 658-1585. Tour Cycliste International (annual organized tour, Chambly to Plattsburgh via Vermont Islands & return); Chambly Canal Nat'l Hist. Site, 800 463-6769/450 447-4888, www. pc.ca/canalchambly

12.2 (19.6)	Bourgone St. @ Ft Chambly	22.1 (35.6)

Turn Northwest on to Bourgone St.

13.2 (21.2)	Martel @ Bourgone St.	21.1 (33.9)

Turn North on to Martel.

14.7 (27.6)	Daigneault @ Martel	19.6 (31.5)

Turn West on to Daigneault.

15.4 (24.8)   Rt. 112/Chemin de Chambly   18.9 (30.4)
               @ Daigneault
Continue straight West on Rt. 112/Ch. de Chambly

16.4 (26.4)   Bellvue @ Rt. 112   17.9 (28.8)
               Rt. 112 changes its name to Boul. Cousineau

18.7 (30.1)   Mountainvue @ Rt. 112   15.6 (25.1)
               Turn South on to Mountainvue.

20.6 (33.1)   Bike path || parallel to Railroad   13.7 (22.0)
               @ Mountainvue
Turn West on to gravel bikepath.
Saint-Hubert: Motels. B&B: Gîte touristique Beu Mont,
5225, rue Raoul, Saint-Hubert J3Y 7P7, 656-2612.

21.6 (34.8)   Boul. Sir Wilfred Laurier @ Bikeway   12.7 (20.4)
End of Bikeway. Turn South on to Boul. Edouard.

Saint-Lambert & Rive Sud du Montréal

Info.: Touisme de la Rive-Sud, 205 ch. Chambly,
Longueuil, QC J4H 3L3, 514 674-2977. You are in the
southern suburbs of Montréal.
Services: All. **Bike Info.**: Bike shops.
Lodging: Motels. B&Bs in Longueuil.
Attractions: Musée Marsil (customs, fibers & textiles),
349, rue Riverside, Saint-Lambert J4P 1A8, 465-3357.

22.4 (36.0)   William St. @ Boul. Edourd   11.9 (19.1)
               Turn Northwest on to William St.

23.2 (37.3)   Montcalm St. @ William St.   11.1 (17.9)
               Turn Southwest on to Montcalm.

23.7 (37.8)   Boul. Taschreau @ Montcalm St.   10.6 (17.1)
               Turn Northwest on to Boul. Taschreau.

24.4 (39.2)   King Edward St. @ Boul. Taschreau   9.9 (15.9)
               Turn Southwest on to King Edward St.

24.6 (36.5)   Simms St. @ King Edward St.   9.7 (15.6)
               Cross Victoria St. to Simms St.

25.9 (41.7)   Wickham St. @ Simms St.   <8.4 (13.5)
               Turn Northwest on to Wickham St.

<26.0 (<41.5) Arran St. @ Wickham St.   8.3 (13.4)
               Turn South on to Arran St.

26.6 (42.3)   Rivermere @ Arran St.   7.7 (12.4)
Turn Northwest on to Rivermere St.

27.5 (44.2)   Ch. Riverside St. @ Rivermere St.   7.6 (12.2)
Cross Riverside St. to Bikeway

27.9 (44.9)   Canal de la Rive Sur @ Bikeway   7.2 (11.6)
Use the Bridge to cross over the Canal.

28.3 (45.5)   Under Pont Victoria @ Bikeway   6.8 (10.9)
Continue traveling Northeast on the Bikeway. Turn on to
Ile Notre Dame.

29.1 (47.3)   Ile Sainte Hélène/Pont de la Concorde   6.0 (9.7)
@ Bikeway
Continue traveling on Bikeway over Fleuve St.-Laurent.

33.6 (54.0)   Rue Riverside   1.5 (2.4)
@ Av. Pierre Dupuy on Bikeway
Turn North towards Montréal on to Rue Riverside

35.1 (46.5)   Square Gallery @ Bikeway   0.0 (0.0)

Montréal

Info.: Greater Montréal CVB, Infotouriste Centre 1001 Square-
Dorchester Street (corner Peel and Ste-Catherine Streets),
Metro Station: Peel. 514 873-2015. Entire travel guides are
written on Montréal. Area code: 514. Postal code: various.

Bike Info.: Bike shops and camping equipment stores galore. Le
Tour de L'Île de Montréal, a huge major bike event.

Services: All. Hospitals. VIA Rail. Airport. Local transit.: Société
de transport de la Communauté urbaine de Montréal, 101
Sainte-Catherine St. West (at Peel), Montréal, QC, 514 873-
2015. Bikes are permitted on Métro trains.

Lodging: Hostel: Auberge de de Jeunesse de Montréal, 1030
Mackay St., Montréal H3G 2H1, 843-3317. Camping:
Camping Alouette, 3449 De L'Industrie, St-Mathieu de
Beloeil, J3G 4S5, 464-1661.

Attractions: Everything! Entire books are written on Montréal's
attractions! 24+ museums, 845-6873. Arts: 2 major
orchestras; opéra; theatre; dance companies; Sports: Expos
baseball, Grand Prix auto racing; MLS Impact soccer.

S to N	Montréal to	N to S
mi. (km.) Read↓	**Saint-Jean sur Richelieu**	mi. (km.) Read↑

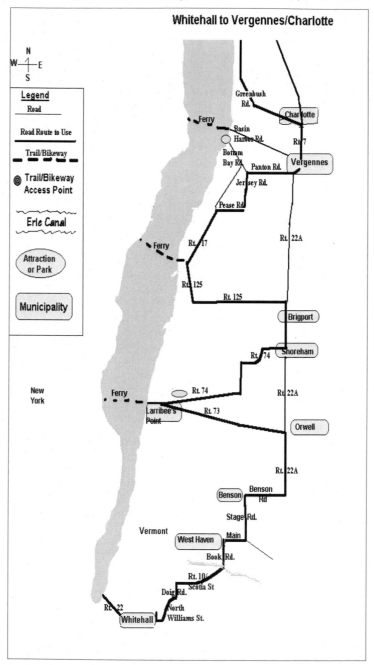

Whitehall to Vergennes/Charlotte

Legend

Road

Road Route to Use

Trail/Bikeway

Trail/Bikeway Access Point

Erie Canal

Attraction or Park

Municipality

New York

Vermont

Whitehall

Rt. 22

Doig Rd.

North Williams St.

Rt. 104

Scotia St.

Book Rd.

West Haven

Main

Stage Rd.

Benson

Benson Rd.

Rt. 22A

Orwell

Rt. 73

Larribee's Point

Ferry

Rt. 74

Rt. 22A

Shoreham

Rt. 74

Brigport

Rt. 125

Rt. 125

Rt. 17

Ferry

Pease Rd.

Jersey Rd.

Panton Rd.

Rt. 22A

Vergennes

Bottom Bay Rd.

Basin Harbor Rd.

Ferry

Greenbush Rd.

Charlotte

Rt. 7

VERMONT

Lake Champlain's eastern shore is primarily in Vermont. Crossing the Lake is relatively easy. Ferries and one mid Lake bridge connect New York and Vermont.
This section is included to allow you to circumnavigate Lake Champlain. Each year Tourism Boards and a host of commercial enterprises in Vermont New York, and Québec sponsor Tour Cycliste International. The Tour's route generally begins at Chambly, QC and turns North at Grand Isle, VT/Plattsburgh, NY.

Round Lake Champlain
Vermont - East Side Route

S to N mi. (km.) Read↓	**Whitehall to** **Saint-Paul de l'Île-aux-Noix**	N to S mi. (km.) Read↑

Vermont

Info.: Lake Champlain Reg. CofC, 60 Main St., Burlington VT 05401, 877 686-5253/802 863-3489, www.vermont.org; Vermont Tourism, www.vermontvacation.com; Vermont Dep't. of Parks, 103 S. Main St., Waterbury, VT 05671-0603, 802 241-3655.

Cycling & Hiking Info.: Cycling: Lake Champlain Bikeways, 60 Main St., Burlington VT 05401. Hiking: The Green Mountain Club, RR1, Box 650, Rt. 100, Waterbury Center, VT 05677.

Services: Most small villages on the route will have a restaurant and a convenience store.

Lodging: Only B&Bs and campgrounds which have noted that they are *bicycle friendly* are listed for Vermont. Only State Parks which permit camping are listed.

0.0 (0.0)   Champlain Canal Lock 12   156.3 (251.5)
              @ Main St.
Travel South along the Canal.
Whitehall, NY: See main route for information.

.1 (.1)   Hall St.   156.25 (251.4)
Turn East and cross the Bridge.

.15 (.2)   North Williams St. @ Bridge   156.2 (251.3)
Turn North on to N. Willams St.

.7 (1.2)   Doig St./Rt. 10 @ N. Williams St.   155.6 (250.4)
Turn North on to Doig St./County Rt. 10.
Doig St./County Rt. 10 is also Scotia St.

1.3 (2.1)   E. Bay Rd. @ Scotia St./Rt. 10   155.0 (249.4)
A *T* intersection. Turn East, continue travelling on Scotia
St./County Rt. 10.

4.1 (6.6)   Pecks Rd. Jct. Scotia St./Rt. 10   152.2 (244.9)
Bear Northwest, continue travelling on Scotia St./County
Rt. 10.

6.9 (11.1)   Book Rd. @ Scotia St./Rt. 10   149.4 (240.4)
Continue travelling North on to Book Rd.

9.5 (15.3)   Main St./Stage Rd. @ Book Rd.   146.8 (236.2)
Turn East on to Stage Rd.

11.0 (17.7)   Main Rd. @ Stage Rd.   145.3 (233.8)
Turn North on Stage Rd. at Y intersection.

13.9 (22.4)   Benson Rd. @ Stage Rd.   142.4 (229.2)
Turn East on to Benson Rd.
Benson: Benson's historic architecture is the result of its
prosperity due to wool trading and shipping via the Lake
Champlain Canal during the 19th century.

14.5 (23.3)   Rt. 22A @ Benson Rd.   141.8 (228.2
Turn North on to Rt. 22A.

22.3 (35.9)   Rt. 73 @ Rt. 22A   134.0 (215.7)
Turn West on to Rt. 73.

Orwell

Info.: Area code: 802. Zip code: 05760.
Lodging: B&Bs: Brookside Farms Country Inn, Rt. 22A,
948-2727; Lake Ledge Far B&B, RR1, Box 70,948-2347;
Buckswood B&B, Rt. 73E, 948-2054.
Attraction: Mt. Independence St. Hist. Site.

28.4 (45.7)   Rt. 74 @ Rt. 73   127.9 (205.8)
Turn East on to Rt. 74.
Ticonderoga Ferry (Pt. Kent Ferry) is at Larribee's Point;
Carillon Cruises, 802 897-5221;

33.2 (53.4)   Rt. 22A @ Rt. 74   123.7 (198.1)
Turn North on to Rt. 22A.
Shoreham: Info.: Area code: 802. Zip code: 05770.
Lodging: B&Bs: Cream Hill Far, PO Box 205, 897-2101;
Indian Trail Farm, Smith St., 897-5292;

40.3 (64.9)   Rt. 125 @ Rt. 22A   116.0 (186.7)
Turn West on to Rt. 125.

47.5 (76.4)   Rt. 17 @ Rt. 125   108.8 (175.1)
Turn North on to Rt. 17.

Addison

Info.: Addison County CofC, 9 Court St., Middlebury, VT
05753, 802 388-7951/800 733-8376.   Area code: 802.
Zip code: Addison VT 05491.
Cycling & Hiking Info.: Bike shop.
Lodging: Camping: Ten Acres Cpgd., Rt. 125, 759-2662;
Sportsman Campgrd., RFD 1, Box 3585, 759-2348.
Attractions: Chimney Point St. Historic Site, Rt. 17, 759-2412.

49.5 (79.7)   Lake St. @ Rt. 17   106.8 (171.9)
Continue travelling straight on to Lake St.   This
intersection is just past the DAR mansion. Rt. 17 makes
a westward turn eventually crossing Rt. 22A. Continue
travelling north along the Lake shore.

55.5 (89.3)   Pease Rd. @ Lake St.   100.8 (162.2)
Turn West on to Pease Rd. Sometimes there is a street
sign, sometimes not.

56.0 (90.1)   Jersey St. @ Pease Rd.   100.3 (161.4)
Turn North on to Jersey St.

56.5 (90.9)   Panton Rd. @ Jersey St.   99.8 (160.6)
Turn East on to Panton Rd. Panton Hamlet.

Button Bay & Basin Harbor

Directions: Continue North on Jersey St.   Turn
Northwest, .25 mi, .3 km, North of Panton on to Button
Bay Rd.
Lodging: Camping: Button Bay St. Pk.
Attractions: Lake Champlain Maritime Mus., RR 3, Box
4092, Vergennes (Basin Harbor) VT 05491, 475-2022.
Button Bay St. Pk.

Vergennes to Colchester

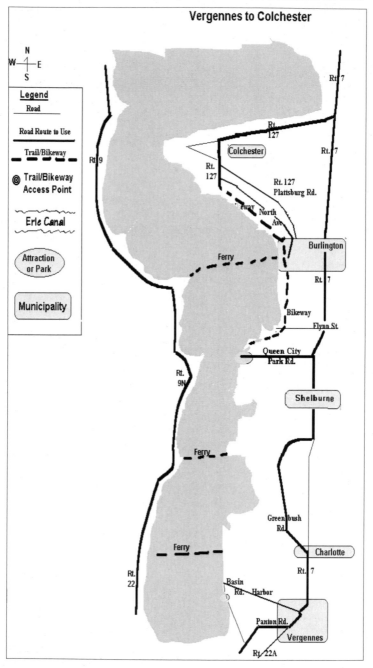

Legend

Road

Road Route to Use

Trail/Bikeway

◉ Trail/Bikeway Access Point

Erie Canal

Attraction or Park

Municipality

N
W — E
S

Rt. 7

Rt. 127

Colchester

Rt. 7

Rt. 127 Plattsburg Rd.

Rt. 127

Bikeway   North Ave

Rt. 9

Ferry

Burlington

Rt. 7

Bikeway

Flynn St.

Queen City Park Rd.

Rt. 9N

Shelburne

Ferry

Greenbush Rd.

Ferry

Charlotte

Rt. 7

Rt. 22

Basin Rd.   Harbor

Panton Rd.

Vergennes

Rt. 22A

61.0 (98.2)   Rt. 22A @ Panton Rd./Water St.   95.3 (153.4)
Turn East on to Rt. 22A.

Vergennes

Info.: Vergennes CofC, PO Box 7, Vergennes VT 05491, 802 877-3111. Area code: 802. Zip code: 05491.
Biking Info.: Bike shop.
Services: Grocery, & other retail stores.
Lodging: Motels. B&Bs: Emersons, Main St., 877-3293; Woodman Hill House B&B, RR2, Box 2507, 877-2720; Whitford House Inn, RR1, Box 490, 758-2704. Camping & Cottages: Hillcrest Cpgd., RR 3, Box 4265 Basin Harbor Rd., 475-2343; Sportsman Cpgd., RFD 3, Box 3585, 759-2348. Button Bay St. Pk., 475-2377; DAR St. Pk., 759-2354.
Attractions: Underwater St. Hist. Preserve.

64.6 (104.0) Rt. 7 @ Rt. 22A   91.7 (147.6)
Turn North on to Rt. 7.

67.5 (108.6) Greenbush Rd. @ Rt. 7   88.8 (142.9)
If you haven't noticed, Rt. 7 is a very busy road. Not fun to walk on or bike on. But it's the only way to get over the River! Away with all those cars and RVs! Just past the Rokeby Museum on the West side of Rt. 7 is Greenbush Rd. Turn West/North on to Greenburgh Rd. Rokeby Museum, Rt. 7, Ferrisburgh, VT 05456, 802 877-3401.

72.7 (117.0) Ferry Rd. @ Greenbush Rd.   83.6 (134.5)
Continue travelling North on Greenbush Rd.
Ferry to Essex, NY.
Charlotte: **Lodging:** Old Lantern Campgrd., Greenbush Rd., 802 425-2121; B&B at Horsford Gardens, N. Greenbush Rd., Charlotte, VT 05445, 802 425-2811.

76.3 (122.8) Greenbush Rd. @ Rt. 7   80.0 (128.7)
Turn North on to Rt. 7. You're about half way up the Lake!
Mt. Philo St. Pk. (hiking trails), Ferrisburgh, VT 05456, 802 425-2390 (not directly on the route, close to Rt. 7).
Many motels and hotels from here to Burlington.

82.3 (132.4) Queen City Park Rd. @ Rt. 7   74.0 (119.1)
Turn West on to Queen City Park Rd.

Shelburne

Info.: Area code: 802. Zip code: 05482.
Lodging: Motels. Shelburne Cpgd. Rt. 7, 985-2540.
Attractions: Shelburne Mus., Rt. 7, PO Box 10, 985-3346; Shelburne Farms, Rt. 7, 985-8442.

83.8 (134.8) Bikeway @ Queen City Park Rd.   72.5 (116.7)
Enter Bikeway and travel North on it!

84.3 (135.7) Ferris St. @ Bikeway   72.0 (115.9)
Continue travelling North on Bikeway.

88.2 (141.9) Burlington Ferry @ Bikeway   68.1 (109.6)
Continue on Bikeway; actually it goes parallel to North St. Take the ferry if you like but you'll be missing the beautiful Hero Islands.

Burlington

Info.: Lake Champlain Regional CofC, 60 Main St., Ste. 100, Burlington, VT 05401.
Area code: 802. Zip code: 05401.
Cycling & Hiking Info.: Bike shops.
Services: All. Hospital. Ferry: Lake Champlain Ferries, 864-9804; Amtrak stop. Trailways and Greyhound.
Lodging: Motels; B&Bs: Burlington, Converse Ct., 862-3646; Tetreault House, Staniford Rd., 862-2781.
Attractions: Ethan Allen Homestead, Rt. 127, 865-4556; Lake Champlain Basin Science Ctr., Burlington Waterfront/Rts. 7 & I 89, 864-1848. Lake Champlain Aquarium, 1 King St., 862-7777. University of Vermont.

94.8 (152.6) Rt. 127/Plattsburgh Rd./Winooski Rd.   61.5 (99.0)
@ Bikeway
Cross River and go North East on Rt. 127.
Colchester: **Info.:** Area Code: 802. Zip code: 05446.
Lodging: Camp Kiniya, 77 Camp Kiniya Rd., 893-7849; Lone Pine Campsites, Malletts Bay, 878-5447; Malletts Bay Cpgd., 863-6980.

97.8 (157.4) Rt. 127 @ Rt. 7   58.5 (94.1)
Turn North on to Rt. 7.

108.8 (175.1) Rt. 7 Jct. With Rt. 2   47.5 (76.4)
Continue travelling North on Rt. 2.

114.7 (184.6)   Sand Bay St. Pk. @ Rt. 2   41.6 (67.0)
Continue travelling on Rt. 2. Yes, Rt. 2 does have a lot
of tourists! It needs a 2 meter wide shoulder!

South Hero Island & Grand Isle

Info.: Area code: 802. Area codes; S. Hero Is., 05486;
Grand Isle, 05458.
Lodging: B&Bs: Paradise Bay, LightHouse Rd., South
Hero, 372-5393; Farmhouse on the Lake, West Shore
Rd., Grand Isle, 372-8849; Camping: Appletree Bay
Cpgd., Sand Bar Bridge, South Hero, 372-4398; Camp
Skyland on Lake Champlain, Allen Point, South Hero,
372-4200; Grand Isle St. Park, Grand Isle, 372-4300;
Champlain Adult Cpgd., Rt. 314, Grand Isle, 372-5938.

120.8 (194.4)   Rt. 314 @ Rt. 2   35.9 (57.8)
S to N: A short side loop to take you away from the cars,
RVs and trucks! You could continue on Rt. 2, ha, ha!
Turn West on to Rt. 314.

126.6 (203.7)   Rt. 2 @ Rt. 314   29.7 (47.6)
N to S: A side loop to relax your muscles. Turn North on
to Rt. 2.

132.0 (212.4)   North Hero Island @ Rt. 2   24.3 (39.1)
Continue North on Rt. 2.

North Hero Island

Info.: Area code: 802. Zip code: 05474.
Lodging: B&Bs: Charlies Nothland Lodge, Rt. 2, 372-
8822; Shore Acres Inn; Rt. 2, 372-8722; North Hero
House, Rt. 2, 372-8237. Camping: Knight Island St. Pk.,
524-6353; North Hero Island St. Pk., 372-8727; Carry
Bay Cpgd., Rt. 2, 372-8233.

140.5 (226.1)   Rt. 129 @ Rt. 2   15.8 (25.4)
Continue on Rt. 2 or use Rt. 129 to zip loop around Isle
La Motte!

Isle La Motte

Info.: Area code: 802. Zip code: 05463.
Lodging: B&Bs: Ruthcliffe Lodge, Old Quarry Rd., 928-
3200. Camping: Lakehurst Cpgd., RR2, Box 30, 928-
3266; Summerplace Cpgd., Box 30, 928-928-3300.

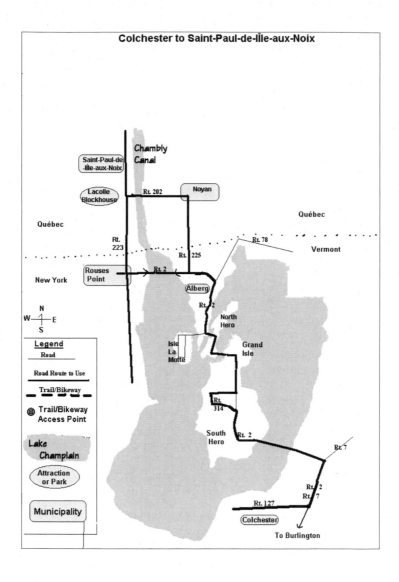

Colchester to Saint-Paul-de-Île-aux-Noix

145.9 (234.8)   Rt. 78 @ Rt. 2   10.4 (16.7)
Continue on Rt. 2. St. Albans is Southeast on Rt. 2.

Alberg

Info.: Area code: 802. Zip code: 05440.
Lodging: B&Bs: Thomas Mott Homestead, Blue Rock
Rd., 796-3736; Ransom Bay Inn B&B, Center Bay Rd.,
796-3399; Camping: Alburg RV Resort, Blue Rock Rd.,
Box 50, 796-3733; Goose Point Cpgd., Rt. 2, 796-3711.

149.0 (239.8)   VT Rt. 225 @ Rt. 2   7.3 (11.7)
Turn North on to Rt. 225. A sign will state: *To Nolan.*

150.7 (242.5)   Border on VT Rt. 225/QC Rt. 225   5.6 (9.1)
Continue North on QC Rt. 225. See main route for
border crossing information.

154.4 (248.5)   Rt. 202 @ Rt. 225   1.9 (3.1)
Turn West on to Rt. 202

156.3 (251.5)   Rt. 223 @ Rt. 202   0.0 (0.0)
You've done it! Circled Lake Champlain!
Lacolle Blockhouse.
See main route for information regarding
Saint-Paul-de-l'Île-aux-Noix.

Round Lake Champlain
Vermont - East Side Route
S to N   **Saint-Paul de l'Île-aux-Noix**   N to S
mi. (km.) Read↓   **to Whitehall**   mi. (km.) Read↑

Kingston to Albany   Albany to Rhinebeck

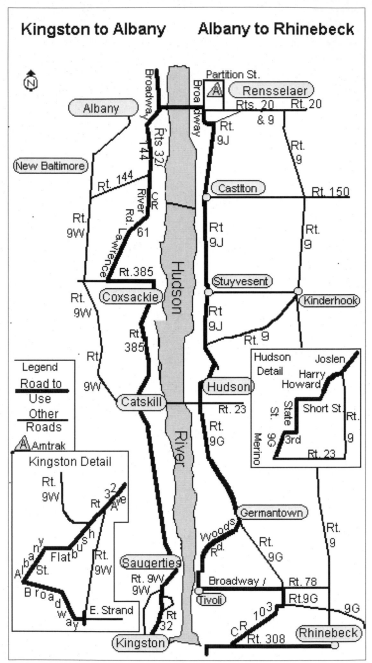

THE HUDSON RIVER VALLEY

This route along the Hudson River from Albany to New York City
completes the major Erie Canal Bicyclist routes.
Technically, New York City is the Southeastern most
terminus of the Erie Canal. The City is the Southeastern
most city on the Erie Canal.

New York City is the point where many goods from Western New
York State and the Great Lakes region were destined.
Likewise it was from New York City that many goods were
shipped to those regions.

When the orginal Erie Canal was opened Atlantic Ocean water
was poured into the Great Lakes by the Governor of New
York State.

This Hudson Valley Route provide visitors from other nations and
other parts of the US who begin to tour in New York City
with a reasonable route to begin on their traverse across the
Continent.   Basic routes from New York City's LaGuardia
and Kennedy Airports allow the bicyclist to go to the main
business and tourist area of Manhattan.

N to S	**Hudson River Valley**	S to N
mi. (km.) Read↓		mi. (km.) Read↑

Route Note
The routes both East and West of the Hudson River from Albany
to New York City are provided. The maps show both routes.

Lodging Note
There are literally thousands of B&Bs in the Hudson Valley.
Some are in the towns and cities along the River. It would
significantly increase the size of this book if all were listed.
Listed B&Bs are those which were easily located via
directories and the web. The web site www.enjoyhv.com and
other in the Hudson Valley categories can help locate
detailed information on communities, attractions and lodging.

Campgrounds are a bit harder to locate. Guerilla campers will find
many sites North of Westchester County on the East side and
North of Rockland County on the West side of the River.

Public Transit Note
As you travel along the eastern shore of the Hudson River you will
encounter many Amtrak and Metro-North railroad stations.
Bicycles are permitted, unboxed or boxed only on specific
Amtrak trains. No permit is needed to transport a bicycle on
an Amtrak trains. Amtrak shares its facilities with Metr-North

commuter trains from NYC to ~Poughkeepsie.

Bicycles are permitted, by permit only, on Metro North RR and Long Island RR commuter lines as well as NYC Subways. A *lifetime* Bike Permit is needed and is good for all three surface rail transit facilities during non-rush hours. Some NYC buses have bike racks.

You will have to contact the MTA (Metropolitan Transportation Authority) about a bicycle permit. Send your permit application form to the MTA as soon as possible, hopefully at least one month in advance of your departure. The Bike Permit is available via mail (most efficient way of obtaining a Bike Permit) or at Pennsylvania and Grand Central Stations (odd office hours). Thus you can not simply go to any station and obtain a Bike Permit before boarding a train. Of course as a non-NYC Metropolitan area resident you could plead ignorance and hope that the conductor will allow you to continue using the train. Metro NYC folks are really very provincial but kindly to folks from outside their area. It's best to say that you're from either a foreign city and nation (Toronto, Canada will do) or from a very distant US city and state (Cheyenne, Wyoming will probably get much sympathy if New York Cityites even recognize that Wyoming is in the USA.) When you request your Bike Permit make certain that you tell them a date you need the permit, ask them to send it via Priority Mail (doubtful that the MTA will do this) and most importantly, request a set of NYC Bicycle Maps for all five boroughs of the City, a Subway Map, a Long Island RR map, and a Metro-North Map. If the MTA is efficient then they will have these maps in a packet ready to send to permit holders.

N to S	**Hudson River Valley**	S to N
	East Side of the Hudson River	
mi. (km.) Read↓	**Albany to Rhinebeck**	mi. (km.) Read↑

0.0 (0.0)   State St. @ Broadway, Albany   59.4 (95.6)
Face the River, behind the SUNY building, on the River
is the Pedestrian Ramp to the Dunn Mem. Bridge. It's
actually located underneath the highway over passes.

0.2 (0.3)   Dunn Mem. Brdg. West Side   59.2 (95.3)
               @ MH Bikeway
Ride up the ramp and cross the Hudson River. Take a
picture! The motorists will envy you.

0.5 (0..8)   Broadway, Rensselear   58.9 (94.8)
               @ Dunn Mem. Brdg. Ramp
Turn South on to Broadway.

0.8 (1.2)   Rtes. 9 & 20/Columbia Tpk.   58.6 (94.3)
               @ Broadway
Cross Rtes. 9 & 20/Columbia Tpk. at the traffic light and
continue traveling on Broadway/Riverside Ave. Some
place along Broadway it changes its name to Riverside
Ave. There are a few motels along Rt. 9 but the hill is long
and steep. You're better off staying in Albany.

2.3 (3.7)   Riverside Ave./Broadway   57.1 (91.9)
               @ Stewart Port Expwy
Turn East on to Stewart Port Expwy. There will be a
guard & a gate in front of you & you'll have to turn East.

3.0 (4.8)   Stewart Port Expwy.   56.4 (90.8)
               @ Rt. 9J/River Rd.
Turn South on to Rt. 9J.

9.9 (15.9)   Rt. 150 @ Rt. 9J   49.5 (79.7)
Continue traveling South on Rt. 9J/River Rd.
Castleton on Hudson: Convenience store.

13.5 (21.7)   CR 2 @ Rt. 9J/River Rd.   45.9 (73.9
Continue traveling South. Hilly areas in the next 9 mi.
(14 km.). Schodack Landing

20.2 (32.5)   Rt. 26A @ Rt. 9J .   39.2 (63.1)
Continue traveling South on Rt. 9J/River Rd.
Stuyvesent
Turn East on to Rt. 26A to go to Kinderhook, 6 mi. (9.6
km.), Pres. Martin VanBuren Nat'l. Hist. Site; Columbia
Co. Mus.; James Vanderpool House; Van Alen House.

25.6 (41.2)   Rt. 9 Jct. Rt. 9J   33.8 (54.4)
Continue traveling South on Rt. 9/BR 9. Rossman

29.1 (46.9)   Joslen Blvd. @ Rt. 9/BR 9   30.3 (48.8)
Bear Southwest at Joslen Blvd. You might just miss this
intersection. Landmark: Landsman's Motors. It's just
after CR 20 which goes to Sottsville.. If you miss this
intersection you'll go through a busy section of Rt. 9.

30.9 (49.7)   Joslen Blvd. @ Harry Howard Ave.   28.5 (45.9)
Bear Southwest on to Harry Howard Ave. which begins
at the high School.

31.7 (51.0)   Harry Howard Ave. Jct. Short St.   27.7 (44.6)
Bear South on to Short St.

31.9 (51.4)   State St. @ Short St.   27.5 (44.3)
Turn West on to State St.

32.1 (51.7)   N. 3rd St. @ State St.   27.3 (44.0)
Turn South on to N. 3rd St.

Hudson

Info.: Area code: 12534. Zip code: 518.
Services: All. Amtrak station.
Lodging: Motels. B&Bs: Hudson City, 326 Allen St.,
822-8044; Inn at Blue Stores, 2323 Rt 9, 537-4277; Pine
Tree Inn B&B, Rt.. 9.
Attractions: Olana St. Hist. Site, Rt. 9G, 828-0135; Am.
Mus. of Firefighting, 125 Harry Howard Ave., 828-7695;
Robert Jenkins Home (Federal period), 113 Warren St,
828-9764.

32.2 (51.8)   Rtes. 9G/23B Jct. N. 3rd St.   27.2 (43.8)
Continue traveling South on Rtes. 9G/23B/S. 3rd. St. A
few hills going through Hudson.

33.1 (53.3)   Mt. Merino Rd. @ Rtes 9G/23B   26.3 (42.3)
Bear Southeast on to Mt. Merino Rd. If you miss this
turn off, continue traveling on Rt. 9G. Mt. Merino Rd. is
shady and almost devoid of traffic. Rt. 9G has a wide
shoulder and is trafficked.

36.0 (58.0)   Rtes. 23/9G @ Mt. Merino Rd.   23.4 (37.7)
Turn West on to Rt. 23. Use caution Rt. 23 becomes a 4
lane highway leading to the Rip Van Winkle Brdg.

36.2 (58.3)   Rt. 9G Jct. Rt. 23   23.2 (37.4)
Travel South on Rt. 9G. You will have to be very careful.
You will have to go from the right lane or shoulder to a
crossing point & across all 4 lanes of traffic. Fortunately,
except for rush hours and special events there isn't too
much traffic. Rt. 9G is also termed Rhinebeck-Hudson
Rd. from this point South. We'll use Rt. 9G!

37.1 (59.7)   Olana Entrance   22.3 (35.9)
              @ Rt. 9G/Rhinebeck Rd.
Olana St. Hist. Site, The home of Frederick Church,
Hudson River School painter. Well worth the 1.3 mi. (2
km.), trip up a fairly steep hill on a not so well maintained
chip sealed road.

40.6 (65.4)   Northern Blvd./CR 35A @ Rt. 9G   18.8 (30.3)
Continue traveling on Rt. 9G. Tired of 9G? Turn West on
to CR 35A/Northern Blvd. which loops close to the River.
But do note that Northern Blvd. changes its name at its
southern end to Anchorage Rd.

41.8 (67.3)   Anchorage Rd./Northern Blvd./CR 35A   17.6 (28.3)
          @ Rt. 9G
Continue traveling on Rt. 9G.
Northbound travelers: Tired of 9G? Turn West on to CR
35A/Anchorage Rd./Northern Blvd. which loops close to
the River. But do note that Northern Blvd. changes its
name at its southern end to Anchorage Rd.

43.0 (69.2)   CR 8 @ Rt. 9G   16.4 (26.4)
Continue traveling on Rt. 9G. Just past the center of Germantown
is CR 35/Woods Rd. It is a poorly marked intersection so look for
it as you leave the Village.

Germantown

Info.: Area code: 518. Zip code: 12526.
Services: Restaurant, general retail stores.
Lodging: B&Bs: Delaneys' at Strawberry Hill, Rt. 9G,
537-4391; Fox Run, 936 CR 6, 537-6945.
Attractions: Clermont St. Hist. Site, 1 Clermont Ave.,
537-4240.

43.2 (69.6)   Woods Rd./CR 35 @ Rt. 9G   16.2 (26.1)
Bear Southwest on to Woods Rd./CR 35. This is a very
nice road with negligible traffic. OR continue traveling
South on Rt. 9G.

46.9 (75.5)   CR. 6 @ Woods Rd./CR 35   12.5 (20.1)
Turn West on to CR 6. You are now in Clermont St. Pk.

47.0 (75.7)   Woods Rd./CR 6   12.4 (20.0)
          @ Clermont Ave./CR 6
Turn South on to Woods Rd./CR 6. Confused about this
jog in Woods Rd. Yup! You guessed it. You've crossed
into another county. From Columbia County to Dutchess
County. Turn West on to Clermont Ave. to go to
Clermont St. Hist. Site, a grand house on the Hudson.
Nice place for a picnic.

48.9 (78.7)   Broadway/CR 78 @ Woods Rd. CR 6   10.5 (16.9)
Turn East on to Broadway/CR 78. Tivoli:
Restaurants, convenience store: Lodging: Birds Nest
B&B,21 Clay Hill Rd., Tivoli, 12583, 757-4279; Lily of the
Valley B&B, 21 Old Rt. 9G, Tivoli, 12583, 757-5120.

49.7 (80.0)   Rt. 9G @ Broadway/CR 78   9.7 (15.6)
Turn South on to Rt. 9G.

51.9 (83.6)   CR 103/Annandale Rd./River Rd.   7.5 (12.1)
          @ Rt. 9G

Turn West on to CR 103. CR 103 goes through Bard College. If you miss this turn off simply enter Bard College and meander West to Annandale Rd./CR 103 and travel South. Annandale Rd. is renamed River Rd. South of Bard College.

54.1 (87.1)   CR 82/Barrytown Rd.   5.3 (8.5)
               @ CR 103/River Rd.
Through travelers continue traveling South on CR 103/ River Rd.
Folks who want to stop can turn East on to Barrytown Rd. and go to Red Hook.
Directions to Red Hook: Turn East on to Barrytown Rd./ Old Rt. 199. At. Rt. 9G, turn North for .2 mi. (.3 km.). At Rt. 199 turn East on to Rt. 199. Total distance to Red Hook: ~2 mi. (3.2 km.)

Red Hook

Info.: Area code: 914. Zip code: 12571.
Services: All.
Lodging: Motels. B&Bs: 1821 House, Old Post Rd., RD 1, Box 1, 758-5013; Gaslight Inn, RR 3, Box 491, Rt. 9, 758-1571; The Grand Dutchess, 50 N. Broadway, 758-5818; The Lombards Lodgings, RD 3, Box 79, Spring Lake Rd., 758-3805; River Dance, Rt. 9, RD 3, Box 491, 758-0120.

56.2 (90.5)   Rt. 199/Bridge overpass   3.2 (5.2)
               @ CR 103/Annandale/River Rd.
Continue traveling South on CR 103.
No bikes allowed on the Rhinebeck-Kingston Bridge. If you want to cross the Hudson River here you'll have to go back about a mile to Rokby Rd. and then go to Rt. 9G. At the Bridge you'll have to call for a pickup truck to take you across. Don't bother. Just travel South!

59.4 (95.6)   Rt. 308   0.0 (0.0)
               @ CR 103/River Rd./Annandale Rd.
Turn East on to Rt. 308. Travel 1.2 mi. (1.9 km.) to the heart of Rhinebeck.
Through travelers turn West on to Rt. 308 to go to Rhinecliff. Rhinecliff Info in Rhinebeck-Rhinecliff to Bear Mt. Rhinecliff is just 1 mi. (1.6 km) Southwest of this intersection.

Rhinebeck

Info.: Area Code: 914. Zip code: 12572.
Bike Info.: Bike shop.
Services: All.
Lodging: Motels. B&Bs: Beckrick House on Chumley's Pond, 2258 Rt. 9G, 876-6416; Beekman Arms, 4 Mill St., Rt. 9, 876-7077; Betty's, 2 Mill Rd., 876-7334; The Bitter Sweet,53 Wurtemburg Rd., 876-7777; Bryndelbrook, 38 River Rd., 876-6618; Chestnut Suite, 11 Chestnut St., 876-6203; Delamater Inn & Conference Center, 44 Montgomery St., Rt. 9, 876-7080; Heller's, 91 Astor Dr. 876-3468; Hideaway,36 Lake Dr., 266-5673; Jenny's Country Manor Lodge, 423 Rt. 199, 800-859-8978; MacPherson House, 37 Knollwood Rd., 876-6221; Mansakenning Carriage House, 29 Ackert Hook Rd., 876-3500; Mulberry Street Guest House, 25 Mulberry St., 876-5478; Olde Rhinebeck Inn, c. 1745, 37 Wurtemburg Rd., 871-1745; Schoolhouse, 112 River Rd., 876-3194; Sepascot Farm, 301 Rt. 308, 876-5840; Sleeping Beauty, 30 Chestnut St., 876-8986; Veranda House, 82 Montgomery St., 876-4133; Village Inn of Rhinebeck, 6 Rt. 9 S.,876-7000; WhistleWood Farm, 11 Pells Rd., 876-6838.
Attractions: Rhinebeck Aerodrome Mus., 44 Stone Church Ave., 758-8610; Wilderstein Preservation, 64 Morton Rd., 876-4818.

N to S	Hudson River Valley	S to N
	East Side of the Hudson River	
mi. (km.) Read↓	**Rhinebeck to Albany**	mi. (km.) Read↑

Bear Mt. to Kingston   Rhinebeck to Bear Mt.

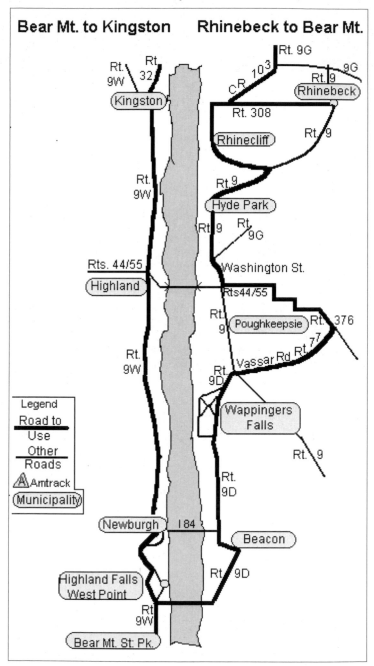

N to S	Hudson River Valley	S to N
	East Side of the Hudson River	
mi. (km.) Read↓	**Rhinebeck to Bear Mt.**	mi. (km.) Read↑

0.0 (0.0)   Rt. 308   **52.8 (85.0)**
@ CR 103/River Rd./Annandale Rd.
Turn West on to Rt. 308.
OR Turn East to go to Rhinebeck. Rhinebeck info. is the
last entry in the Albany to Rhinebeck chapter.

1.0 (1.6)   Hutton St. @ Rt. 308   **51.8 (83.4)**
Continue traveling South on Charles St. which becomes
Kelly St. Rt. 308 ends here in Rhinecliff. Don't panic! In
less than the blink of an eye, Kelly St. becomes CR 85.
CR 85 has many names: Kelly St. becomes Morton Rd.
which becomes South Mill Rd. all of which go under the
local nom de plume of Fishing Ground Rd.
Rhinecliff: Rhinecliff B&B, PO Box 167, 12574, 876-
3710.

1.5 (2.4)   Kelly St. @ CR 85/Morton Rd.   **51.3 (82.6)**
Continue traveling South on CR 85/Morton St.

2.7 (4.3)   CR 85/Morton Rd. .   **50.1 (80.7)**
@ CR 85 South Mill Rd
Bear Southwest on to South Mill Rd./CR 85.

4.9 (7.9)   Rt. 9 @ CR 85/South Mill Rd.   **47.9 (77.1)**
Turn South on to Rt. 9.

5.7 (9.2)   Old Post Rd.   **47.1 (75.8)**
@ Rt. 9/Albany Post Rd.
Turn West on to Old Post Rd.
Or you can continue traveling South on Rt. 9.

Staatsburg

Info: Area code: 914. Zip code: 12580.
Lodging: Motel. B&Bs: Belvedere Mansion, Rt. 9, 889-
8000; Cozy Rest, 912 Rt. 9, 889-4320; Half Moon, 284
Meadowbrook Ln., 266-5296. Camping: Margaret Lewis
Norrie St. Pk., Rt. 9, 889-4545
Attractions: Mills Mansion St. Hist. Site & Mills St. Pk.,
Old Albany Post Rd., 889-8851.

8.5 (13.7)   Vanderbilt Mansion Nat'l. Hist. Site   **44.3 (71.3)**
@ Rt. 9
Continue traveling South on Rt. 9 or go for a visit,
Vanderbilt Mansion, 229-9115.

9.2 (14.8)   Market St./CR 41   43.6 (70.2)
               @ Rt. 9/Albany Post Rd.
Continue traveling South on Rt. 9. This is a busy section
of Rt. 9. Use extreme care. There are many tourists
looking for tourists attractions, lodging, etc.

Hyde Park

Info.: Area code: 914. Zip code: 12538.
Cycling & Hiking Info.: Bike shop.
Services: All.
Lodging: Costello's Guest House, 21 Main St., 229-
2559; Fala, E. Market St., 229-5937; Inn at Hyde Park,
537 Albany Post Rd., Rt. 9, 229-9161; Inn the Woods, 32
Howard Blvd. Ext., 229-9331; Journey Inn, 1 Sherwood
Pl. 229-8972; Roosevelt Inn, 616 Albany Post Rd., Rt. 9,
229-2443; The Saltbox, 255 Ruskey Ln. 266-3196;
Village Square Country Inn, Rt. 9, 229-7141; The
Willows, 53 Travis Rd. 471-6115.
Attractions: Franklin D. Roosevelt Library, 511 Albany
Post Rd., 229-8114; Franklin D. Roosevelt, Eleanor
Roosevelt & Vanderbilt Nat'l. Hist. Sites, 229-9115.
Culinary Inst. of Am., 471-6608. Marist Coll.

10.8 (17.4)   FDR Home NHS @ Rt. 9   42.0 (67.6)
Continue South on Rt. 9. Visit the President's home &
library. Eleanor's is 3 mi. (4.8 km.) East.

14.1 (22.7)   Rt. 9G/Washington St. @ Rt. 9   38.7 (62.3)
Bear Southeast on to Rt. 9G. Rt. 9 becomes a fast
moving semi-limited access road. You can use it and
save some mi./km. going through Poughkeepsie but it is
more fun wandering through a city.

14.8 (23.8)   Parker St./Rt. 9G   38.0 (61.2)
               @ Washington St./Rt. 9G
Continue South on Washington St. Rt. 9G goes off to
the Northeast.

15.1 (24.3)   Mill St./Rtes. 44/55 @ Washington St.   37.7 (60.7)
Continue South on Washington St.

15.4 (24.8)   Church St./Rtes. 44/55   37.4 (60.2)
               @ Washington St.
Turn East on to Church St./Rtes. 44/55. It's just 3 pedal
strokes to the next turn. Turn West on to Church St./
Rtes. 44/55 to cross the Hudson via the Mid-Hudson
Bridge to Highland and the West Side of the Hudson Rt.

Poughkeepsie

Info.: Area Code: 914. Zip code: 12601.

Cycling & Hiking Info.: Bike shop. Mid-Hudson Bicycle Club, PO Box 1727.

Services: All. Hospital. Mid-Hudson Bridge. Amtrak.

Lodging: Motels.

Attractions: Frances Loeb Lehman Art Ctr., Vassar Coll., 124 Raymond St., 437-5632; Samuel F. B. Morse Nat'l. Hist. Site, 370 South Rd., 454-4500; Clinton House St. Hist. Site, 549 Main St., 471-1630; River Boat Tours, 310 Mill St., 473-5211.

15.5 (25.0)   Market St. @ Church St./Rtes. 44/55   37.3 (60.1)
Turn South on to Market St. You might even see some BR 9 signs. Follow them, for a while at least.

15.6 (25.1)   Noxon St. @ Market St.   37.2 (59.9)
Turn East on to Noxon St. The only way you can go.

15.8 (25.4)   Academy St. @ Noxon St.   37.0 (59.6)
Turn South on to Academy St.

15.9 (25.6)   Montgomery St. @ Academy St.   36.9 (59.4)
Turn East on to Montgomery St.

16.1 (25.9)   Hooker Ave. @ Academy St.   36.7 (59.1)
Turn Southeast on to Hooker Ave. You're ready to roll.

18.1 (29.1)   New Hackensack Rd./Rt. 376   34.7 (55.9)
              @ Hooker Ave.
Turn Southeast on New Hackensack Rd./Rt. 376.

20.3 (32.7)   CR 77/Vassar Rd. & Rt. 113   32.5 (52.3)
              @ Rt. 376/New Hackensack Rd.
Travel due South on to CR 77/Vassar Rd.   Busy intersection.

24.0 (38.6)   Rt. 9D & Rt. 9 @ CR 77/Vassar Rd.   28.8 (46.4)
Cross Rt. 9 to Rt. 9D.
Northbound travelers: Rt. 9 becomes a fast moving semi-limited access road here. You can use it and save some mi./km. going through Poughkeepsie but it is more fun wandering through a city.

25.6 (41.2)   Market St. @ Rt. 9D/Main St.   27.2 (43.8)
Southbound travelers: Rural Road Route Turn West on to Market St. This rural road route will add ~6 mi. (9.6 km.), to your distance vs. using Rt. 9D. It is also hillier. OR continue traveling South on Rt. 9D.

Wappingers Falls: Bike Info.: Bike Shop: Attractions: Renegades Baseball, 838-0094.

26.1 (42.0)   Market St. @ CR 91/Creek Rd.   26.7 (43.0)
Continue traveling South on Market St. It becomes CR 91/Creek Rd. after leaving the Village boundary.

27.3 (44.0)   Rt. 28/New Hamburg Rd.   25.5 (41.1)
              @ CR 91/Creek Rd.
Continue traveling South on to Old Troy Rd. CR 91 ends here. For less than 2 pedal strokes you'll be traveling on Rt. 28. To return to Rt. 9D, turn East on to Rt. 28, then South on Rt. 9D to continue your tour. To catch a train, follow Rt. 28, West to New Hamburg.

28.0 (45.1)   Wheeler Rd. @ Old Troy Rd.   24.8 (39.9)
Continue traveling South on to Wheeler Rd. Remember that the Hudson flows South.

28.5 (45.9)   Wheeler Hill Rd. @ Wheeler Rd.   24.3 (39.1)
Turn Southeast on to Wheeler Hill Rd.

29.1 (46.9)   Old State Rd. @ Wheeler Hill Rd.   23.7 (38.2)
Turn South on to Old State Rd. It's 2 pedal strokes to the next turn. If you're tired of these rural roads then keep traveling South on Old State Rd. to reach Rt. 9, in .3 mi. (.5 km.)

29.2 (47.0)   River Rd. N. @ Old State Rd.   23.6 (38.0)
Turn Southwest on to River Rd. North. The sign says to Chelsea.

30.9 (49.7)   CR 92 @ River Rd. N./Market St.   21.9 (35.3)
Continue South on Market St.
OR turn East on to CR 92/Fishkill Ave. to return to Rt. 9D. At Rt. 9D turn South. CR. 92/Fishkill Ave. changes its name along the way traverse to Rt. 9D to Chelsea Rd. Turning South on 9D you will pass Stony Kill Environmental Ed. Ctr., 914 831-8780. If you cross 9D, CR. 92 becomes CR 34 and goes into Fishkill, 2.6 mi. (4.2 km.) from Rt. 9D.
Fishkill: Services: All. Bike Info.: Shops: Wheel & Heel, 2275 Rt. 9, 914 896-7591; Fitness Concepts, 914 896-9131. Lodging: Motels. B&B: Star Mill Farm B&B, PO Box 421 Old Grange Rd., 914 897-5443.

31.0 (49.9)   Spring St. @ Market St.   21.8 (35.1)
Turn West (towards the River) on to Spring St.

31.1 (50.1)   River Rd. S./Old Castle Point Rd.   21.7 (34.9)
             @ Spring St.
At the River/Railroad, Spring St. makes a right angle turn
and transforms itself into River Rd. South. As you travel
South to Rt. 9D, River Rd. S. becomes Old Castle Point
Rd.

33.0 (53.1)   Rt. 9D @ Old Castle Point Rd.   19.8 (31.9)
Turn South on to Rt. 9D.
Northbound travelers: Continue traveling North on Rt.
9D or turn West here to use a Rural Road Route. The
Rural Road Route will add ~6 mi. (9.6 km.) to your
distance vs. using Rt. 9D. It is also hillier. Castle Point
Pk.

35.5 (57.2)   Commerce St. @ Rt. 9D/North Ave.   17.3 (27.9)
Continue traveling South on Rt. 9D through Beacon. Rt.
9D uses several different streets to go through the City.
Just follow the 9D signs.

Beacon

Info.: Area code: 914. Zip code: 12508.
Bike & Hike Info.: Bike shop. Amtrak.
Services: All. Newburgh Beacon Bridge (Interstate.)
Lodging: Motels.
Attractions: Mt. Gulian Hist. Site, 145 Sterling St., 831-
8172; Hudson Highlands St. Pk., undeveloped (no
camping), hiking & scenic views, 225-7207.

37.0 (59.6)   Rt. 9D/Wolcott Ave.   15.8 (25.4)
             @ Rt. 9D/Howland Ave.
Turn South on to Howland Ave.
Northbound travelers: Rt. 9D uses several streets
through Beacon. It really isn't turning, just going with the
flow of the street. Follow the 9D signs.

41.0 (66.0)   County Border @ Rt. 9D   11.8 (19.0)
Continue traveling South on Rt. 9D. Hudson Highlands
St. Pk. (no camping), 225-7207.
Dutchess County-Putnam County.

42.9 (69.1)   Main St./Rt. 301 @ Rt. 9D   9.9 (15.9)
Continue traveling South on Rt. 9D. Of course there are
street names to Rt. 9D.
Cold Spring: Foundry School Mus., 63 Chestnut St.,
Cold Spring, 265-4010.

46.8 (75.3)   Rt. 403 @ Rt. 9D   6.0 (9.7)
Continue Traveling South on Rt. 9D.

Garrison

Info.: Area code: 914. Zip code: 10524.
Attractions: : Boscobel Restoration, Rt. 9D, 265-3638;
Manitoga, 424-3812, hist. homes.

51.2 (82.4)   Bear Mt. Bridge, E. side @ Rt. 9D   1.6 (2.6)
Continue traveling South on Rt. 9D.
Southbound travelers: If you are planning to go South
on the East side of the Hudson, be prepared for a very
steep climb on Bear Mt. Bridge Rd. South of the Bridge.
The roadway going South from the Bridge is narrow with
a negligible shoulder. There are many cars with tourists
looking at the view and not paying attention to the road.
The view is magnificent. To put it another way, Rt. 1, in
Northern California barely rivals this scenic stretch of
road.
OR cross the Bridge to Bear Mt. St. Pk., to the West of
the Hudson Route and NYS's Bike Route 9.

52.0 (83.7)   Rt. 9W @ Bear Mt. Bridge, W. side   0.8 (1.3)
Turn South on to Rt. 9W.

52.8 (85.0)   Bear Mt. St. Pk./Lodge @ Rt. 9W   0.0 (0.0)
of the Hudson or returning to the East side.
Relax. Bear Mt. St. Pk. & Lodge: Bear Mt. Lodging:
Bear Mt. Lodge, Bear Mt. 10911, 914 786-2731;
camping. Beaver Pond Cpgd., Harriman St. Pk., ~9 mi.
(14.5 km.) South of this point. Book both Lodge and
camping reservations at least 1 week in advance, more if
you're traveling on a weekend.
You have a choice to continue traveling South on the
West side using the offical Bike Route 9 (and a few
variations of it or going back to the East side of the
Hudson

N to S	**Hudson River Valley**	S to N
	East Side of the Hudson River	
mi. (km.) Read↓	**Bear Mt. to Rhinebeck**	mi. (km.) Read↑

N to S	**Hudson River Valley**	S to N
	East Side of the Hudson River	
mi. (km.) Read↓	**Bear Mt. to New York City**	mi. (km.) Read↑

0.0 (0.0)　　　Bear Mt. St. Pk. @ Rt. 9W　　　　50.8 (81.8)
Turn North on to Rt. 9W.

0.8 (1.3)　　　Bear Mt. Bridge Rd. @ Rt. 9W　　　50.0 (80.5)
Turn East on to Bear Mt. Bridge Rd. & cross the Hudson
River.

1.6 (2.6)　　　Bear Mt. Bridge East side　　　　49.2 (79.2)
　　　　　　　@ Bear Mt. Bridge Rd./Rt. 9D
Turn South on to Bear Mt. Bridge Rd., Rt. 9D goes North.
Southbound travelers: If you are planning to go South
on the East side of the Hudson, be prepared for a very
steep climb on the Bear Mt. Bridge Rd. The roadway is
narrow with a negligible shoulder. There are many cars
with tourists looking at the view and not paying attention
to the road. The view is magnificent.
Use extreme caution on this road. Lights on! There is
an overlook about ½ way up the Mt.

4.6 (7.4)　　　Hook Rd. @ Bear Mt. Brdg. Rd.　　46.2 (74.4)
Really just a turn in the road & a roadway name change.

5.2 (8.4)　　　Rt. 9/Annsville Rd./Jan Peek Brdg.　45.6 (73.4)
　　　　　　　@ Hook Rd
Cross the Bridge on Rt. 9. I must warn you that
theoretically bicycles may not be permitted on Rt. 9 at
this point & you must exit Rt. 9 either on to Hallenbeck
St. (just over the bridge or at Main St.) Frankly its easier
using Rt. 9's shoulder and taking your chances than
using Annsville Rd., which is fraught with inclines.
OR continue traveling East on Rt. 9/Annsville Rd. The
Annsville Rd. Rt. is listed in detail since the Rt. 9 Rt. is
obvious.
Bear right at Sprout Brook Rd. A steep decline.

6.0 (9.7)　　　Highland Ave. @ Annsville Rd.　　44.8 (72.1)
Turn South on to Highland Ave.

6.5 (10.5)　　　Bear Mt. St. Pkwy. @ Highland Ave.　44.3 (71.3)
Continue traveling South on Highland Ave.

7.2 (11.6)　　　Division St. @ Highland Ave.　　43.6 (70.2)
Continue traveling South on Division St.

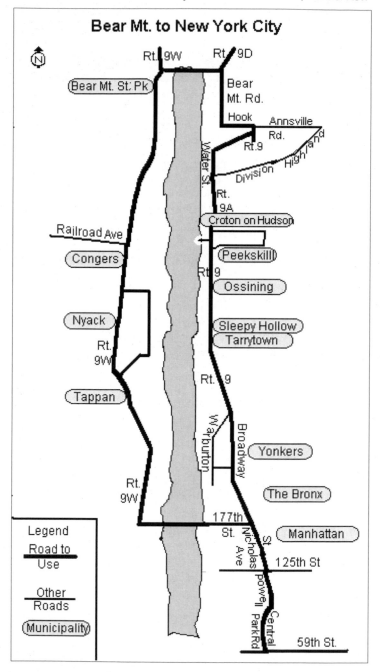

Bear Mt. to New York City

7.4 (11.9)   Central Ave. @ Division St.   43.4 (69.9)
Turn West on to Central Ave.

Peekskill

Info.: Peekskill/Cortlandt CofC, 1 S. Division St., 737-3600. Area code: 914. Zip code:
Services: All. Metro North railroad to NYC.
Lodging: Motel.
Attractions: Peekskill Mus., 124 Union Ave., 737-6130, Hudson River boat tours, 788-4000; MS Commander, 534-7245.

7.8 (12.6)   Water St. @ Central Ave.   43.0 (69.2)
Turn South on to Water St. If you chanced using Rt. 9 from Hook Rd. [4.6 (7.4) above.] and exited Rt. 9 either on to Hallenbeck St. or at Main St. you'll meet us here at Water St.
Northbound travelers: Either turn West on to Central Ave. OR continue traveling North on Water St. Water St. melds into Hallenbeck St. at Annsville Creek. Continue traveling to the Rt. 9 Bridge over the Creek and cross there. See warning at Rt. 9/Annsville Rd./Jan Peek Brdg. @ Hook Rd. above. The Annsville Rd. route is fraught with steep inclines. Rt. 9 is fraught with cars.

8.2 (13.2)   Requa St. @ Water St./South St.   42.6 (68.6)
Continue traveling South on South St.

9.4 (15.1)   Rt. 9A @ Water St.   41.4 (66.7)
Continue traveling South on Rt. 9A/Albany-New York (City) Post Rd.

13.8 (22.2)   S. Riverside Ave. & Old Post Rd.   37.0 (59.6)
          @ Rt. 9A

Croton-On-Hudson

Info.: Area code: 914. Zip code: 10520.
Services: Metro-North railroad/Amtrak.
Lodging: Camping: Croton Pt. Pk., Croton Pt. Ave., 271-3293.
Attraction: Van Cortlandt Manor, S. Riverside Ave., 631-8200; Alexander Hamilton House, 49 Van Wyck St., 271-6737.

     A V in the road & a choice.
Choice A: Bear South on to S. Riverside Ave.
.2 (.4)   Rt. 129 @ Riverside Dr.   4.7 (7.6)
     Continue traveling South on S. Riverside Dr.
.7 (1.1)   Croton Pt. Ave.   4.2 {6.8}

@ S. Riverside Ave.
Travel South towards Van Cortlandt Manor.
OR Turn West on to Croton Pt. Ave to go to Croton Pt.
Pk. (family camping).
OR go under the Rt. 9 overpass, enter Rt. & cross the
Croton River. Then just continue to travel straight on
Rt. 9/Albany-NY Post Rd. Which of course changes its
name to Highland Ave. a bit further on.
Choice B. Continue traveling East on to Old Post Rd.
.6 (.9)   North Old Post Rd.   4.1 {6.6)
           @ Old Post Rd.
Continue East on North Old Post Rd.
.8 (1.3)   Grand St. @ North Old Post Rd.   3.9 (6.3)
Continue North East on Grand St./Rt. 129.
1.8 (2.9) Quaker Bridge Rd.   2.9 (4.7)
           @ Grand St./Rt.129
Turn East on to Quaker Bridge Rd. This is a very steep
decline/incline.
2.3 (3.7) Bridge @ Quaker Bridge Rd.   2.4 (3.7)
Cross the bridge & travel South on Quaker Bridge Rd.
Do not go on Quaker Bridge Rd. E.
4.7 (7.6) Rt. 9 @ Quaker Bridge Rd.   0.0 (0.0)
Continue traveling South on Rt. 9/Albany-NY Post Rd.

17.5 (28.2)   Rt. 9   33.3 (53.6)
           @ Highland Ave./Quaker Bridge Rd.
Continue traveling South on Rt. 9/Albany Post Rd.
Somehow you made it across the Croton River. If you
took the Highland Ave. route then you're tired from the
hills. If you took Rt. 9, then the traffic annoyed you.
Sorry about that.

19.0 (30.6)   Main St. @ Rt. 9   31.8 (51.2)
Continue South on Rt. 9.

Ossining

Info.: Visitors Ctr, 95 Broadway, Ossining, 10562, 914
941-3189. Area code: 914. Zip code: 10562.
Bike Info.: Bike Shop.
Services: All. Metro-North Railroad.
Lodging: Motel. Attractions: Hudson Riverboat Co.,
941-3295. NYS Correctional Inst. (Sing Sing Prison)
display & mus. at Visitors Ctr.

23.9 (38.5)   Rt. 448 @ Rt. 9   26.9 (43.3)
Continue South on Rt. 9.

Sleepy Hollow

Info.: Area code: 914. Zip code: 10591.

Attractions: Kykui, Rockefeller House & Gardens, 631-8200; Philipsburg Manor, 631-3992; Sleepy Hollow Cemetery, 430 N. Broadway, 631-1123; Tarrytown Lighthouse, Kingsland Pt. Pk., 242-6300.

Tarrytown: Tarrytown is actually larger than Sleepy Hollow; has more services (Grocery, etc.); and Motels.

30.4 (48.9)   Warburton Ave. @ Rt. 9/Broadway   20.4 (32.8)
Continue traveling South on Rt. 9. You can use Warburton Ave. if you desire a bit of a change.

34.6 (55.7)   Glenwood Ave. @ Rt. 9/Broadway   16.2 (26.1)
Continue traveling South on Rt. 9. Turn on to Glenwood Ave. to go to Warburton Ave. & the Hudson River Mus.

Yonkers

Info.: City of Yonkers, 40 S. Broadway, Yonkers NY 10701 914 377-6000
Area code: 914. Zip code: various.
Bike Info.: Bike shops.
Services: All.
Lodging: Motels. Metro-North railroad.
Attractions: Hudson River Mus., 511 Warburton Ave., 963-4550; Philipse Manor Hall, Warburton Ave. at Dock St., 965-4027; Yonkers Raceway.

37.5 (60.4)   New York City @ Rt. 9/Broadway   13.3 (21.4)
Continue traveling South on Rt. 9/Broadway. In New York City it is rare for streets to be numbered with route numbers. Names or street numbers are more commonly used. You are entering The Bronx, the northern most County of NYC. It's also the only part of NYC which is not an island. In NYC the counties are usually termed boroughs. There is a reason and it deals with politics.

The Bronx

Info.: Bronx Tourism Council, 880 River Ave., Bronx 10452, 718 590-3518.
Area code: 718. Zip code: various.
Bike Info.: Bike shops.
Services: All.
Attractions: Yankee baseball, Yankee Stadium, 161st St. at River Ave., 293-6000; Wave Hill Gardens & Mansion, W. 249th St. at Independence Ave., 549-3200. The Bronx Zoo, NY Botanical Gardens, Bronx Hist. Mus. 3309 Bainbridge Ave., 881-8900.

40.7 (65.5)   Broadway Bridge   10.1 (16.3)
              @ Broadway/The Bronx
Continue South by crossing the Broadway Bridge into Manhattan (New York County). Travel South on Broadway.

43.5 (70.0)   179th St. @ Broadway   7.3 (11.8)
Continue South on Broadway. Geo. Washington Brdg. Bus Term. Inter-city buses to everywhere, including across the George Washington Bridge to New Jersey and the West of the Hudson Route.
Directions to cross the George Washington Bridge under your own pedal power.

To George Washington Bridge Walkway
We are talking about a distance of .4 mi. (.6 km.) from W. 179th St. @ Broadway to W. 178th St. @ Cabrini Blvd. However, there are one way streets in the way and the lower deck of the Bridge.
Travel South on Broadway to W. 177th St. Turn West on to W. 177th St. Travel 2 blocks to Cabrini St. Turn North on Cabrini St. to 178th St. @ Cabrini St. On the West side of Cabrini St. will be the entrance to the Bridge walkway. You must walk your bike on the Bridge walkway. It is 1 mi. (1.6 km.) across the Bridge to Rt. 9W/BR 9 in Fort Lee, New Jersey.

44.2 (71.2)   St. Nicholas Ave. @ Broadway   6.6 (10.6)
Bear Southeast on to St. Nicholas Ave. An on street bike lane begins here. Please use extreme caution. New York City, in particular, Manhattan streets, are not a place for recreational bicyclists to ride. Use the subway to go to your lodging.

45.2 (72.8)   W. 155th St. @ St. Nicholas Ave.   5.6 (9.0)
Continue traveling South on St. Nicholas Ave. If you
want to go to Yankee Stadium and The Bronx, turn East
here. Yankee Stadium is just over the Macombs Dam
Bridge.

46.9 (75.5)   W. 126th or W. 125th St.   3.9 (6.3)
          @ St. Nicholas Ave.
Continue traveling South on St. Nicholas Ave.
If you are going to NYC's LaGuardia or Kennedy Airports
turn East on to W. 126th St. or W. 125th St. W. 126th St.
is one way going East and a side street. W. 125th St. is
a major E<->W street and as such has a good deal of
traffic. The route to LaGuardia is at the section after you
arrive in mid-town Manhattan.

47.0 (75.7)   W. 124 St. @ St. Nicholas Ave.   3.8 (6.1)
Continue traveling South on St. Nicholas Ave.

47.5 (76.5)   Adam C. Powell Ave.   3.3 (5.3)
          @ St. Nicholas Ave.
Turn South on to Adam C. Powell Ave.

47.9 (77.1)   Central Park Rd.   2.9 (4.7)
          @ Adam C. Powell Ave.
Go counterclockwise via the on street bikeway.

50.8 (81.8)   W. 59th St. @ Central Park W.   0.0 (0.0)
Exit Central Park Rd. on to W. 59th St. This is just after
rounding the Zoo. If you find yourself going North again.
Exit. You are in mid-town Manhattan and on your own!
Entire books are written on NYC's myriad attractions,
lodgings, etc. I won't even try to describe them.

N to S	**Hudson River Valley**	S to N
	East Side of the Hudson River	
mi. (km.) Read↓	**New York City to Bear Mt.**	mi. (km.) Read↑

W to E	**Manhattan to**	E to W
mi. (km.) Read↓	**LaGuardia Airport**	mi. (km.) Read↑

To Triboro Bridge & NYC's LaGuardia Airport

0.0 (0.0)W. 126th or W. 125th St. @ St. Nicholas Ave.   5.0 (8.1)
Turn East on to either W. 126th St. or W. 125th St.

.6 (.9)   5th Ave. @ W. 126th/125th St.   4.4 (7.1)
Continue traveling East. 5th Ave. is the dividing line
between East & West in Manhattan.

1.1 (1.8)   2nd Ave. @ E. 126th/125th St.   3.9 (6.3)
If you used 126th St., the entrance to the Triboro Bridge
walkway to Randall's Island and Queens is just across
2nd Ave. If you used 125th St. turn either North or South
& go 1 block to the bridge walkway entrance.

1.6 (2.6)   Randall's Island   3.4 (5.5)
@ Manhattan Triboro Brdg. walkway
Use the bikeway route on Randall's Is. to the Queens
section of the Triboro Bridge.

4.4 (7.1)   Queens Triboro Bridge @ Randall's Is.   .6 (.9)
Use the South walkway on the Bridge.

5.0 (8.1)   Hoyt Ave. S.   0.0 (0.0)
@ Triboro Brdg. Walkway Entrance
It's about 3 mi. (5 km.) to LaGuardia Airport from this
point via Use the NYC Queens Bike Map from here.

W to E	**LaGuardia Airport**	E to W
mi. (km.) Read↓	**to Manhattan**	mi. (km.) Read↑

To Kennedy Airport
It is a much longer bike ride to Kennedy Airport. I suggest that
you use the Subway to go to Kennedy Airport. With a Bike
Permit you'll be able to go to the Aqueduct Race Track
Subway stop on the A Line.(Far Rockaway/Rockaway Blvd.).
Bicyclists should not follow the MTA's directions to Howard
Beach.
Upon exiting at the Aqueduct Race Track station, use the
southern most exit point on to N. Conduit Ave./Southern
Pkwy. Follow N. Conduit Ave. East to Lefferts Blvd. & the
northern entrance to the Airport. You'll have to weave around
the Airport to the North or South Service Rds. to get to the
terminal areas. Total Time needed: ~1 hr. 30 min..

S to N   **Hudson River Valley**   N to S
                    West Side of the Hudson River
mi. (km.) Read↓   **New York City to Bear Mt.**   mi. (km.) Read↑

Map Note

The maps for this section, *Hudson River Valley: West Side of the Hudson River* are the same maps used for the segments on the East side of the Hudson River

Lodging Note

There are literally hundreds of B&Bs in the Hudson River Valley. Some are in the towns and cities along the River. It would significantly increase the size of this book if all were listed. Listed B&Bs are those which were easily located via directories and the web. I suggest that you search the web, especially, http://www.enjoyhv.com before you begin your tour.

Campgrounds are a bit harder to locate. Guerilla campers will find many sites North of Westchester County on the East side of the River and North of Rockland County on the West side.

Travelers Note

You can use any route to go to the George Washington Bridge Bus Terminal in Upper Manhattan. A route to the Terminal is provided in the East Side of the Hudson Route. Hopefully you have obtained a Bike Map for each of the five Boroughs of New York City from the NYC Dep't. of Planning, Transportation Div., Bicycle Network Program, City Hall, NY, NY, 212 442-4640.

0.0 (0.0)   179th St. @ Broadway   0.0 (0.0)
                 George Washington Brdg. Bus Terminal.

To George Washington Bridge Walkway

We are talking a distance of .4 mi. (.6 km.) from W. 179th St. @ Broadway to W. 178th St. @ Cabrini Blvd. However, one way streets and the lower deck of the Bridge are in the way.

Travel South on Broadway to W. 177th St. Turn West on to W. 177th St. Travel 2 blocks to Cabrini St. Turn North on Cabrini St. to 178th St. @ Cabrini St. On the West side of Cabrini St. will be the entrance to the Bridge walkway. You must walk your bike on the Bridge walkway. It is 1 mi. (1.6 km.) across the Bridge to Rt. 9W/BR 9 in Fort Lee, New Jersey.

0.0 (0.0)   Rt. 9W/BR 9   34.1 (54.9)
@ Geo. Washington Brdg. Walkway
Turn North on Rt. 9W/BR 9. This is New York's BR 9.

Fort Lee, New Jersey

Info.: Ft. Lee CofC, Ft. Lee Hist. Pk. Visitors Ctr.,
Hudson Terr., Fort Lee NJ 07624, 201 461-1776, www.
Fortlee.com; Bergen Co. Dep't. of Parks, 21 Main St.,
Hackensack NJ 07601; Palisades Interstate Park, PO
Box 155, Alpine NJ 07610.
Services: Bus Terminal. George Washington Bridge.
Lodging: Motels.
Attractions: Fort Lee Hist. Pk., Hudson Terr, 201 461-
1776. George Washington Bridge.

10.9 (17.5)   Palisades Interstate Pkwy.   23.2 (37.4)
@ Rt. 9W/BR 9
Continue Traveling North on Rt. 9W.

13.1 (21.1)   Rockland Ave. @ Rt. 9W   21.0 (33.8)
Continue traveling on Rt. 9W.
OR turn East on to Rockland Ave. The distances are
about the same.
You are now in New York State, Rockland County.
Tappan: Leo's Bicycle Shop, 27 Route 303, 914 359-
0693. Attractions: Tallman St. Pk. (no camping).

13.7 (22.1)   Piermont Ave. @ Rockland Ave.   20.4 (32.8)
Cross the bridge and turn Northeast on to Piermont Ave.
You will be traveling along the riverfront.

16.3 (26.2)   Broadway @ Piermont Ave.   17.8 (28.7)
Turn West on to Smith Ave. then North on to Broadway.
Smith Ave. is very short.

17.3 (27.9)   Main St. @ Broadway   16.8 (27.0)
Turn West on Main St.

17.8 (28.7)   Highland Ave./Rt. 9W @ Main St.   16.3 (26.2)
Turn North on to Highland Ave./Rt. 9W/BR 9.

Nyack

Info.: Area code: 914. Zip code: 10960.
Bike & Hike Info: Mt. biking in St. Parks. Bike shops:
Nyack Bicycle Outfitters, 72 No. Broadway, 353-0268;
Piermont Bicycle Connection, 215 Ash St., 365-0900.
Lodging: Motels.   Inn At Clarksville Corners, 11
Strawtown Rd., West Nyack 10994, 353-5356.

Attractions: Blauvelt St. Pk., Clausen Mt. St. Pk. (Long Trail), no camping in either park; Helen Hayes Perf. Arts Ctr., Main St, 358-6333; Hudson Valley Children's Mus., Nyack Seaport, 21 Burd St., 358-2191.

23.5 (37.8)   Rt. 9W/Congers Rd. @ Rt. 9W   10.6 (17.1)
Continue traveling on Rt. 9W. Just a renaming of 9W.
Congers: Bike & Hike Info: Congers Bike Shop, 107 Lake Rd., 268-3315. Attractions: Hook St. Pk. & Rockland Lake St. Pk. (no camping.)

26.9 (43.3)   Railroad Ave. @ Rt. 9W   7.2 (11.6)
Continue traveling on Rt. 9W.
Bear Mt. St. Pk. does not have camping facilities.
Turn West on to Railroad Ave. if you want to camp.
Travel, 2.6 mi. (4.3 km.), West on R ailroad Ave., (which changes its name to Suffern Ln. and then to Letchworth Village Rd.)
Turn West on to Willow Grove Rd. Willow Grove Rd. becomes Gate Hill Rd. and leads in another 3.4 mi. (5.5 km.) to Beaver Pond Cpgd. in Harriman St. Pk., 786-2701. Total dist. = 6 mi. (9.6 km.)
Haverstraw: Lodging: Thomas Avenia Bike Shop, 914 947-3237; Attraction: Stoney Pt. St. Hist. Site, 786-2521.

34.1 (54.9)   Bear Mt. Lodge @ Rt. 9W.   0.0 (0.0)
Book accommodations at the Lodge at least two days in advance; a week if you are arriving on a weekend.
Info.:
Bike & Hike Info: Hiking: Park trails. Appalachian Trail, Appalachian Mt. Club, NY-NoJ Chapter, 5 Tudor City Pl., NY NY 10017, 212 986-1430.
Lodging: Only at the Lodge. No camping. Camp at Beaver Pond Cpgd. ~14 mi. (22 km.) South off Rt. 9W, see above entry.
Relax.
You have a choice to continue traveling South on the West side of the Hudson or returning to the East side. I must warn you that Southbound travelers: If you are planning to go South on the East side of the Hudson

S to N	Hudson River Valley	N to S
	West Side of the Hudson River	
mi. (km.) Read↓	Bear Mt. to New York City	mi. (km.) Read↑

S to N	**Hudson River Valley**	N to S
	West Side of the Hudson River	
mi. (km.) Read↓	**Bear Mt. to Kingston**	mi. (km.) Read↑

0.0 (0.0)   Bear Mt. St. Pk. @ Rt. 9W   50.9 (81.9)
Turn North on to Rt. 9W.
East side of the Hudson travelers Warning: The East side route traveling South from the Bear Mt. Bridge on Bear Mt. Bridge Rd. is an extremely steep climb. Bear Mt. Bridge Rd. is narrow; without a shoulder; heavily trafficked with tourists not paying attention to the road but very scenic. Use extreme caution if you intend to go South on the East side of the River. Make certain that your headlight and rear red flashing light are on. East side travelers going North: Bike Route 9 actually continues on the East side of the Hudson River. Bear Mt. Bridge Rd. going North from the Bridge is a climb but not impossible. It is trafficked with tourists looking at the scenery rather than the road; narrow; and has a marginal shoulder. Use extreme caution. Make certain your lights, front & rear are on.

0.8 (1.3)   Bear Mt. Bridge Rd. @ Rt. 9W   50.1 (80.7)
Continue Traveling North on 9W.
East side of Hudson travelers: Turn East on to Bear Mt. Bridge Rd. & cross the Hudson River.

2.5 (4.0)   Rt. 218 @ Rt. 9W   48.4 (77.9)
Rt. 218 & Rt. 9W weave back and forth. The distance is approximately the same no matter which road you use. Rt. 218 is the scenic route with more hills and less traffic. Rt. 9W the direct route with a bit more traffic. Continue traveling on Rt. 9W/BR 9
OR turn on to Rt. 218 and follow it into Highland Falls and to West Point, the U. S. Military Academy, 914 938-2638. Motels.

5.3 (8.5)   Rt. 9W Jct. Rt. 218   45.6 (73.4)
Continue traveling on Rt. 9W.
Southbound travelers can turn on to Rt. 218 to go to West Point & Highland Falls.

5.9 (9.5)   Rt. 218 @ Rt. 9W   45.0 (72.5)
Continue traveling on Rt. 9W.
OR turn East on to Rt. 218 North. Rt. 218 is a more scenic way to go to North from here.
Cornwall on Hudson: Attractions: Mus. of the Hudson

Highlands, 25 The Boulevard, 534-7781, Kenridge Farm, Rt. 9W, 534-7781.

12.2 (19.6)   Rt. 9W @ Rt. 218   38.7 (62.3)
Turn North on to Rt. 9W.
Southbound travelers: Rt. 218 & Rt. 9W weave back and forth.
The distance is approximately the same no matter which road you use. Rt. 218 is the scenic route with more hills and less traffic.
Vails Gate: Attractions: Edmonston House, Rt. 94, 561-5073; Knox's HQ St. Hist. Site., Forge Hill Rd., Rt. 94, 561-5498; The Last Encampment of the Continental Army, Rte 300, 561-0902; New Windsor Cantonment State Historic Site, Temple Hill Rd., Rte 300, 561-1765.

13.5 (21.7)   River Rd./Water St. @ Rt. 9W   37.4 (60.2)
Continue traveling on Rt. 9W. Or bear Northeast on to River Rd. The distances to Newburgh are about the same either road you use. Rt. 9W does become more heavily trafficked as you approach Newburgh. River Rd. runs near the River. One caveat about using River Rd. is that you will have to descend to the River and then climb back up to Rt. 9W.

16.3 (26.2)   Water St./River Rd. @ South St.   34.6 (55.7)
Turn West on to South St.

Newburgh

Info.: Orange Co. TO, Corner of Union (Route 300) & Stewart Aves., Newburgh NY 12550, 914 567-1467. Area code: 914. Zip code: 12550.
Services: All. Hospital. Newburgh-Beacon Brdg. (Interstate Hwy.)
Lodging: B&Bs: Early Settler, 562-7548; Kelsay's House of Nations, 2 Scenic Dr., 562-1477; Morgan House, 12 Powelton Rd., 561-0326; Stockbridge Ramsdell House, 158 Montgomery St., 561-3462; Orange Co. B&B Assoc., 12 Powelton Rd., 800 210-5565.
Attractions: Crawford House, 189 Montgomery St., 561-2585; Washington's HQ St. Hist. Site, 84 Liberty St., 561-1195.

17.1 (27.5)   South St. @ Rt. 9W/Robinson Ave.   33.8 (54.4)
Turn North on to Rt. 9W/Robinson Ave.

24.5 (39.4)   CR 14 @ Rt. 9W.   26.4 (42.5)
Continue traveling on Rt. 9W.

Marlboro: Attractions: Gomez Mill House c. 1714, Millhouse Rd., 236-3126. Riverview Winery, 1338 Rt. 9W, 236-3164; Benmarl Vineyards, 156 Highland Ave., 236-4265

32.0 (51.5)   Rtes. 44/55 @ Rt. 9W   18.9 (30.4)
Continue traveling on Rt. 9W.
Turn East on to Rtes. 44/55 to cross the Mid-Hudson Bridge to Poughkeepsie and the East Side of the Hudson River Route.
Highland: Services: Mid-Hudson Brdg., NYS Bridge Auth., PO Box 1010, 691-7245. Grocery. Lodging: Motels. Black Creek Cottage, 227 South St., 883-6446; Fox Hill B&B, S. Chodikee Lake Rd., 691-8151.

34.5 (55.5)   Rt. 299 @ Rt. 9W   16.4 (26.4)
Continue traveling on Rt. 9W. Turn West to go to New Paltz and the Shawangunk Mts., ~6 mi. (9 km.)

42.5 (68.4)   CR 24/River Rd. @ Rt. 9W   8.4 (13.5)
Continue traveling on Rt. 9W. Turn East on to CR 24/ River Rd. if you want a diversion.
Esopus: Attractions: Black Bear Mus., 1075 Broadway, 384-6786; Klyne-Esopus Hist. Soc. Mus., 764 Rt. 9W, 338-8109.

45.5 (73.3)   River Rd./CR 24 @ Rt. 9W/Broadway   5.4 (8.7)
Continue traveling on Rt. 9W. Turn East on to CR 24/ River Rd. if you want a diversion.

47.8 (77.0)   Broadway @ Rt. 9W   3.1 (5.0)
Rt. 9W becomes a semi-limited access highway a bit further North. You can continue traveling on Rt. 9W.
OR exit here at, Broadway/East Strand St., and turn West on to Broadway. Broadway makes several twists and turns.

49.7 (80.0)   Albany Ave. @ Broadway   1.2 (1.9)
Continue traveling on Rt. 9W. Turn East on to CR 24/ River Rd. if you want a diversion.

50.3 (81.0)   Albany Ave. @ Flatbush Ave.   0.6 (1.0)
Turn West on to Flatbush Ave.

50.9 (81.9)   Rt. 9W Jct. Flatbush Ave.   0.0 (0.0)
Continue traveling Northeast on Flatbush Ave./Rt. 32. OR turn North on to Rt. 9W. Rt. 32 is the scenic route. Rt. 9W the more direct route. The distances are about the same using either road.

Kingston

Info.: Kingston Visitor Ctr., 20 Broadway, Kingston 12401, 914 331-7517.

Area code: 914. **Zip code:** 12401.

Services: All.

Lodging: Motels. B&Bs: Cordt's Mansion, 132 Lindsley Ave., 331-3921; Black Lion, 124 W. Chestnut St., 338-0410; Miss Gussie Bug, 37½ Broadway 334-9110; Rondout B&B,88 W. Chester St., 331-8144; Cordts Mansion, 132 Lindsley Ave., 331-3921. Camping: Hidden Valley Lake Cpgd. (cabins only), 290 Whiteport Rd., 338-4616.

Attractions: Fred Johnston Mus.,63 Main St., 339-0720; Old Dutch Church & Mus., 272 Wall St., 338-6759; Hudson River Maritime Mus., 1 Rondout Landing, 338-0071; Rondout Lighthouse, Rondout Creek, 338-0071; Senate House St. Hist. Site, 312 Fair St., 338-2786; Trolley Mus., 89 E. Strand, Rondout Landing, 331-3399; Vol. Fireman's Mus., 265 Fair St. 331-0866; Van Steenburgh House, 97 Wall St. Henry Sleight House, Green & Crown Sts., 338-8327; Mus. of Kingston, 266 Fair St., 331-0866; Wildlife Discovery Center, 881 Rt. 28, 338-6680; Wine Cave, 77 McEntee St. 340-9466; Woodstock Brewing Co., 20 St. James St. 331-2810; Hudson River Cruises, Rondout Landing 255-6618; North River Cruises on the Teal, W. Strand Pk., Broadway, 679-8205.

S to N	**Hudson River Valley**	N to S
	West Side of the Hudson River	
mi. (km.) Read↓	**Kingston to Bear Mt.**	mi. (km.) Read↑

S to N	**Hudson River Valley**	N to S
	West Side of the Hudson River	
mi. (km.) Read↓	**Kingston to Albany**	mi. (km.) Read↑

0.0 (0.0)   Albany Ave./Rt. 32 @ Broadway   57.9 (93.2)
Continue traveling on Rt. 9W to go North. OR Turn East
on to CR 24/River Rd. if you want a diversion. Kingston
Info. in Bear Mt. to Kingston Chapter

0.6 (1.0)   Albany Ave. @ Flatbush Ave./Rt. 32   57.3 (92.3)
Turn West on to Flatbush Ave./Rt. 32.

1.5 (2.4)   Rt. 9W @ Flatbush Ave.   56.4 (90.8)
Continue traveling Northeast on Flatbush Ave./Rt. 32.
OR Turn North on to Rt. 9W. Rt. 32 is the scenic route.
Rt. 9W the more direct route. The distances are about
the same using either road.

3.4 (5.5)   Ulster Landing Rd./CR 37 @ Rt. 32   54.5 (87.7)
Continue traveling on Rt. 32.   OR turn on to Ulster
Landing Rd./CR 37 for a diversionary loop of 5.12 mi. (8.2
km.)   Be forewarded, using Ulster Landing Rd. means
going down and then up to the River. You can cut this
loop a bit by exiting back on to Rt. 32 via Kukuk Ln.

7.4 (11.9)   Rt. 32 @ Ulster Landing Rd./CR 37   50.5 (81.3)
Continue traveling North on Rt. 32.
Southbound travelers can take a diversion via Ulster
Landing Rd. Read next entry, first.

10.1 (16.3)   Rt. 9W Jct. Rt. 32   47.8 (77.0)
Continue traveling North on Rtes. 9W/32. As you enter
Saugerties Rt. 9W travels along several different named
streets. Simply follow the 9W signs.
Southbound travelers can use Rt. 32 to go to Kingston.
The distance using Rt. 32 or Rt. 9W is about the same.

12.3 (19.8)   Rt. 9W/Main St.   45.6 (73.4)
              @ Rt. 9W/W. Bridge St.
Turn Northeast on to Main St./Rt. 9W.

Saugerties

Info.: Area code: 914. Zip code: 12477.
Lodging: Motels. B&Bs: Bed by the Stream, George
Sickle Rd., 246-2979; Evergreen Country Inn, 6711
Hommelville Rd., 247-0015.
Attractions: Saugerties Lighthouse, 246-1380;
Quarryman's Mus., 7480 Fite Rd., 246-3400.

12.9 (20.8)   Rt. 9W/Main @ Rt. 9W/Malden Ave.   45.0 (72.5)
Continue traveling on Rt. 9W, street name change.
Malden Tpk., CR 34, to Malden.

22.8 (36.7)   W. Bridge St./Rt. 9W @ Rt. 9W   35.1 (56.5)
Continue following Rt. 9W/W. Bridge St.
Ulster-Greene County Border.

23.2 (37.4)   Rt. 9W/Maple St.   34.7 (55.9)
               @ Rt. 385/W. Bridge St.
Traveling East on W. Bridge St./Rt. 385.
OR Continue traveling North on Rt. 9W/Maple St. Using
Rt. 385 to go North will add a negligible distance, and its
more scenic.

24.0 (38.6)   Main St. @ Rt. 385/Bridge St.   33.9 (54.6)
Continue traveling on Bridge St./Rt. 385.

Catskill
Info.: Area code: 518. Zip code: 12414.
Services: Grocery & other retail stores.
Lodging: Motels. B&Bs: Alden House, 242 Main St.,
943-5526; Caleb's Street's Inn, 251 Main St.,-943-0246;
The Catskill's, 23 Thompson St.,-943-3967; The Oaks,
166 High Falls Rd. Ext., 678-5555; Alden House, 242
Main St., 943-5526. Camping: Brookside Cpgd., 4952
Rt. 32,-678-9777; Catskill Cpgd., 79 Castle Rd. (Route
32, west 1 mile on Game Farm Road),-678-5873; Cedar
Grove Cpgd., 1226 Schoharie Tpk., 945-1451; Woods
Road Cpgd., 152 Vedder Rd., 943-9118
Attractions: Ulster & Delaware RR, www.udrrhs.org;
Catskill Game Farm, 400 Game Farm Rd., 678-9595;
Ted Martin's Reptile Land, 5464 Rt. 32, 678-3557.

24.2 (39.0)   Rt. 385/Bridge St. @ Rt. 385/Spring St. 33.7 (54.3)
Turn on to Spring St./Rt. 385.

28.9 (46.5)   1st St. @ Rt. 385/Washington St.   29.0 (46.7)
Continue traveling on Rt. 385.
Athens: Lodging: Stewart House B&B, 2 N. Water St.,
12015, 518 945-1357. Juniper Woods Cpgd., PO Box 1,
12015, 518-945-1399.

35.6 (57.3)   Mansion St./Rt. 385   22.3 (35.9)
               @ Washington St./Rt. 385
Continue on Rt. 385.
Coxsackie: Lodging: Motels: B&B: Honey Locust
Hollow, Bronck Mill Rd., West Coxsackie 12192, 731-

2240.
Attractions: Bronck Mus., Rt. 9W at Peter Bronck Rd.,
731-6490; Hudson River Is. St. Pk., (accessible by boat
only) 872-1674.

36.3 (58.4)   CR 61/Lawrence Ave./River Rd.   21.6 (34.8)
              @ Rt. 385/Mansion St.
Turn North on to CR 61 at Lawrence Ave.   CR 61
changes its name to River Rd. in about .5 mi. (.8 km.)
OR continue West on Rt. 385/Mansion Ave. for
another .9 mi. (1.5 km.) to reach Rt. 9W and then travel
North on Rt. 9W to New Baltimore.   The distance is
about the same. Neither road is heavily trafficked. Rt.
9W does have fewer hills, a wide shoulder and a
smoother surface than CR 61.

43.0 (69.2)   CR 61/River Rd. @ Washington St.   14.9 (24.0)
Northbound: Continue traveling on CR 61/Main St.
through New Baltimore to Rt. 144 North. If you want to
use Rt. 9W, turn West on to Washington St. which
becomes New Baltimore Rd. and reaches Rt. 9W in ~1.5
mi. (2.4 km.)
Southbound: Follow the CR 61 Route or continue on Rt.
144 for ~2 mi. (3.2 km.) to use Rt. 9W South.

43.2 (69.6)   Rt. 144 @ Washington St.   14.7 (23.7)
Continue North on Rt. 144.
New Baltimore: Lodging: Motels. B&B: River Hill II, PO
Box 253, New Baltimore, NY 12124, 518756-3313.

45.2 (72.8)   Rt. 143 @ Rt. 144   12.7 (20.4)
Continue on Rt. 144. Turn West on to Rt. 143 to go to
Ravena & Rt. 9W, .8 mi. (1.3 km.).

49.0 (78.9)   Rt. 396 @ Rt. 144   8.9 (14.3)
Continue on Rt. 144. Turn West on to Rt. 396 to go to
Selkirk

54.6 (87.9)   Rt. 32 Jct. Rt. 144   3.3 (5.3)
Continue on Rtes. 144/32/River Rd.
Glenmont: Motels.

55.7 (89.7)   Rtes. 144/32/South Pearl St./River Rd.   2.2 (3.5)
Continue traveling on Rtes./32/144. River Rd. becomes
South Pearl St. as you cross into the City of Albany. Rt.
144 ends. Rt. 32 becomes the Route number to follow.
But we will use street names to get you to the Mohawk
Hudson Bikeway in downtown Albany.

56.3 (90.6)   I 787 Overpass mess   1.6 (2.6)
                  @ South Pearl St. Rt. 32
       Follow Rt. 32.

56.8 (91.4)   Church St. @ Rt. 32   1.1 (1.8)
       Turn towards the River and go to Broadway.

57.0 (91.8)   Broadway @ Church St.   .9 (1.4)
       Continue traveling towards the River and then North on
       Broadway. Weave around under the Interstate to State
       St.

57.9 (93.2)   State St. @ Broadway   0.0 (0.0)
       You're here!

S to N	**Hudson River Valley**	N to S
	West Side of the Hudson River	
mi. (km.) Read↓	**Albany to Kingston**	mi. (km.) Read↑

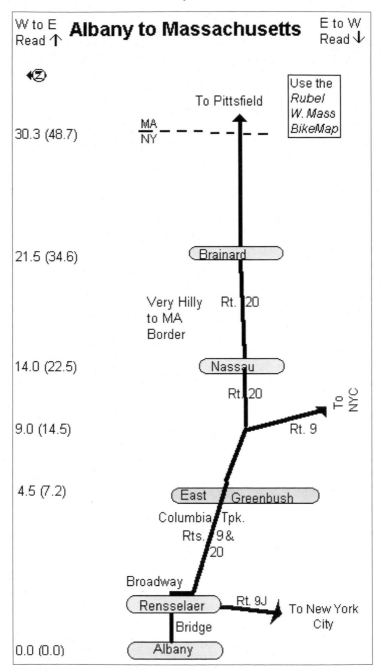

W to E
Read ↑

Albany to Massachusetts

E to W
Read ↓

To Pittsfield

$\frac{MA}{NY}$

Use the
*Rubel
W. Mass
BikeMap*

30.3 (48.7)

21.5 (34.6)   Brainard

Very Hilly   Rt. 20
to MA
Border

14.0 (22.5)   Nassau

Rt. 20

To NYC

9.0 (14.5)   Rt. 9

4.5 (7.2)   East   Greenbush

Columbia Tpk.
Rts. 9 &
20

Broadway

Rensselaer   Rt. 9J   To New York
City

Bridge

0.0 (0.0)   Albany

BIBLIOGRAPHY

Adirondack Mountain Club, Inc. *1994 Mountain Bike Preliminary Trail and Route Listing.* Glens Falls, NY: The Club. 1995.

Ehling, William P. *Fifty Hikes in Central New York.* Woodstock, VT: Backcountry Publications. 1990.

Ehling, William P. *Fifty Hikes in Western New York.* Woodstock, VT: Backcountry Publications. 1990.

Finch, Roy G. *The Story of the New York State Canals.* Albany, NY: New York State Engineer and Surveyor. 1925.

Fitzgerald, John R. *The New Erie Canal: Travel Guide & History.* Saratoga Springs: Quest Press. 1993.

Frankel, Jeremy G. *Erie Canal Guide.* Skeneateles, NY: Mid-Lakes Navigation. 1991.

Lake Champlain Bikeways. *Lake Champlain Bikeways Test Map Sections 1, 3 & 4.* Crown Point, NY: Lake Champlain Bikeways. 1996.

Lake Champlain Visitors Center. *Directory of Bicycle-Friendly Accommodations and Services.* Crown Point, NY: The Center. 1999.

Lake Placid/Essex County VB. *Mountain Bike Trails in the Adirondack Mountains of Essex County, NY.* Lake Placid, NY: The Bureau. May, 1996.

Lewis, Clarence O. *The Erie Canal 1817-1967.* Lockport, NY: Niagara County Historical Society. 1967.

National Maritime Historical Society. *URGER on the Erie Canal.* Croton on Hudson: The Society. Summer, 1991.

Rosenberg-Naparsteck, Ruth. *Runnin Crazy.* Rochester, NY: Corn Hill Waterfront & Navigation Foundation. 1996.

Scheller, William. *New York: Off the Beaten Path.* Chester, CT: Globe Pequot Press. 1994.

Van Diver, Bradford B. *Roadside Geology of New York.* Missoula, MT: Mountain Press. 1985.

APPENDIX

---

[1] You can rip out this letter and mail it from any Post Office. Ask the Postal clerk for a small stamped envelope; address the envelope and drop it in the post box.

COMMENTS

I appreciate your comments. Please feel free to add comments.

Dates you toured _____.

Which chapters or information did you find most useful in:

Erie Canal Bicyclist & Hiker Tour Guide, 2nd Ed. Rev.

- ◯ Tour Preparation
- ◯ The Route
- ◯ Distance Information
- ◯ Lodging Information
- ◯ Municipal Information
- ◯ Other: _____

Lodging Recommendations

Attractions Recommendations

Restaurant/Bakery/Grocery Recommendations

Route Recommendations

Other Comments:

Your Name: _____

Your Address: _____

City, State/Prov., Zip/PC: _____

E-mail: _____

The name of a friend who might be interested in receiving our brochure:

Name: _____

Address: _____

City, State/Prov., Zip/PC: _____

E-mail: _____

We do not sell or rent our mailing list.

Please return this Comment Form to:
Cyclotour Guide Books, PO Box 10585, Rochester, NY 14610

Thanks,   Harvey

SURVEY FORM

One of the most significant problems facing bicycling advocates is the the lack of data on cyclotourism and cyclotourists. It is almost impossible to make a case for improving roadway and general bicycle touring conditions unless cycling advocates have data on bicycle tourists.

This Survey is anonymous. You do not have to provide your name, etc. and I will not compare this Form to the *Comment Form*. That's why there are two separate forms.

I have tried to make this Survey Form easy for you to complete. Check the boxes or fill in the spaces, almost all of which are on the right side of the page. Sorry lefties!

Erie Canal Bicyclist & Hiker Tour Guide, 2nd Ed. Rev.

I'll use the data when I lecture and write articles on bicycle touring.

How many people were in your touring party? _____

Demographic data of cyclotourists

Your age? _____ Sex? _____
Spouse's age? _____ Sex? _____
Child's age? _____ Sex? _____
Child's age? _____ Sex? _____
Friend's age? _____ Sex? _____
Friend's age? _____ Sex? _____
Friend's age? _____ Sex? _____

Your per annum income range, measured in:

○ US $ ○ CAN $ ○ EURO ∈   ○ Other _____

Teenager on allowance?   ○
Below US$20,000   ○
US $20,001 - $30,000   ○
US $30,001 - $40,000   ○
US $40,001 - $50,000   ○
US $50,001 +   ○

Enough of this demographic stuff but It is important for presenting a case for better bicycling conditions.

What was the total distance you toured on this tour? _____mi.

The average daily distance you traveled on this tour? _____mi.

Did you tour in segments? _____ How many? ____

Average amount of money expended each day, per person?
In ○ US $ ○ CAN $ ○ EURO ∈   ○ Other _____

Less than US$10.00	○
US $10.01 - 15.00	○
US $15.01 - 25.00	○
US $25.01 - 35.00	○
US $35.01 - 45.00	○
US $45.01 - 55.00	○
US $55.01 - 65.00	○
US $65.01 - 75.00	○
US $75.01 - 85.00	○
Over US $85.01	○

Average Amount of money expended each day for these items:
In ○ US $ ○ CAN $ ○ EURO ∈   ○ Other _____

Amount	Lodging	Food, Incl.	Attractions	Misc.
Less than $5.00				
$5.01 - 10.00				
$10.01 - 20.00				
$20.01 - 25.00				
$25.01 - 30.00				
$30.01 +				

How did you cyclotour? General description.

Loaded touring?	○
Camping & mainly eating in restaurants?	○
Sagwagon camping?	○
○ B&Bs ○ Motels & preparing own meals?	○
○ B&Bs ○ Motels & eating in restaurants?	○
Other: _____	○

Other Comments or data:

Please return this form to: Cyclotour Guide Books, PO Box, 10585, Rochester, NY 14610. Thanks, Harvey.

————— YOUR ADDRESS —————

————— CITY STATE ZIP/PC —————

————— DATE —————

Mr. David L. Gunn
President and CEO
Amtrak
National Railroad Passenger Corporation
Washington Union Station
60 Massachusetts Avenue, N. E.
Washington, DC 20002

Dear Mr. Gunn,

I urge you to expand Amtrak's carriage of unboxed bicycles to all trains.

I suggest that Amtrak establish a special Empire Service multi-day fare for bicyclists and hikers who want to traverse New York State in segments. This type of fare is applicable to other areas in the United States where Amtrak intersects significant outdoors facilities, *e. g.*, between Chicago, Illinois and Michigan City, Indiana.

Thank you for considering these marketing enhancements to Amtrak's service.

Sincerely yours,

EQUIPMENT LISTS

✓ Clothing
- ○ Cycling Short
- ○ Cycling Shorts
- ○ Cycling Shorts
- ○ Cycling Gloves
- ○ Off Cycling Shorts
- ○ Tee Shirts
- ○ Tee Shirts
- ○ Socks #_____
- ○ Short Socks #_____
- ○ Underwear
- ○ Jacket
- ○ Sweater/Fleece top
- ○ Dress pants
- ○ Long (thermal) Tights
- ○ Jeans
- ○ Rain Gear
- ○ Shoes
  - ○ Cycling
  - ○ Off-cycling
- ○ Dress
- ○ Blouse #_____
- ○ Shirt #_____
- ○ Wicking base layer
- ○ Bathing Suit
- ○ Scarf (*do rag*)
- ○ Belt
- ○ Clothes Pins
- ○ Sewing Kit
- ○ Hat

- ○ Other _____

- ○ Other _____

✓ Tools
- ○ Combination tool
- ○ Patch Kit
- ○ Screwdriver(s)
  - ○ Philips
    - ○ # 0
    - ○ # 1
    - ○ # 2
  - ○ Flat
    - ○ 5mm/ ^{3}/8 in
    - ○ 8mm/ ^{5}/8 in
- ○ Wrenches
  Hex, Open, Box
  or Sockets
  - ○ 4mm-H O B S
  - ○ 5mm-H O B S
  - ○ 6mm-H O B S
  - ○ 8mm-H O B S
  - ○ 9mm-H O B S
  - ○ 10mm-H O B S
- ○ 11mm-H O B S
  - ○ 12mm-H O B S
  - ○ 13mm-H O B S
  - ○ 14mm-H O B S
  - ○ Other_____
- ○ Pliers
- ○ Vise Grips
  - ○ 3in
  - ○ 5in
- ○ Cone Wrenches
- ○ Screws
- ○ Freewheel Remover
- ○ Crank Remover
- ○ Electrical Tape

EQUIPMENT LISTS

✓ **Bicycle**
- ○ Rear Rack
- ○ Front Rack
- ○ Low Riders
- ○ Rear Panniers
- ○ Handlebar Bag
- ○ Front Light
- ○ Rear Flashing Red
- ○ Light Other Color
- ○ Wiring for Lights
- ○ Generator
- ○ Batteries
- ○ Extra Batteries
- ○ Cables
  - ○ Brake
  - ○ Gears
- ○ Other_____
- ○ Special Screws
- ○ Special Screws
- ○ Cyclometer
- ○ Bungie Cords #_____
- ○ Other _____

- ○ _____
- ○ _____
- ○ _____
- ○ _____
- ○ _____
- ○ _____
- ○ _____

✓ **Personal**
- ○ Watch
- ○ Towel
- ○ Sunglasses
- ○ Helmet
- ○ First Aid Kit
- ○ Soap
- ○ Tooth Brush
- ○ Tooth Paste
- ○ Cosmetics
- ○ 2nd pair of Eyeglasses
- ○ Shaving Equipment
- ○ Medical Prescriptions
- ○ Eyeglass Prescription
- ○ Contact Lens Solutions
- ○ Journal
- ○ Citizenship ID
- ○ Pen
- ○ Stamps
- ○ Sun Screen
- ○ Medicine
- ○ Calculator
- ○ Flashlight
- ○ 25¢ (for phone)
- ○ Credit Cards
- ○ Passport & Visas
- ○ Tickets
- ○ Maps
- ○ Camera & Film
- ○ Photographs (self)

EQUIPMENT LISTS

✓ Camping
- ○ Tent
  - ○ Tent stakes
  - ○ Tent Poles
  - ○ Ground cloth
- ○ Rope (3m/10ft)
- ○ Sleeping Bag
- ○ Mattress
- ○ Day pack
- ○ H$_2$0 Purifier/Filter
- ○ Toilet Paper
- ○ Candle
- ○ Flashlight
- ○ Other
- ○ _____

- ○ _____

✓ Food
- ○ Pasta ○ Peanut Butter
- ○ Cereal
- ○ Rice
- ○ Dried Milk
- ○ Fruit
- ○ Cookies
- ○ Snacks

- ○ Other _____

- ○ _____

- ○ _____

✓ Cooking
- ○ Cup
- ○ Pot (Cook Set)
- ○ Knife
- ○ Fork
- ○ Spoon
- ○ Can
- ○ Opener/Cork Screw
- ○ Stove
  - ○ Fuel Bottle
  - ○ Fuel
  - ○ Matches
  - ○ Pre-Starter
- ○ Stove Repair Kit
- ○ Swiss Army Knife
- ○ Wire (2m/2yds)
- ○ Other _____

- ○ Oil or fat
- ○ Vegetables_____
- ○ Vegetables_____
- ○ Vegetables_____
- ○ Other _____
- ○ _____

- ○ _____

- ○ _____

- ○ _____

LESS IS MORE
LESS IS MORE

LESS IS MORE
LESS IS MORE

Cyclotour Expense Log

Date	Odometer	Destination	Brkfast	Lunch	Dinner	Groceries	Snacks	Lodging	Bicycle	Misc.	Daily Total	Running Total
Total												

Cyclotour Expense Log

Date	Odometer	Destination	Brkfast	Lunch	Dinner	Groceries	Snacks	Lodging	Bicycle	Misc.	Daily Total	Running Total
Total												

Order Form

I want to go on the adventure of my life time!

'Round Lake Ontario: A Bicyclist's Tour Guide

A self guided two week cyclotour around this gem of a Great Lake. Riding 50 mi. (80 km.) a day on lightly trafficked rural roads this 600 mile (965 km) tour will leave you plenty of time to loll on the beaches or sight see in Niagara Falls, Toronto or Rochester.

Campgrounds are spaced approximately 50 mi. (80 km.) apart. There are numerous B&Bs, motels, hostels and other places to stay.

Please send me the books I have checked ✓.

O 'Round Lake Ontario: A Bicyclist's Tour Guide	us $24.95
O 'Round Lake Erie: A Bicyclist's Tour Guide	us $24.95
O 'Round Lake Michigan: A Bicyclist's Tour Guide	us $24.95
O 'Round Lake Huron: A Bicyclist's Tour Guide	us $24.95
O 'Round Lake Superior: A Bicyclist's Tour Guide	us $24.95
O Finger Lakes Bicyclist's Tour Guide	us $24.95
O Erie Canal Bicyclist & Hiker Route Guide	us $24.95
O Rubel Massachusetts BikeMaps	ea. us $ 6.95
O Pedaller's Paradise New Zealand Bike Guides	ea. us $24.95
O EDB Guides to the French Canal System	ea. us $24.95
O See the web site for other great hard to find bicycling books	

Shipping:

☑ ADD Standard shipping charge	us $ 4.30
☐ Global Priority Mail current rate	us $13.65
toCanada & Other nations	

Total   **US $**_____

_____
YOUR NAME

_____
STREET

_____
CITY, STATE (PROVINCE), ZIP (POSTAL CODE)

Send your check or money order to:

Cyclotour Guide Books
PO Box 10585
Rochester, NY 14610
www.cyclotour.com   cyclotour@cyclotour.com

INDEX